Praise for *Be Child Wise*

"This book is incredibly complete; a fabulous guide to making families wise and healthy. The book should be in every therapist's, social worker's, and family's hands. I especially like the ending statements for each chapter as a reminder of poignant thoughts and the permission for parents to read as they need and explore chapters that are relevant at a certain part of the child's life. This will remain a classic."

SHARON KAPLAN ROSZIA, MS, *adoption expert*

"*Be Child Wise* offers a marvelous combination of wisdom, science, common sense, and practical advice from a truly trusted source."

ART ULENE, MD, *guardian to a struggling child*

Be Child Wise

A Dynamic Approach to Raising and Caring for Emotionally Distressed Children

DEVELOPED BY

and presented by

ChildWise Institute Parent Handbook

Published by ChildWise Institute and Intermountain in the United States of America

For information, please write:
ChildWise Institute
PO Box 1170
Helena, MT 59624
www.childwise.org

ISBN 978-0-9979641-0-3

Be Child Wise

A Dynamic Approach to Raising and Caring for
Emotionally Distressed Children

Acknowledgments

This book began as the brainchild of Jim FitzGerald, CEO of Intermountain, who brought many of these principles of care to Intermountain thirty-three years ago. Morgan Adams had the Herculean task of taking the experience that was in the heads of various Intermountain professionals and putting those ideas into writing for the first time. Only then could Kate Cremer-Vogel, MS, LCPC, therapist, writer, and teacher extraordinaire, take that material and create the book that you now read. This book has served as the primary text for the online course that Kate developed and taught, Morgan facilitated, and Intermountain sponsored—"Relational Development"—which has been taught at University of Montana and Montana State University.

Although Morgan and Kate wrote the text, the actual content and ideas came from several of our staff and colleagues. Thanks to Elizabeth Kohlstaedt, Jim FitzGerald, Edward Gray, Jann Petek, Twila Costigan, Morgan Adams, and Kate Cremer-Vogel for their seminal ideas about how to understand and be present for children. Thanks to our many sources of inspiration and training: Daniel Hughes, our friend and mentor, who created Dyadic Developmental Psychotherapy; Sharon Kaplan-Roszia, our guide in all things adoption; Circle of Security gurus Kent Hoffman, Glen Cooper, Bert Powell, and Bob Marvin; Bruce Perry of the Child Trauma Academy; Toni Cavanagh Johnson, who taught us about sexual development in children; Robert Anda, principal co-investigator of the Adverse Childhood Experiences study; and our dear friends and early mentors at Forest Heights Lodge, whose values, philosophy, and approaches are woven throughout this work. These individuals are leaders in psychological and developmental thought, and they also have been our friends, mentors, colleagues, and teachers.

Prologue

This book represents the wisdom of many professionals from Intermountain, the oldest child welfare agency in Montana. In its 105-year existence, Intermountain has developed a way of understanding children and families that helps them heal. Our treatment approach has at its center the principle that *what is harmed by relationship must be healed by relationship.* It is our job as adults to be the healing agent for children by understanding the need that the child is expressing. The science of child development acknowledges that each age of development can represent growth and regression, and this is particularly true of children who have experienced loss, trauma, or emotional distress. The understanding of child development, particularly as it may go askew, is crucial in understanding how to frame and proceed in the healing relationship. We call Intermountain's approach, which developed over the past thirty-three years, a *developmental/relational* approach.

The understanding and interventions represented in this book come from the knowledge and experiences of our staff, as well as from what we have learned from other professionals. Some of the stories are written in the first person for clarity, yet each story is the voice of a different professional or a different child. By the end of this book, you will see *how to heal by relationship what has been harmed by relationship.*

Our hope is that parents might read this book before adopting or fostering, but we realize that the heart often leads the head, so you may be coming to this book after you have made the heroic decision to bring a child into your home. We want this book to give you the tools to understand yourself and your child, so you can become the strongest family you can be.

The first chapters are designed to help you see yourself and your own strengths and weaknesses, and then to see the world through your child's eyes, for only then will your relationship with your child be a healing one. The second part of the book provides methods to help your child negotiate the world and your relationship in positive ways.

Intermountain provides direct services for thousands of children each year, but we needed a way to share what we have learned with others in the community and to advocate for the well-being of all children. Thus we created ChildWise Institute, the publisher of this book. ChildWise, an independent, charitable, social-profit organization, has a threefold mission: to advance awareness of child well-being issues, to accelerate knowledge and understanding of best practices around child well-being issues, and to advocate for change in funding, protection, treatment, and well-being of children and their families.

Intermountain is committed to understanding and healing the whole child, as opposed to treating the child's symptoms. Each child must be seen and understood within the context of his specific history, including understanding how the quality of his early nurturing experience affected his unique genetic nature. In order to grow and thrive, a child must reside within a stable culture of caring and nurturing. The child's relationships with adults in this setting must reflect the value of trust, which is conveyed through a continuity of care by providers who communicate with him openly, honestly, and directly.

At Intermountain, treatment emphasis is on learning and growth, which takes place within a structure based on defined values, including supporting strong feelings, providing a means to address problems, creating an environment of fun, and promoting personal accountability. Above all, Intermountain is dedicated to providing stability and a permanent home for each child, which requires a significant commitment to each child. For that reason, Intermountain requires parents to invest a significant amount of time in preparation to ensure that they have the tools to handle the responsibilities this commitment brings with it.

So, we invite you into the world of your own hopes, fears, wants, and needs, and those of your child. These may be two very different worlds at first, but they can come together and coalesce into one compassionate, forgiving, and loving world. For simplicity, throughout the book we will refer to the caregiver as "she" and the child as "he."

Be Child Wise

1.
Who Are You?

Understanding Your Desires, Your Hopes, and Your Achilles' Heel in Parenting

**Parents need to be someone for their child,
not do something to him.**

JIM FITZGERALD, CEO, INTERMOUNTAIN

NATALIE, AGE SIXTEEN, sobbed as she rocked in the overstuffed rocker with her adoptive mother. She had just finished her weekly telephone call with her biological mother. Each time Natalie spoke with her biological mother, the hurt, pain, and shame of being abandoned came rushing back to her. But Lisa, her adoptive mother, said nothing; she just opened her arms and let Natalie come sit on her lap in the rocking chair. There were no words to take the hurt away; there was only Lisa's understanding that Natalie just needed Lisa to be the loving mother who was there to soothe and nurture the hurt two-year-old inside of Natalie's sixteen-year-old body. Lisa had to put aside her own hurt that after all of these years, Natalie still wanted her biological mother. There were no words, no techniques that would make this okay. Natalie just needed Lisa to be someone for her.

Our Approach to Parenting

What is harmed through relationship must be healed through relationship (Kohlstaedt, 2010). A relationship—a singular entity consisting of two intertwined world views—is the place where two unique persons connect with one another. The drive to seek relationship is instinctual and part of our genetic code. Relationship is essential to our survival as individuals, couples, families, communities, and the human race. Creating a relationship is a give-and-take process in which each participant engages with the other from his or her individual perspective, while seeking to "get" the other and his or her *unique* viewpoint sufficiently enough to communicate genuine understanding.

The challenge of helping a hurting child is that the parent must carefully direct the formation of a relationship with the child, and in doing so, accept that as a parent, she will be giving much more than she is taking.

The adult in the relationship must reconcile unfinished business from her own past and understand and take care of her own needs in the present in order to have the objectivity she needs as she seeks to understand the child and his needs, to teach the child who he is, and to help him organize his experience of the world. In short, *she must be someone for this child* (FitzGerald, 2015). The therapeutic adult-child relationship is more about give than take, and it begins as the adult facilitates the child's development while fostering his ability to connect.

There is no teachable formula that we can give parents to follow as they navigate the interpersonal process of creating a union with their child. Therefore, this parent handbook does not serve as a collection of techniques, but rather as a guide that promotes the understanding of how a child came to see the world as he does, how his previous experiences have colored his view of relationship, and how his parents can use their hearts and minds to create a safe and meaningful connection with their child. Our approach is not aimed at changing or curing a child; it is designed to help parents fulfill the previously unmet core needs of an emotionally distressed child. We assist parents in developing healthy and fruitful ways of being with their child and in actively demonstrating their commitment to him so he can begin to internalize their promise to him that giving up is not an option.

So, let's start this journey with an inward look at who *you are*, since you are the most important part of the puzzle of parenting.

Who Am I? Starting from the Inside

You are the agent of change in your child's life; therefore, the impact of who you are and what you bring to the relationship with your child is central to his healing process. Parents who are able to courageously explore their own history and look at how it may affect their parenting are generally better prepared to partner with their child in the healing process for the long term. It's never too late to become who you want to be!

As parents, we need to understand that we do not see things objectively; rather, we see things through the lens of *ourselves*. In other words, who we *are* is what we *see*. It is not always easy to remember that our perspective is not *the* perspective, that it is only *one* perspective. In addition, it is tempting to want to see ourselves as whole, resolved, and without any issues because "digging into your stuff" is neither easy nor usually

WHO ARE YOU? 5

To guide your child toward healing, you need to know the healing path yourself

very pleasant. However, you cannot avoid yourself when you are in relationship with *anyone*, especially your child, who you will discover has an uncanny ability to find those places in you that are vulnerable.

You may try to convince yourself to delay exploring these hidden parts that everyone has, or you might try to bypass the process entirely. Just know that if you take the chance *now* to look within, before a crisis, everything and everyone can be your teacher. So, pay attention, reduce your resistance to change, and make the commitment to understand yourself. Become aware of the explanations and excuses you have chosen to immobilize your power. You are equal to life. You need to be able to thoroughly answer the question, "What do I bring to the relationship?"

As challenges and issues with a child arise, it is common for parents to assume that the problem—and accordingly, the solution—lies completely within the child: "If only the child would change." This hope disempowers you, and it is futile. Parents must remind themselves continually that the problem and the solution lay within their *relationship* with their child. Blaming the child only further prolongs the pain and frustration of the situation and does not address the problem. While honest and critical self-evaluation is vitally important early on in the adoption process, it is never too late for parents to start looking "inside" to ask themselves the right questions. You will find there are things you *can* do and things you *cannot* do as you begin to look at yourself.

Unavoidably, when you take an emotionally distressed child into your home, he will bring your unresolved issues of grief and loss, past abuse and neglect, addiction, and health problems to the surface. Your child's

YOU CAN
➤ own your personal mistakes and do things better the next time around
➤ recognize and address your triggers
➤ improve your role in communication and relationship
YOU CANNOT
➤ change another person

deep needs can trigger these unresolved issues in you because his pain vibrates within you to stir them up. Your issues will eventually become the roadblock to deepening your relationship with your child and to your being able to guide him through his healing. *You cannot help him go where you cannot go.* Pushing your issues away ultimately results in you pushing your child away. When we dig to the bottom of placement disruptions to see why they happen, it is the parents' unresolved issues that are most often at the core of the festering wound. It may seem counterintuitive, but therapy for the *parents* is the most helpful intervention when there are problems with the child. The following are examples of unresolved issues in your past that can prevent you from being fully engaged in the relationship with your child.

Examples of Unresolved Issues of Parents
➤ death of a parent or sibling during childhood
➤ alcoholism, drug addiction, or mental illness of a parent during childhood
➤ childhood trauma, neglect, or abuse
➤ death of a spouse or child in adulthood
➤ infertility
➤ divorce, family estrangement in adulthood

Now it is time for self-evaluation. There are many roads that can lead to your discovering the hidden parts of yourself. You can find an individual therapist who works from a psychodynamic or attachment-focused perspective to explore your issues. You could enter group therapy or begin by finding a self-help group that focuses on self-exploration. You could start by reading self-help books.

Parenting from the Inside Out by Daniel J. Siegel and Mary Hartzell (2003) is an excellent resource for parents beginning the journey into self. The premise of this book, that the parenting journey begins within, has the same foundation as our approach. We recommend you get a copy of this book for yourself, read it thoroughly, and complete the questionnaires

Parents must start their parenting journey from the inside

Looking Inside: Who Am I?

1. What was it like growing up? Who was in your family?

2. How did you get along with your parents early in your childhood? How did the relationship evolve throughout your youth and up until the present time?

3. How did your relationships with your mother and father differ, and how were they similar? Are there ways in which you try to be like, or try not to be like, each of your parents?

4. Did you ever feel rejected or threatened by your parents? Were there other experiences you had that felt overwhelming or traumatizing in your life, during childhood or beyond? Do any of these experiences still feel very much alive? Do they continue to influence your life?

5. How did your parents discipline you as a child? What impact did that have on your childhood, and how do you feel it affects your role as a parent now?

6. Do you recall your earliest separations from your parents? What were they like? Did you ever have prolonged separations from your parents?

7. Did anyone significant in your life die during your childhood, or later in your life? What was that like for you at the time, and how does that loss affect you now?

8. How did your parents communicate with you when you were happy and excited? Did they join with you in your enthusiasm? When you were distressed or unhappy as a child, what would happen? Did your father and mother respond differently to you during these emotional times? How?

9. Was there anyone else besides your parents in your childhood who took care of you? What was that relationship like for you? What happened to those individuals? What is it like for you when you let others take care of your child now?

10. If you had difficult times during your childhood, were there positive relationships in or outside of your home that you could depend on during those times? How do you feel those connections benefited you then, and how might they help you now?

11. How have your childhood experiences influenced your relationship with others as an adult? Do you find yourself trying *not* to behave in certain ways because of what happened to you as a child? Do you have patterns of behavior that you'd like to alter but have difficulty changing?

12. What impact do you think your childhood has had on your adult life in general, including the ways in which you think of yourself and the ways you relate to your children? What would you like to change about the way you understand yourself and relate to others? ◆

and exercises within. We would like you to get started right away on beginning to identify your personal unresolved issues by answering the questions on page 7, excerpted from *Parenting from the Inside Out*.

Who Are You for Your Child?

You have begun to explore how you came to see the world as you do. Now, we will help you explore who you are today. Parents often struggle with the difference between how they wish their child would act and feel and the reality of how their child truly acts and feels. Meanwhile, your child is struggling to let go of his preconceived negative beliefs or fantasies about who you are. A child whose past experience included neglect, abuse, or trauma caused by his former caregiver brings with him fears, doubts, and anger that he will often project onto his present caregiver. In striving for a feeling of predictability, your child will attempt to make his present experience match his past. With off-putting behaviors, your child will try to elicit from you the kind of negative treatment and reactions he was used to receiving from his former caregiver. Therefore, parents need to be clear and confident about who they are and who they want to be for their child. They need to be able to recognize the child's projections and avoid being drawn into the reaction trap.

Here is an opportunity for you to look more closely at the "ingredients" you bring to your parenting from your past experiences. This is not a test, but rather a way for you to get clear about what your areas of strength are and to identify those areas that may need improvement. The more honest you are, the better picture you will have of your present ability to handle the parenting of challenging children. Likewise, honesty will give you a more accurate accounting of the aspects of your parenting you may decide to work on to better meet the demands of the job. Use the self-assessment on page 9 to get a clearer view of yourself and of what you presently bring to parenting.

Rate your *current* abilities as a parent. Circle the number that corresponds with your perception of yourself with respect to each item. Focus on *your abilities*, *not* whether your child is receptive to the interaction. Notice your areas of strength as well as areas that may need improvement. Then, put a check mark next to those items you rated as a "1," "2," or "3." These are the items that describe how you *intend or want* to be as a parent. These items can serve as your goals for self-improvement.

Parenting Skills Self-Assessment: My Perceptions of Myself as a Parent

None of the time	Some of the time	Half of the time	Most of the time	All of the time
1	2	3	4	5

1.	I'm able to set and keep realistic expectations	1 2 3 4 5
2.	I'm able to make and keep a commitment	1 2 3 4 5
3.	I had effective, appropriate parenting in childhood	1 2 3 4 5
4.	I had shaming-free parenting in my childhood	1 2 3 4 5
5.	I'm able to maintain appropriate boundaries	1 2 3 4 5
6.	I'm able to maintain objectivity	1 2 3 4 5
7.	I'm able to nurture	1 2 3 4 5
8.	I'm able to look at myself objectively	1 2 3 4 5
9.	I'm able to create and maintain routine and structure	1 2 3 4 5
10.	I'm able to maintain parent-in-charge hierarchy	1 2 3 4 5
11.	I'm able to convey modest self-assurance	1 2 3 4 5
12.	I'm able to maintain self-control under stress	1 2 3 4 5
13.	I'm able to maintain self-control most of the time	1 2 3 4 5
14.	*I'm able to maintain a sense of humor	1 2 3 4 5
15.	*I'm comfortable with giving physical affection	1 2 3 4 5
16.	*I'm comfortable receiving physical affection	1 2 3 4 5
17.	*I'm ready to comfort my child in his distress	1 2 3 4 5
18.	*I'm able to be playful with my child	1 2 3 4 5
19.	*I'm ready to listen to my child's thoughts/feelings	1 2 3 4 5
20.	*I'm able to be calm and relaxed much of the time	1 2 3 4 5
21.	*I'm patient with my child's mistakes	1 2 3 4 5
22.	*I'm patient with my child's misbehaviors	1 2 3 4 5
23.	*I'm patient with my child's anger and defiance	1 2 3 4 5
24.	*I'm patient with my child's most difficult behaviors	1 2 3 4 5
25.	*I'm comfortable expressing love for my child	1 2 3 4 5
26.	*I'm able to show empathy for my child's distress	1 2 3 4 5
27.	*I'm able to show empathy for my child's anger	1 2 3 4 5
28.	*I'm able to set limits, with empathy, not anger	1 2 3 4 5
29.	*I'm able to give/follow through with consequences	1 2 3 4 5
30.	*I'm able/willing to give my child much supervision	1 2 3 4 5
31.	*I'm able/willing to give my child a lot of time	1 2 3 4 5
32.	*I'm able to express anger quickly and to the point	1 2 3 4 5
33.	*I'm able to quickly get over a conflict with my child	1 2 3 4 5
34.	*I'm able to let my child experience consequences	1 2 3 4 5
35.	*I'm able to accept the thoughts/feelings of my child	1 2 3 4 5
36.	*I'm able to accept the behavior of my child	1 2 3 4 5
37.	*I'm able to receive parenting support from others	1 2 3 4 5
38.	*I'm able to acknowledge parenting failings/mistakes	1 2 3 4 5
39.	*I'm able to ask for help from people I trust	1 2 3 4 5
40.	*I'm able to let my child's problems be his own	1 2 3 4 5
41.	*I'm able to cope with parenting criticism	1 2 3 4 5
42.	*I'm able to not feel shame/rage over parenting failures	1 2 3 4 5
43.	*I'm able to remain focused on the long-term goals	1 2 3 4 5

*(Hughes, 2007)

Parents will often unconsciously emulate both positive and negative parenting behaviors they experienced in childhood. In readying themselves for the challenge of parenting, parents will also consider those parental attributes they *wished* they had experienced. Knowing the reality of who you are as a result of your upbringing and your intention of who you want to be for your child are essential as you enter into and pursue the job of being a parent.

It may seem easier to avoid facing the truth by running from it, but the problem with this approach is that eventually the store of energy used for running will get depleted and reality will catch up. Furthermore, the wear and tear that results from running in fear takes its toll and leaves the runner without inner resources to deal with the reality that will inescapably return. Born of fear, negative thoughts and feelings inevitably cannot be resisted, avoided, or "weeded out." What *does* work, however, is to begin to open up and observe all thoughts and feelings, no matter their type, and then to gradually accept and eventually start to love those thoughts and feelings. Oftentimes, this process requires developing a relationship with a therapist who "gets it" and who can offer the support necessary to bring fear-based realities out for observation and transformation.

As you continue to consider your intentions and who you want to be for your child, it might be helpful to think about and write out your responses to the following.

Who Do You Want to Be for Your Child?
➤ When you considered adopting/fostering/parenting, what parental attributes were you relying upon to help you raise your child?
➤ Think of a person who was strongly influential in your life. How was she/he there for you?
➤ How did that person's belief in you change your view of yourself?
➤ Who are you for the child now in your care? Look at the difference between who you want to be for the child and how he sees you. Does he see you as his worst fear or his greatest hope?

You have now looked at your current parental strengths and weaknesses in relation to those parental attributes you would like to have. Are your desired and intended attributes realistic and achievable? If not, can you amend them so that they are achievable? The key to becoming the parent you would like to be is knowing and accepting who you are *now*

Successful parenting of children with serious emotional distress comes with parents knowing themselves and being clear about who they intend to be for the child

and creating and committing to a viable plan for achieving your goal for becoming who you want *to be*.

Exploring Your Motivation

You've just examined your own history, vulnerabilities, and struggles. Now it's time to see how these translate into your motivations, expectations, and tolerances for your child. In understanding your desire to parent an emotionally distressed child, it is essential to assess your *motivation* for parenting, the *level of commitment* you are willing and able to make, and your *expectations* about what you will likely experience. After a past of experiencing failure and rejection, a hurt child will not be convinced by words that parents will always accept and be there for him. A for-better-or-worse commitment is the greatest gift a parent can give a hurt child, and the only way to prove that commitment is through persistent trials, tribulations, and striving to improve your own understanding of yourself and of your child. Even parents with this commitment may find themselves challenged, so it is vital that we seek what is beneath our motivations.

Many of us find out the hard way what our incentives for becoming a parent were when we run up against a child's difficult feelings. For example, a parent who was motivated by her desire to be known as a good parent may become flustered, angry, and embarrassed when her child throws a tantrum at the grocery store. This realistically unavoidable event "proves" to her that she is not a good parent because, in her mind, the child of a good parent never acts out in public.

A parent who is motivated to bring a child into her home to become a better parent than her own parents may feel like a failure on a day she is exhausted and unable to meet her whining child's need for affection and attention. Or she may become angry if the child seems "ungrateful" for all of her hard work. Even a child's normal behavior may cause a parent to trip on a piece of unfinished business from her past, which may undermine her core reason for becoming a parent.

Is your desire to adopt a child more about you, or is it about making an unconditional commitment to the child?

The goal of uncovering your motivation for becoming a parent is to develop a keen awareness of any intention that eventually may get in the way of deepening your relationship with your child. We really cannot get rid of our unconscious motivations any more than a child can get rid of his past experiences; they are a part of us. Yet we can maintain an *awareness* of how this motivation is playing out. Is it getting in the way of understanding and seeing your child? If so, then let go of the motivation, even temporarily, and hold on to the child.

Although there are personal rewards that come with parenting, choosing to parent an emotionally distressed child must ultimately be more about the child than it is about the parent. In the process of considering becoming parents, it is essential that prospective parents ask themselves difficult questions and provide honest answers to ensure that they are appropriately motivated and capable of committing for the long term. A sustainable motivation must be rooted in the loving desire to give unconditionally to a child for a lifetime. This love cannot simply be a sentiment or feeling, but rather a true commitment of the heart, mind, body, and soul. Unconditional love—accepting the child for better or worse—is the key ingredient necessary for parents to partner with their child as they build a healthy and trusting forever relationship.

Prospective parents are typically emotionally captivated by their desire to bring a child into their lives, and are caught up with excitement about expanding their family. Setting aside your positive feelings of expectation to make way for objectivity may feel like a diversion, yet in considering taking on what is bound to be the most important endeavor of your life, doing so is necessary. For that reason, we will assist you in investigating your motivation for parenting and help you decide if your reason for wanting to parent a hurt child and your level of commitment have the potential to stand the test of time.

We are all motivated by personal needs of one sort or another. These are not *bad* motivations; after all, they are inducing you to parent a child.

Understanding why you chose to parent this child is an important first step

What could be better? But there is a way that each of these motivations can trap us into rejecting that very child when the relationship turns out to be different than we expected. In the process of raising a hurt child, challenges inevitably arise that shake a parent's confidence and even her sense of competence. When a parent is faced with the feeling of inadequacy, her natural tendency is to try to avoid the feeling. She may react by pushing away what she sees as the cause of that unwanted feeling—her child—rather than interpreting her feeling of inadequacy as a signal that the child has an unmet need in the moment. When the measure of how well a child is doing becomes the measure of his parent's worth or a judgment of her competency, the child's needs can go unmet. Therefore, we will help you look at your motivations so that you can be a better parent.

Below, cross out those items you can easily dismiss as not being part of your motivation to parent a child at this time, and put a check mark next to those items that contribute more strongly to your motivation or feel more tenacious in deciding to parent this child at this time. If you already have a child in your care, check those items that may have prompted you to parent your child.

Evaluating My Motives for Wanting to Adopt
- [ ] I want to make a difference in the world.
- [ ] I see taking in a hurting child as a religious obligation.
- [ ] I want to rescue an orphan.
- [ ] I want to fix a broken child's life.
- [ ] I've always had a need to be a parent.
- [ ] This child really needs a good home and we can provide one.
- [ ] Seems like everyone I know has adopted or is adopting a child.
- [ ] Bringing a child into our home will give us something to focus on.
- [ ] Living life just as a couple feels like something's missing.
- [ ] I don't want a partner, but I do want to become a parent.
- [ ] My spouse really wants to adopt a child, so I'll go along with the idea.
- [ ] I want to give a child the love and attention I did not receive when I was a child.
- [ ] I want to do a better job with this child than I did with my own.

Next, review the list you have created. Then take some time to write about those motivations you have checkmarked and talk them over with a trusted friend, spouse, or professional. You may discover some unfinished business from either childhood or the present that will take time to work through. Honest self-examination is a vital part of parenting because some motivations, when left unexamined or when relied upon solely, can lead to great disappointment, hurt, and heartache for everyone involved. Can you imagine what situations might trigger the trap of each of these motivations?

If you are coming to this self-assessment after you have already gotten tripped up by your motivations, try to think through what they are and let go. It is important that both parents are able to say, individually and as a couple, "We accept this child into our lives as a completely equal member of our family." One parent described her commitment as, "This is a weird child, but he is *my* weird child." Commitment is a choice we make regardless of the outcome. Once the commitment is made, the question is no longer about whether the child belongs. It is not about changing the child. The question is, "How can we be a family that supports this child?" In answering this question, we teach children what it takes to thrive in this world and how to have a close, intimate connection with another human being. Children learn that no matter what happens in their life, they have a place where they can belong and be safe.

Managing Expectations

In anticipation of adding a child to their family, parents understandably become excited, confidently assuming that the future will be positive and that their child will thrive in their care. However, parents need to acknowledge that this is their *expectation*—their *belief* about or *mental picture* of a future they would *like* to have—one that may or may not be realistic. It is essential that parents temper their excitement with knowledge to avoid romanticizing their family's future, lest unrealistic expectations lead to disappointment or, worse, failure.

A wise woman and an expert in adoption, Sharon Kaplan Roszia cautions all of us: "Remember, adoption is usually about loss"—loss for the child of not growing up with his biological parents or growing up in a foreign and frighteningly different culture; loss for the adopting parents in not having the perfect family or biological offspring (Silverstein and Roszia, 1999).

As family relationships evolve, there will undoubtedly be positive times, the achievement of major milestones, and breakthrough experiences filled with joy as the child begins to receive and respond to the parents' love and care. There will also certainly be frustration, disappointment, and pain for the parents and child as well. As parents embark upon the adventure of becoming a family, it is difficult for them to believe they will be receiving anyone other than "the perfect child." Equally so, it may not occur to them that they might not possess the parenting skills or "healing powers" that will cure whatever problems their child may have. Rationally, however, no child will ever be perfect, nor will his parents be infallible. Therefore, parents need to ground themselves purposely in realistic expectations in order to be prepared for the challenges that inevitably lie ahead. The truth is that no family is immune from encountering problems.

Consider the following questions that can help you examine your expectations. You may have already confronted challenges to your expectations. If so, you are ahead of the game! Spend some time talking with your spouse and/or loved ones about your responses to the questions. Then, ask them to consider the questions and discuss their responses with them.

Examining My Expectations

➤ What issues or challenges do I expect to encounter as I parent my children?

➤ How do I plan to deal with those issues and challenges?

➤ How will I respond if things don't turn out as I had planned after my child is in our home?

➤ What issues or challenges do my friends and family expect me to encounter?

➤ How might they react if things happen that they don't expect?

➤ How will I feel if the reactions of friends and family are not supportive?

➤ Are there issues in my past such as unresolved grief, loss, abuse, or trauma that I have not adequately dealt with? If so, how do I plan to address and deal with those issues?

For some families, challenges can begin right away with unrealistic expectations being the reason for an ultimately negative outcome. After months, and in many cases years, of waiting, anticipating, and lovingly imagining the arrival of a child, parents may unrealistically expect the child to connect with them instantaneously. They may find it very difficult to put themselves in their child's shoes—a child whose experiences with adults, parents, or family may have been neglectful, frightening, or abusive. If the child is old enough to anticipate the prospect of "getting parents," it is likely his core expectations are anything but positive. When this child first meets his new parents, he may be scared and standoffish, while they may be expecting a "mommy-daddy moment." Alternatively, a child may seem to instantly "attach" to his new parents, when in fact it may be that his display of indiscriminate friendliness is an indication that he has some level of attachment disorder.

In adding an older child to the family, parents may experience a "honeymoon" period with the child, fueling their expectations of a smooth transition and adjustment, only to be knocked off guard when the child seems suddenly to become ungrateful and noncompliant as it sinks in that everything familiar and "safe" to him is now truly gone. Parents may then find themselves struggling with the child's lack of desire to communicate, his unwillingness to follow the rules and cooperate, and his seemingly purposeful poor decision-making. Their challenge then becomes an all-encompassing task, helping the child experience and fully understand what it means to be part of a family—something perhaps beyond their expectations and outside what they had anticipated or even desired.

In setting expectations, it is essential that parents realize that parenting is an ongoing act of investing in a child's life. This investment will take place slowly, over time, and whatever successes might be achieved will be the result of parents having established a long-term commitment to be in relationship with the child. No overnight return exists on the investment of raising an emotionally distressed child. In the modern world, we are accustomed to living a fast-paced life that is full of instant gratifications. We are so immersed in this pace that we hardly know that there is an alternative. The slower tempo of the child's needs will likely be foreign to you and will take time to identify and even more time to adjust.

When an infant comes into a family through birth, parents and relatives

To *be someone* for your child, you must begin to move at the pace of the *child's needs*, not at the pace of your expectations

have grown naturally to expect several months of sleepless nights, loads of diapers, hours of holding, feeding, and rocking, and constant attention to the baby's needs. As surprising as it is to some, when a *child* comes into a family through adoption, parents and relatives should expect to spend an equal amount of time and attention in service of the child's needs. Expressing this level of care and attention may not be an intuitive response for parents as they bring a child who is no longer a baby into the family, but it can and needs to be a learned response. The set of parenting tasks will differ with the child's presenting developmental age, yet the amount of time a parent needs to spend with a new child is comparable to the time a parent needs to spend with an infant.

As you evaluate your expectations about what it might be like to bring an emotionally distressed child into your home, consider the following recommendations offered to help parents achieve success (Cremer-Vogel, Richards, and Richards, 2008).

Recommendations for Nurturing Success in Adoption

➤ Consider taking time off work for an extended period when your child comes home in order to help cement his connection with you and his new family.

➤ Delay or discard the plan to put your child in day care or school to allow your child to have maximum time with you and the family.

➤ Create and maintain a connection with other adoptive families— those who are willing to be honest and open about both the highs and the lows of their experiences—through a local parenting group or adoptive ministry, and join an online forum to learn more about what you can realistically expect as well as how other families are dealing with the challenges they have in common.

➤ Read books about raising hurt and challenging children and biographies written by adoptive parents who openly share their experiences, including the difficulties and rewards.

➤ As you prepare yourselves for your parenting endeavor, consider working with an experienced adoption therapist to get as clear as possible about your hopes and dreams as they compare to the plausible realities of your desired undertaking.

➤ Recognize that some of your expectations will be unmet.

➤ Know that your expectations will need modification, and be willing to adjust them.

**It is not a matter of *if* there will be challenges;
it is a matter of *when* they will surface**

➤ Identify and accept the new normal toward which your life is shifting.
➤ Keep the lines of communication in your family open and honest.
➤ Accept yourself and your child on your bad days, for you and your child will have them.
➤ Allow yourself and your child to start over every day without yesterday's baggage.

Parents who are able to generate realistic expectations and maintain them throughout their entire journey are far more likely to thrive, to feel competent amidst the challenges that arise, and to experience success. Unmatched expectations can lead to disappointment, to feelings of failure, and sometimes to disruption of the child's placement. Parents must be able to give up their attachment to their "dream child" to be free to attach to their *actual* child. As you move along in the process of bringing a new child into your home, you will need to readjust your expectations based on your unfolding relationship with your child.

What Can I Tolerate?

Understanding *the need beneath the behavior* is vital in parenting distressed children. We will explore in the next several chapters why distressed children do what they do, but now is the time to evaluate yourself. What can you handle? What are your triggers? Preparing yourself beforehand to know what your triggers are can help you not react to them later when they happen. Just like your motivations and expectations, you can come to know your tolerances and you can be alert to your more tender areas.

Look at the list of behaviors on page 20. They are ways that some children behave when they are distressed. The distress can come from trauma, from loss, from fear of this new relationship, or from shame. The child's behavior may have nothing to do with you, but it can certainly feel personal. *No emotionally distressed child has all of these behaviors*, but most have some of them.

Put an "X" in the boxes next to the behaviors that seem to you now to be "deal breakers" and an "O" in the boxes next to the ones that you think you could overcome through your relationship with the child by seeing and meeting the need beneath his behavior. Do you have more Os than Xs? When you consider those behaviors marked "X," what might be the origin of your sense that they are deal breakers for you? Can you imagine someday being able to resolve the issues that underlie your feelings about these behaviors being deal breakers?

Building an Army of Two

If you are parenting as a couple, nothing is more important than establishing and maintaining your bond with your partner. Before you consider bringing a child into your home, your marital bond must be solid, tested, and durable. The next step as a couple who is preparing for a child to come home is assessing parenting philosophies—how they are similar and how they are different. You and your spouse can use the results of the individual self-assessments you completed above in the areas of motivation, expectations, and parenting attributes as the groundwork for comparing your readiness for parenting, as well as your approach to parenting. You may find you agree on some aspects of parenting and do not agree on others. The goal is to come up with a workable, joint approach that has its foundation in cooperation, commitment, and flexibility. The parenting approach you agree to begin with may need to be amended as you go about responding to your child's unique needs. The key is to parent as a team and, when differences arise, to stay unified in front of your child while sequestering your working through of any disagreements to private parent time.

Parenting as a team is even more critical when it comes to adoption because of the testing an adopted child inevitably needs to do to feel safe. If your child is able to "split" your team by keeping you and your spouse at odds with one another, he will feel more in control in the moment. In the past, when your child experienced inadequate parental care, fear drove him to try to maintain the locus of control within himself to survive. He learned to rely upon himself, not others, to stay alive. In a two-parent family, the phrase "divide and conquer" describes this child's unconscious motive—to control the adults in charge of him to keep them from hurting or neglecting him.

Exploring My Tolerances

What if my child

	is very different from me; for example, he may be high energy and on the go all of the time while I am low energy and enjoy peace and quiet activities?
	reminds me of someone I very much dislike or someone of whom I am frightened?
	is physically repulsive to me despite attempts to accept him?
	gets angry with me and defies just those values that I hold most dear?
	has negative behaviors that make me angry, not just once a day, but ten or more times a day?
	continues negative behaviors for many days in a row?
	embarrasses me in public, causing me to look bad to others and feel bad about myself?
	takes all of my attention by endless whining and clinging, but is not able to respond to my soothing and nurturing?
	ends up not being at all like the biological child I had imagined but could not have?
	does not appreciate all that I give him, but instead acts ungrateful?
	is unable to give and receive love and avoids or resists my physical closeness and touch?
	longs for his birth parents and holds them in an ideal light?
	destroys those possessions that are most precious to me?
	physically hurts me, my spouse, another one of my children, or a family pet, or is cruel to animals?
	brings about anxiety and differences in child rearing between me and my spouse that threaten to fracture the marriage?
	gives only me his most painful and/or hateful feelings while acting "perfectly" with others?
	elicits feelings of incompetence, inadequacy, helplessness, and uncontrollable anger in me?
	is emotionally phony, hollow, or empty?
	is manipulative or controlling and will not take my direction or follow the rules?
	has frequent and/or intense angry outbursts?
	is shut down, will not talk to me, and is unreachable?
	cannot be trusted so I feel the pressure to keep a constant eye on him?
	has little or no conscience and does not feel remorse when he hurts me or others emotionally or physically?
	physically hurts himself or is destructive to property?
	steals?
	lies often, including lying about the obvious (crazy lying)?
	gorges on or hoards food?
	is preoccupied with fire, blood, or violence?
	is an incessant chatterbox or asks nonsense questions persistently?
	sexually acts out toward himself, me, my spouse, other children, other adults, or animals?
	cannot maintain in school?
	cannot entertain himself?

When a child is able to split his parents apart, he feels momentarily stronger and more in control than the parents who are supposed to be there to protect him and keep him safe. However, when a child feels stronger and more in control than the adults present, this upside-down heirarchy ultimately leads him into feelings of deep insecurity. Therefore, be aware that allowing your child to divide and manipulate you and your spouse ultimately will tap into his insecurity, will rouse his fear and anger, and may ignite his rage or give way to challenging behaviors. To learn interdependence so he can participate fully in relationship, your child will need for you to help him shift his locus of control from within himself to you, his parents. For this shift to happen, your child will need to experience your consistent, loving parental care over a significant period of time to begin to allow himself to trust you and to allow him to trust *himself* in giving up control to you.

For example, if a child is giving mom an especially hard time, dad can come to her side to support her in responding in a healing way. This can be done in person when dad is home, by phone if dad is at work, or as promised when dad gets home. The more consistent the parents can be as a team when working with their child, the quicker he will start to feel safe and thus decrease his testing behaviors. It is harder for your child to cause rifts between you and your spouse if you *demonstrate* your trust in one another. Parents sharing affection and fun with one another in general is an effective way to boost the feeling of safety their child cultivates by being with them. A little bit of a "Romeo and Juliet" mentality—the commitment that you will not let anyone divide the two of you—goes a long way when it comes to your children.

In establishing future relationships, children raised by their birth parents naturally tend to follow the example set by their birth parents, whether positive or negative. Therefore, one of the best things birth parents can do to help their child have healthy, successful relationships is to cultivate more unity within their marriage. Unfortunately, in the case of adopted children whose birth parents were neglectful, abusive, or constantly engaging in conflict the same propensity endures—to emulate the

---

The less control the child has over your emotions and your relationship with your spouse, the more secure he will feel in the end

relational example of their *birth* parents, even though their adoption offers them a healthier alternative. The more time the child has spent with his birth parents, the more this is likely to be the case.

Nevertheless, parents still need to strive to help their child set aside acquired negative relational models because that negative example will still influence their child to some degree. Still, the most powerful leverage you have as an adoptive parent is cultivating a responsive, nurturing, individual relationship with your child. There is no doubt that your marital relationship will stand as a good example for your child; however, it is *your child's experience in the relationship with you* that remains the strongest catalyst for changing his negative mind-set about and behavior within relationships, setting the course for the kinds of relationships he will have in the future.

One caution for parents developing a relationship with their child is that they must remain oriented toward getting their emotional needs met *outside of the relationship with their child*. If a parent looks to her child instead of to herself and her spouse to meet her needs, she is giving her child power over her, which once again leads to her child feeling insecure and fearful. Furthermore, a parent needs to allocate an adequate but appropriate amount of her attention to the needs of her child while reserving enough time and energy to attend to herself and her marriage. When a parent's total focus is on the needs of the child, she is denying not only her partner's needs but also her own. When examined more closely, total focus on a child's needs is, in fact, a sign that the parent is actually trying to meet *her own unmet needs* through the child. This imbalance will not go unnoticed by the child, and once again, his insecurity will be roused.

Getting Real, Together

Making a commitment with your spouse to work together in raising your child is the initial step in the process of developing your teamwork approach. Successfully following through with your commitment to work as a team day to day requires adhering to a particular set of practical guidelines. Discuss the following list with your partner.

Parenting Teamwork

How willing is each of you to . . .

➤ be frank about your expectations of yourself and your spouse, revising them as necessary to keep them aligned with reality?

➤ maintain good communication: be open, honest, and respectful?

➤ develop sensitivity to one another's vulnerabilities to avoid being destructive?

➤ seek to understand your partner's perspective and empathize with his feelings?

➤ be good to your spouse even when you are frustrated?

➤ remember that you and your partner are on the same team even when you disagree?

➤ attack the problem instead of each other?

➤ NOT bring up the past? It is a dead-end alley and a waste of time.

➤ avoid accusations such as "You never . . ."?

➤ focus on your contribution to the problem? You can only have power over your 50 percent of the relationship.

➤ accept your partner instead of criticize her?

➤ know your partner's triggers; avoid tripping them and step in as needed when your child trips them?

➤ remember that your partner is not your mommy: take care of yourself and ask for what you need in your relationship.

➤ be demonstratively grateful for your partner? You may be surprised by how much more caring she can be.

➤ maintain your integrity regardless of what your partner does?

➤ develop a pattern of repair? An honest apology strengthens your bond.

➤ take time each day with no distractions to focus on each other, e.g., schedule a weekly childless date night?

➤ be aware that when you are currently the parent more strongly bonded with the child, your partner may feel left out?

➤ tell your spouse the positive things you notice about him and his actions as a parent?

➤ not take your spouse for granted, even though she may be a "rock" of security for you? Express your appreciation for her every day.

➤ delight in your spouse and the things that make him unique?

➤ give each other the opportunity for alone time? Each of you needs to recharge.

A Note about Parenting Roles

Your child was born from his birth mother's womb; therefore, for better or worse, she remains a central figure in your child's life. Consequently, upon separation from his birth mother, your child's expectations, resentments, and neediness will naturally fall upon his adoptive mother. Generally, the role of primary caregiver is fulfilled by the adoptive mom, while the role of the adoptive father is to be the primary support person for the adoptive mother in her work as primary caregiver. If the parents are a same-sex couple, it is important that these roles be "assigned" and adhered to for the sake of the child, who needs a singular primary caregiver in order to develop a primary attachment.

The father's role includes supporting mom in regulating her mood so that she can be present and capable of regulating their child. As the father fulfills mom's need for emotional and physical support, the quality of his response influences the development of their child's attachment pattern. If the father is calm, supportive, and consistent, mom will have a stable foundation upon which to rely as she goes about responding to their child's needs. If the father is dismissive of the mother's need for support, the psychological environment is altered negatively, and the child may be more likely to develop an insecure attachment. In the worst-case scenario, if the father is hostile or physically and verbally abusive toward the mother, the child will experience fear and unpredictability from his mother, which may lead to the development of a disorganized attachment pattern.

The father's role includes creating a father-child relationship in accordance with the child's developmental needs. The father's interactional style with the child will differ from that of the mother and may fulfill a different function. While the mother's relationship with the child is focused on regulating and responding to his physical and emotional needs, the father's relationship tends to be more stimulating and educative. *Both* regulation and stimulation are critical.

The "father-supports-mother-supports-child" arrangement provides the psychological environment necessary for the formation of a secure attachment

The key to successful single parenting is cultivating and maintaining an available support system, including an experienced family therapist

Single-Parenting an Adopted Child

As in a parenting partnership, getting members of your support system on the same team is essential. Single parents may have family members or close friends who will commit to making themselves available as needed. There may be neighbors or other adoptive families who would be willing to be part of your team. Churches can often rally members who would be interested in supporting the efforts of a single adoptive parent. If your child attends school outside your home, it is essential that you bring the child's teachers, school principal, and school counselor on board so that your team's continuity extends into your child's community.

Creating and committing to following a consistent self-care practice needs to be included in the groundwork as you are working toward parenthood. You will need a plan that will provide for self-renewal, relaxation, and regeneration of your energy to be built into your weekly schedule. Securing a trusted respite provider for your child, along with establishing and adhering to a monthly respite schedule, will ensure you get the alone time you need to rejuvenate. Locating and beginning a relationship with an experienced family therapist who is trained to help adoptive families is recommended. This relationship can be the hub around which you gather other professionals you may need on your support team. All of this preparation serves to give you a firm foundation for parenting your child, as well as a reminder that you cannot successfully raise your child without the support of others.

Your role as an adoptive parent will include elements of the roles of the primary *and* secondary caregiver. Chiefly, you will focus on being your child's primary caregiver, fulfilling your child's need for a consistent, nurturing, trustworthy mother (even if you are male). Secondarily, you will provide the stimulation and educative experiences for your child that a father would (even if you are female). It is essential that you closely consider your unique child's core needs as you evolve in your parental role. The reality is that you may not be able to provide your child with many "extras," especially if you are also working outside the home. Remembering that

> The question is not *whether* you set aside time
> for yourself, your adult interests, adult friends, and spouse,
> but rather *when and how* you are going to do so

you are only one person, and thus you can only do what one person can do, may be your biggest challenge as a single parent.

If Momma Ain't Happy, Ain't Nobody Happy

You will need to establish and commit to a self-care plan if you are to become a successful parent. As a child, you were probably unaware that your parents (if they were securely attached themselves) considered their own needs and consciously took time for themselves. Young children, tweens, and teens generally are self-centered and tend to notice the things their parents are *not doing for them*, rather than what their parents are *not doing for themselves*. As much time as you spend thinking about your child and planning for your adventure of parenting is the same amount of time you need to spend considering your own needs. You are a grown-up, and no one but you is going to look out for your needs in the way you will be looking out for your child's needs.

Parents need not lose themselves in thoughts of selflessness and gallantry when they are considering how they will carry out their parental roles. Just as you must put on your own oxygen mask before helping others (including your children) with theirs in the event of airplane cabin pressure failure, you must provide yourself with the "oxygen" you need to be able to perform your duties as a parent. It will not be sufficient to consider taking time for yourself "when you have time." Parents who deprioritize their needs inevitably succumb to exhaustion and feelings of defeat. Take the time to create a self-care plan that will not only sustain you but also energize and renew you. Parenting is a creative venture: a well-rested and relaxed brain and body will give you the energy and motivation you will need to get up tomorrow and give it your all.

Some Words of Encouragement

As you form an attachment with your child, you will begin to see him embody some of your most important values—those you are teaching him as you live together within your relationship. As you experience your child beginning to accept your love and care, you may find that bringing him into relationship with you has enriched both his life and yours. You will begin to uncover the true breadth of your own positive and negative traits. Your tolerance of others will broaden because you will have experienced and accepted that which has come from the depths of yourself.

Despite your child's antics and struggles, you will begin to feel the joy of raising him in all of his uniqueness. You will be there as he begins to experience and know his place in the world—a place that you have helped him to achieve. Due to your increasing ability to share control and be open to your child's inner world, you will begin to realize that your own capacity for intimacy has grown. You will experience the deepening of your relationship with your spouse as you see and meet each other's needs in a more open and responsive way.

You will feel your own healing taking place as you carry forth your resolve to revisit and reintegrate those parts of your own past that are most painful, a choice you made in part because you knew you couldn't take your child where you couldn't go. As you resolve and integrate your own unfinished business that was stirred up as a result of your child's needs, you will find a new peace. In the process of forming a relationship with your child, you will come to have a more accurate and accepting sense of yourself and of others. You will see that if you fail or do the wrong thing sometimes, you can still be a good parent, and that your child can embarrass and anger you sometimes and still be a good child.

No doubt there will be challenging times, surprising experiences, tears, laughter, and times you will feel defeated. Yet you will not lack for excitement or feel you are leading a life without meaning. If you have given yourself the care you need and are well grounded in a good partnership and/or support system, the work of giving an emotionally impoverished child the nurturance he needs so he has a chance to reach his potential can become the most important and meaningful work you will do in your adult life.

Key Points for Chapter 1

1. Understanding why you chose to parent this child is an important first step.
2. It is not a matter of *if* there will be challenges; it is a matter of *when* they will surface.

3. To guide your child toward healing, you need to know the healing path yourself.

4. You *can* own your personal mistakes, do things better the next time around, recognize and address your triggers, and improve your role in communication and relationship.

5. You *cannot* change another person.

6. Successful parenting of children with serious emotional distress comes with parents knowing themselves and being clear about who they intend to be for the child. This means that the start of the parenting journey is *inside* of the parent.

7. Exploring your motivations, expectations, and tolerances is a good place to begin this journey.

8. The less control the child has over your emotions and your relationship with your spouse, the more secure he will feel in the end.

9. The "father-supports-mother-supports-child" arrangement provides the psychological environment necessary for the formation of a secure attachment.

10. The key to successful single parenting is cultivating and maintaining an available support system, including an experienced family therapist.

11. The question is not *whether* you set aside time for yourself, your adult interests, adult friends, and spouse, but rather *when and how* you are going to do so.

2.
Who Is Your Child?

To Parent and Heal a Child,
You Must First Understand Him

Do not free a camel of the burden of his hump;
you may be freeing him from being a camel.

G. K. CHESTERTON

~ WE ALL STOOD PROUDLY at the adoption ceremony in which Marta and Lewis adopted Max. They had parented Max in foster care for two years, had gone through a lot with him, and now were making the commitment to be his permanent family. As we, the helping professionals, reflected on their progress and how far they had come as a family, Marta said "You know, he may be a weird child, but he is *my* weird child," and the whole family, including Max, smiled. She and Lewis had accepted all parts of Max and most of the time could really see the world through his eyes.

Your Unique Child

To parent, teach, or heal a child you must first understand him. Understanding a child involves perceiving him simultaneously on several levels, and the next few chapters will examine the fixed features, brain development, attachment, and developmental changes across several domains that are influenced by relationships. Children can move through the stages or get "stuck" depending on the nature of their resilience and their relationships.

Developmental change is influenced by species- and child-specific genetic factors ("nature," or fixed factors) as well as relational/environmental factors ("nurture," or variable factors). Species-specific genetic factors include the propensity to trust and seek relationship, to adapt to change, and to reason. Child-specific genetic factors include those traits inherited from his immediate familial pool that determine temperament and physical, cognitive, and emotional potential. In this chapter, we will be examining "fixed" aspects of your child's temperament.

Relationship and environmental influences (nurture) potentiate the

Genetically encoded temperament and resilience factors
determine physical, cognitive, and emotional *potentials*,
but it is relationships that guide the unfolding of the potentials

genetic factors (nature) that are present, either by turning them on or off or by not being present to turn them on or off. For example, if an infant is abandoned at birth, his species-specific genetic predisposition for trust in care will not be activated. On the other hand, if an infant is adequately nurtured by his primary caregiver, his species-specific genetic predisposition for trust in care will be activated, potentiating his trust in care.

Looking through a developmental lens, we can observe a child at any specific moment in his growth across a spectrum of domains. The goal of viewing a child developmentally is to identify and meet the age-specific need he is demonstrating with his behavior, which is his primary language. If we observe the child and his behavior solely with respect to his chronological age, we may miss the message he is trying to relay to us about his present need through his behavior. A caregiver facilitates her child's growth through correctly identifying and meeting his *developmental* need in any given moment. We will show you how to accomplish this in the next two chapters.

Before we proceed with seeking an understanding of your child from a developmental point of view, we first need to look at the core parts of him—those permanent factors that make him uniquely and unchangeably who he is. These include his genetically encoded temperament and his genetically determined physical, cognitive, and emotional potentials. We also need to identify the variable factors that have impacted your child's development to date—his relational and environmentally induced handicaps. The most influential relational/environmental factors include early interactions with the mother or primary caregiver, and those that relate to exposure to the elements beginning at the time of conception.

Fixed Factors: Your Child's Temperament

Children are neither good nor bad; they have varying temperaments or dispositions and attachment patterns. Your child's temperament is the inborn genetic disposition that underlies and modulates all aspects of his existence. Temperament is defined by the following parameters, each of which lies on a continuum: activity level, persistence, distractibility, initial reaction, adaptability, mood, intensity, sensitivity, and regularity. Temperament is, in effect, the "color of the lens" through which your child experiences and responds to his inner world, or internal environment, and to the outer world, his external environment. Temperament is the combination of traits that arrive with your child at birth that are then honed by his physical, social, and emotional environment and by his physical condition. Your child's temperament colors his overall behavioral style.

The type of temperament a child has is not attributable to how he is parented. Temperament is an entity in and of itself that is essential for parents to identify in their child so they can gauge their parenting approach to him individually. Parents cannot change or determine their child's temperament style; therefore, they need to mold their parenting around his temperament if they are to feel and actually be successful. *Differences in children's temperaments need to be accommodated instead of worked against to maximize harmony and minimize stress.* Understanding your child's temperament is critical to knowing how to work effectively with him. Especially if your child's temperament happens to differ greatly from yours, it is essential that you strive to understand and see the world as your child does.

A child's temperament affects the way parents feel about themselves personally and as parents. It affects the child's view of himself and shapes his perspective on the world. There is a "fit" that occurs between parent and child, and its quality is dependent upon both the parent's temperament and the child's. This fit can be comfortable, awkward, or difficult depending on the types of temperaments that are combined. In general, however, parents with children who have an easygoing temperament will feel happier, more successful, and more competent than will parents who are raising a child with a difficult temperament. Children with certain temperament traits will do better in school than will children without

---

Temperament is the inherited predisposition that is the core of your child's way of being in the world. You can *accommodate* your child's temperament, but you cannot *change* it.

these same traits. Particular temperament types can influence a child's health and make him more vulnerable to illness, accidents, and abuse. Recognizing your child's temperament is essential to understanding him fully and parenting him with success.

Since a child's temperamental disposition cannot be altered, it is necessary to be aware of his "fit" not only with his caregivers but also with his environment. Children whose temperaments do not mesh with their surroundings or adult expectations will display behavioral problems. If a child's temperament is not understood, parents and others may "medicalize" him in reaction to problematic behavior that results from the clash between his temperament and a particular environment. Unfortunately, this practice can lead parents astray and confuse the situation further. A child may have a challenging temperament *and/or* a medical condition. Since a child's temperament is part of him, it always needs to be taken into consideration when looking at other factors.

To determine your child's temperament, you can see a child specialist who will administer a formal assessment. However, you can begin here by looking at the lists of the three temperament types and nine temperament traits to get an idea about where your child might be on the temperament spectrum. These traits and types were standardized through the work of Drs. Alexander Thomas, Stella Chess, and Herbert Birch of New York University in their 1956 New York Longitudinal Study (NYLS) (Chess, et al., 1960; Chess, et al., 1965). These researchers found that 65 percent of children fit one of these three types, with the other 35 percent fitting combinations of these types.

Temperament Types and Traits

The three temperament types are:
➤ Easy or flexible (40 percent of all children)
➤ Difficult, active, or feisty (10 percent of all children)
➤ Slow to warm up or cautious (15 percent of all children)

The nine temperament traits that combine to form these types are:
➤ Activity level—the amount of physical motion exhibited during the day
➤ Persistence—the extent of continuation of behavior with or without interruption
➤ Distractibility—the ease of being interrupted by sound, light, other activity

➤ Initial reaction—response to novel situations, whether approaching or withdrawing

➤ Adaptability—the ease of changing behavior in a socially desirable way

➤ Mood—the quality of emotional expression, positive or negative

➤ Intensity—the amount of energy exhibited in emotional expression

➤ Sensitivity—the degree to which the person reacts to light, sound, and so on

➤ Regularity—the extent to which patterns of eating, sleeping, elimination, and so on are consistent or inconsistent from day to day

You can use this trait list yourself to make an informal assessment of your child. One way to do this is to plot how much each trait fits your child on a number line that goes from one to ten, with one being none of the time and ten being all of the time. The list of nine traits appears again on page 35 with a number line below each for rating the extent to which your child exhibits each trait. Rate your child's traits by placing a mark (▼) on the number line at the location that corresponds most closely to the measure of each trait of your child.

After plotting your child's traits, determine which *three traits most* characterize your child by picking those three ratings you have made that are *closest to either one or ten*. Use the example that Max's parents completed, page 34, to guide you in this process.

The example shows that Max rates *closest to one or ten* on the following three traits: activity (highly active), persistence (not persistent), and distractibility (easily distracted). In this example, these three traits, when combined, would place Max in the "difficult, active, or feisty" type temperament category. When you look at the results from the chart you make for your child, decide which three traits of your child's temperament fall closest to one or ten. Take these three traits as a whole and compare them to the three types of temperament: easy or flexible; difficult, active, or feisty; or slow to warm up or cautious. You may or may not be able to logically place your child's top three traits into a singular temperament type. Remember that 35 percent of all children do not fit neatly into one of the three types, but rather into some combination of types.

It is not necessary that you actually pinpoint your child's exact temperament type. Rather, you can use the results to hone in on your child's *outstanding temperament traits* so that you can see more accurately *who he*

Max's Temperament Traits

Activity level—my child is in physical motion the following amount during the day:

NONE OF THE TIME		SOME OF THE TIME		HALF OF THE TIME		MOST OF THE TIME		ALL OF THE TIME	
1	2	3	4	5	6	7	8	9 ▼	10

Persistence—my child sticks with the thing he is doing (whether interrupted or not) to this extent:

NONE OF THE TIME		SOME OF THE TIME		HALF OF THE TIME		MOST OF THE TIME		ALL OF THE TIME	
1	2 ▼	3	4	5	6	7	8	9	10

Distractibility—my child is easily interrupted by sound, motion, light, or another's activity:

NONE OF THE TIME		SOME OF THE TIME		HALF OF THE TIME		MOST OF THE TIME		ALL OF THE TIME	
1	2	3	4	5	6	7	8 ▼	9	10

Initial Reaction—my child tends to withdraw in response to novel situations:

NONE OF THE TIME		SOME OF THE TIME		HALF OF THE TIME		MOST OF THE TIME		ALL OF THE TIME	
1	2	3	4	5 ▼	6	7	8	9	10

Adaptability—it is easy for my child to change from one situation to another:

NONE OF THE TIME		SOME OF THE TIME		HALF OF THE TIME		MOST OF THE TIME		ALL OF THE TIME	
1	2	3	▼ 4	5	6	7	8	9	10

Mood—my child is in a good mood:

NONE OF THE TIME		SOME OF THE TIME		HALF OF THE TIME		MOST OF THE TIME		ALL OF THE TIME	
1	2	3	4	5	6	▼ 7	8	9	10

Intensity—the amount of energy my child exhibits in his emotional expression is:

NONE		SOME		MODERATE		HIGH		EXTREME	
1	2	3	4	5	6	7 ▼	8	9	10

Sensitivity—my child is sensitively affected by light, sound, touch, smell, and taste:

NONE OF THE TIME		SOME OF THE TIME		HALF OF THE TIME		MOST OF THE TIME		ALL OF THE TIME	
1	2	3	4	5	6	▼ 7	8	9	10

Regularity—my child's patterns of eating, sleeping, elimination, etc., are consistent from day to day:

NONE OF THE TIME		SOME OF THE TIME		HALF OF THE TIME		MOST OF THE TIME		ALL OF THE TIME	
1	2	3	4 ▼	5	6	7	8	9	10

Your Child's Temperament Traits

Activity level—my child is in physical motion the following amount during the day:

NONE OF THE TIME		SOME OF THE TIME		HALF OF THE TIME		MOST OF THE TIME		ALL OF THE TIME	
1	2	3	4	5	6	7	8	9	10

Persistence—my child sticks with the thing he is doing (whether interrupted or not) to this extent:

NONE OF THE TIME		SOME OF THE TIME		HALF OF THE TIME		MOST OF THE TIME		ALL OF THE TIME	
1	2	3	4	5	6	7	8	9	10

Distractibility—my child is easily interrupted by sound, motion, light, or another's activity:

NONE OF THE TIME		SOME OF THE TIME		HALF OF THE TIME		MOST OF THE TIME		ALL OF THE TIME	
1	2	3	4	5	6	7	8	9	10

Initial Reaction—my child tends to withdraw in response to novel situations:

NONE OF THE TIME		SOME OF THE TIME		HALF OF THE TIME		MOST OF THE TIME		ALL OF THE TIME	
1	2	3	4	5	6	7	8	9	10

Adaptability—it is easy for my child to change from one situation to another:

NONE OF THE TIME		SOME OF THE TIME		HALF OF THE TIME		MOST OF THE TIME		ALL OF THE TIME	
1	2	3	4	5	6	7	8	9	10

Mood—my child is in a good mood:

NONE OF THE TIME		SOME OF THE TIME		HALF OF THE TIME		MOST OF THE TIME		ALL OF THE TIME	
1	2	3	4	5	6	7	8	9	10

Intensity—the amount of energy my child exhibits in his emotional expression is:

NONE		SOME		MODERATE		HIGH		EXTREME	
1	2	3	4	5	6	7	8	9	10

Sensitivity—my child is sensitively affected by light, sound, touch, smell, and taste:

NONE OF THE TIME		SOME OF THE TIME		HALF OF THE TIME		MOST OF THE TIME		ALL OF THE TIME	
1	2	3	4	5	6	7	8	9	10

Regularity—my child's patterns of eating, sleeping, elimination, etc., are consistent from day to day:

NONE OF THE TIME		SOME OF THE TIME		HALF OF THE TIME		MOST OF THE TIME		ALL OF THE TIME	
1	2	3	4	5	6	7	8	9	10

is. Please remember that this is an informal, rough measure of your child's temperament, not an official assessment. The purpose of including this temperament chart is to help you "get" your child in a way that will more clearly inform your parenting. It is here for your interest and as a way for you to take a closer look at your child's "unbendable" parts. Hopefully, in working with this chart, you will have further pinpointed some valuable pieces of the puzzle that is your whole child.

Fixed Factors: Capacity for Resilience

Resilience is the genetically encoded potential to rebound readily from illness, depressed mood, and/or adversity. When a child is born with the capacity for resilience, he may be able to bounce back from the most horrendous experiences and go on to live robustly despite his past. Resilience also enables a child with a poor primary caregiver relationship to benefit greatly from contact with the well-attuned care of another adult, such as a teacher, neighbor, or extended family member, even if that contact is infrequent or irregular. It is possible for a child with such a relationship to attain a greater level of attachment than he has been able to with his primary caregiver.

The capacity for resilience is, like temperament, an inborn trait that can greatly affect the quality of the child's relationship with his caregiver, especially if that caregiver is abusive. If resilient, a child who is enduring physical, psychological, emotional, and even sexual abuse may be able to hold on to the sense that he is okay and that it is the abuser who has the problem. Functioning almost like a physical barrier, resilience can deflect an abuser's actions or words so that the projected shame does not sink into the child's psyche. The positive reflection of self that such a child can get from other adults, however, can penetrate and positively help define the child's sense of self.

Children who are not born with the capacity for resilience tend to suffer more in life, especially if they have been abused or neglected. These children tend to interpret their experience as a reflection of themselves; therefore, any negativity directed at them is absorbed and taken as a definition of self. Stress more deeply affects the non-resilient child, drawing down his reserves and making him more susceptible to suffering from illness and adverse experiences. Take a child who is resilient and a child who is not and expose them to the same experience, and there likely will

**Resilient children tend to bounce back more easily
in the face of adversity, but *non-resilient children fare much better
when they receive excellent care***

be two entirely different outcomes. Determining if a child is resilient or not can help permanent caregivers more closely gauge the level of intervention and prevention that the child needs, as well as more precisely attune to him.

On the other hand, there is increasing evidence that if you supply non-resilient children with exceptional care, they can do even better than resilient children who received adequate care (Dobbs, 2009). There is hope for your child, even if he might be considered non-resilient.

Fixed Factors: Your Child's Physical, Cognitive, and Emotional Genetic Potential

Whether your child came to you through birth or adoption, he carries a unique set of genes that determine everything from hair color to general IQ to emotional propensity. Even though the variables of relationship and environment have influenced and can continue to influence the unfolding of your child's genetic potential, he nevertheless can only progress as far as his genetic potential will carry him. You may or may not have information on members of your child's extended family that can give you clues as to what his potential might be. You also may or may not have the results of physical, cognitive, and emotional testing that has been done with your child or results from his completed years in school. Whatever they may be, your child's "fixed factors" can point to both his unrealized potential and his realized limitations.

The more information you can gather about your child's genetic makeup, the more accurately you can hone your expectations of him. Although it is often better to encourage and support your child in reaching beyond his present capabilities than not to do so, being realistic about his *potential* will keep you more closely attuned to who he is. Parents can be overzealous when it comes to providing their child with experiences and enrichment opportunities to the point of "missing" who their true child is. For instance, if college was really important in your life, but your child

Be realistic about your child's potential. Are you missing who he really is? Are your expectations harming or helping your relationship with him?

has a learning disability or a low cognitive potential, he may struggle in school emotionally, not only because school is hard but because he is unable to meet your expectations. Rather than critiquing his teacher or his initiative, parents must tune in to how difficult school is for him. Focus instead on those things your child *is* good at and those things he feels most confident doing.

Misattunement with regard to genetic potential can be the opening of what may become a great crevasse separating parent and child. If your child has a naturally excitable temperament, and you thrive on peace and quiet, it may be that you have to "up *your* game" rather than expecting the child to quiet down. In accepting your child for exactly who he is, you can ground yourself realistically in a solid place from which you can see and meet his needs accurately and build a solid relationship with him.

Variable Factors: Relational/Environmental Influences on Development

From the moment of conception, a child can have positive as well as detrimental experiences that affect his growth and development. These experiences act upon the child's genetics as well as on the course of his physical, moral, cognitive, sexual, social, and emotional maturation. Again, you may or may not know your child's complete history, but even small bits of information can help you to see your child more clearly.

In utero, multiple factors can negatively affect a growing fetus: the birth mother's lack of daily self-care; trauma or abuse suffered by the birth mother; exposure to environmental toxins, bacteria, or viruses; maternal depression; substance abuse on the part of the birth mother; her feelings of not wanting the child; and the birth mother receiving inadequate nutrition. Perinatal influences that can temporarily or permanently damage the infant just before, during, and after birth include preeclampsia, placenta previa, oxygen deprivation, and premature birth.

In infancy and early childhood, relational and environmental deficits that can affect growth include complications at birth; early orphanage

What emotional, physical, and relationship factors influenced your child's development?

placement; having multiple caregivers and/or placements; enduring chronic neglect, abuse, and/or trauma; having drug or alcohol-addicted parents; being "raised" by one's self or siblings; enduring a significant illness that separates a child from his mother; deprivation in learning environment; abandonment of a child by his birth mother; and profound poverty.

Some of the deficits resulting from negative experience can be healed or largely healed, while others cannot. For example, a birth mother's abuse of alcohol while her child is in utero can cause permanent and irreparable developmental damage that handicaps her child for life, while a child whose need for nurturing was insufficiently met may have suffered damage that can be greatly remedied through reparative parenting. The key is knowing as much as possible about a child's experiences so you can see him clearly for who he is in the present, and from there understand what parts of him you most likely can or cannot heal. Your child is who he is, *and yet* some aspects of your child remain more malleable than do others.

In Chapter 4, you will learn about all of the aspects of child development, and at that time you will have the opportunity to list the specifics that you know about your child's development and earliest years. The great news is that even with genetic and past environmental influences, *you* can have the greatest impact on your child's life, particularly if you understand who he really is. As the quotation at the beginning of this chapter says, do not try to "take the hump off of the camel" or your child will no longer be himself. Love him, understand him, and accept him as he is. You both will be better off for it!

Key Points for Chapter 2

1. Genetically encoded temperament and resilience factors determine your child's physical, cognitive, and emotional *potentials*, but it is the quality of his relationships that guide the unfolding of his potentials.

2. Temperament (whether easy, difficult, or slow to warm up) is the inherited predisposition that is the core of your child's way of being in the world. You can accommodate it but not change it. Be realistic about who you are and who your child is.

3. Resilience is also a heritable trait. Resilient children tend to bounce back more easily in the face of adversity, but there is increasing evidence that *non-resilient children can fare even better than their resilient peers*, if they receive excellent care.
4. Be realistic about your child's potential. Are you missing who he really is? Are your expectations harming or helping your relationship with him?

3.
Seeing the World
through Your Child's Frightened Eyes

Experiences During Early Brain Development
Impact How Your Child Sees the World

We don't see things as *they* are; we see things as *we* are.

ANAÏS NIN

〜 "MARCO USED TO SNEAK OUT of his bedroom in the middle of the night to steal food from the refrigerator. I couldn't understand why he felt he had to 'steal' the food, any more than I could understand why he couldn't sleep through the night but seemed to fall asleep suddenly and deeply in school. After all, we have loved him and given him safety for nine years. When will he ever feel safe?"

Marco was born on the streets of Rio de Janeiro, Brazil, and somehow survived his first nine months of trauma and neglect. His body bore the story of his infancy—cigarette burns, malnutrition, and smallpox scars—but that was only part of his story. Even though he had spent his next nine years in the safety of his adoptive parents' home, he constantly *sensed* danger from frustrated parents, teasing children, and even rainy weather, which used to mean long, wet nights without shelter. Marco *felt* alone—afraid of starving and sleeping deeply, always on the edge of surviving. This primitive survival instinct was "wired in" to the deepest parts of Marco's brain. He did not see the present world as *it* was—safe and secure; he saw the world as *he* was—a starving little boy in a world of danger.

Why We Need to Know about Brain Development

We study the brain to understand that sometimes your child's reaction is not about *you*, it is about *his fear* that has been "wired" deeply into his brain based on long-ago experiences. Your child cannot be talked out of his fear or rage because these traumatizing experiences happened when he had no words. We study the brain to understand the origin of your child's difficulties and to help you create new relational patterns and expectations for him that will help him heal.

Even in the womb, a fetus's nervous system is getting prepared for what life will be like through the rhythm of his mother's heartbeat and movements, the nutrients that flow through the umbilical cord, the level of stress his mother is experiencing, the sound of his mother's voice, and the smell of his mother. This "miracle of two" does not just occur in utero; it continues during the particularly sensitive period of the first three years of life, when the child's brain develops in response to patterned, repetitive experiences he has with his mother (Perry, 1995; Teicher, et al., 2002). If the experiences are most often soothing, correct, and timely (Ainsworth, et al., 1978), then the deepest part of the baby's brain is making connections that say, "It's okay to relax; you are safe and Mom will make sure of it." If the baby, like Marco in the story above, has the patterned, repetitive experience of danger—starvation, illness, and physical assault—his brain says, "Stay alert: danger is everywhere." The earlier these neural connections in the child's brain are established and the more critical they are for survival, the stronger they are. What the infant learns in these early years cannot be "unlearned." The infant's past trauma, which became embedded in his brain in the form of neural pathways, makes him feel as if he were going to die, so his survival instinct is triggered whenever he *perceives* danger. Although this has been a lifesaving feature of your child's brain, it can cause consternation for you, the unsuspecting parent in the present, who wonders why your child is behaving so reactively when the actual "threat," as *you see it*, is so low.

A child's brain development, as stimulated by his relational experience with others (or lack thereof), is the basis for all subsequent functioning. The brain is the organ that contains the self of your child, and it directs every aspect of his development. The kinds of connections that have developed in your child's brain determine the quality of his life, which in turn affect the quality of your life. The building of the neurological matrix in the brain is cumulative. The good news is that the brain is malleable throughout life and responsive to new experience. However, the "go-to" nature of the neural pathways that formed early on in primitive parts of

---

Your emotionally distressed child's behavior may seem irrational and confusing at times. If you understand what *he* is "seeing," you may be able to respond in a way that comforts his deepest fears instead of confirming them.

your child's brain can be difficult to change. New neural pathways must form, and the only way to create these alternative pathways is by providing your child with patterned, repetitive, corrective relational experience over time.

When we are not in danger, the highest part of the brain, the cortex, serves a role akin to that of a conductor of an orchestra. The conductor decides when particular areas of the brain need to be engaged, and for how long. The cortex "waves its baton," directing the players and integrating their parts into a cooperative and harmonious whole, yielding the desirable "top-down" mode of processing that ensures the cortex is in charge.

When we perceive danger, we tend to process information from the bottom of the brain upward, causing primitive reactivity instead of thoughtful responses, which leads to behavioral dysregulation. When your child's brain is operating from a bottom-up state, he is not able to feel trusting of you. Like Marco, your child did not learn to trust his earliest caregivers to keep him safe, and this lack of trust in caregivers became embedded in the primitive part of his brain.

Nonetheless, you will discover that you, as parents, can create new connections in your child's brain even after the natural developmental window has passed. However, a new behavior cannot be established with a singular desirable interaction; it can only be created via abundant, patterned, repetitive interactions. Some days it may frustrate you that even though you feel like you have given your child a million positive experiences, he still can revert to his old distrust. Keep in mind that those old pathways, like well-worn trails in the woods, will still be there, but the increasing strength of the pathways you are helping your child create via the corrective patterned experiences you are giving him are becoming stronger every day. Soon these new neural pathways will become your child's "go-to" patterns, changing the trajectory of your child's life and enabling him to live into his potential.

What Is Normal Brain Development?

An organ of adaptation, the brain develops its structures through interaction with others, whether that interaction is healthy or not. At birth, a baby's brain contains billions of neurons, almost all the neurons his brain will ever have. The arrangement, growth, and connection of these neurons are experience sensitive, with social interactions serving as the primary

**As the brain grows, the child's experiences actually "become flesh"
as the repetition of those experiences with his caregiver
stimulates neural growth and new connectivity**

stimulant. Repetitive, patterned experiences—good or bad—shape the wiring of the brain, whether the experiences happen early in a child's life or later in his recovery.

Our brains start forming prenatally, about three weeks after conception. Genetics (nature) influence the quality, base number, and initial arrangement of the brain cells (neurons) we will have. Genetics hold the potential for the brain to manifest a host of abilities as well as disorders. Meanwhile, experiences (nurture) determine *whether* the genetic code gets activated and, if so, *how* its potentials unfold and influence the growing brain. Nurture is the variable aspect of brain growth that includes all of the experiences a child may have during his lifetime. Therefore, what happens in the baby's life, especially in the baby's interpersonal relationships in those first few years, becomes highly significant.

At birth, the brain is not fully developed; it is only 30 percent of its eventual adult weight. Brain growth occurs as repetitive experiences act on and between neurons, multiplying their connections. For neurons to become fully functional, they need stimulation from the outside environment. Experiences fuel the brain's development, whereas the *absence* of experience, as in severe neglect, leaves the brain shrunken and only partially developed. Interactions with caregivers strongly stimulate a child's brain growth, causing connections to propagate robustly.

In the first three years, as a normal part of brain development, unused connections are "pruned," meaning they wither away, leaving only those connections that are used consistently. If a child repeatedly experienced toxic stress in his early relationships, connections in parts of his brain

**Our early experiences have a disproportionate impact
on brain development because they are the means by which
the brain will grow from 30 percent of adult brain weight at birth,
to 70 percent by age two, to 90 percent by age six**

involving memory and planning may be damaged and their growth potential may become limited even many years later. In the case of a child experiencing neglect, an inordinate amount of pruning may occur due to stress and lack of stimulation.

Godzilla, Fido, and Mother Teresa

A metaphor to help us understand brain development is the concept of the "triune" or three-part brain. Each part of the brain appears to have an experience-sensitive window of development (Chugani, 1998), and an infant's unique experiences determine how and to what each part responds later in life. We will refer to the lower and most primitive part of the brain as the "reptilian brain," the middle, emotional part as the "mammalian brain," and the upper, most sophisticated part as the "human brain." From the bottom up, each part of the brain builds upon the one below it. Therefore, if the lower part of the brain develops in an environment of danger, as in Marco's case, then the higher parts have the tendency to interpret, look for, and prepare for danger even when it does not exist. If all of Marco's energy is consumed by watching for danger, it will be hard for him to learn algebra or play soccer. If his parents become frustrated with him, he is likely to fear that he is on his own and that he needs to protect and fend for himself.

Knowing the function of each of the three parts of the brain will enable you to understand and more closely pinpoint the origin of your child's difficulties. If we can hone in on the area of the brain that is responding to the alarm, we can figure out how your child is seeing the world in that moment and then determine how to help him. Remember, it is not always about you, personally; it is about what your child is seeing and feeling— his *perception* of his experience.

Discovering the part of the brain fundamentally responsible for the particular difficulty the child is having allows us to choose the nurturing interventions he needs to heal

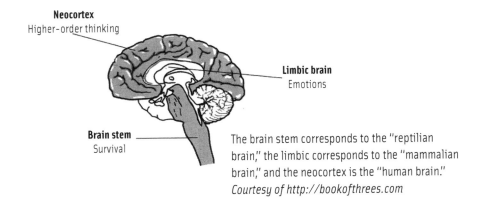

Neocortex
Higher-order thinking

Limbic brain
Emotions

Brain stem
Survival

The brain stem corresponds to the "reptilian brain," the limbic corresponds to the "mammalian brain," and the neocortex is the "human brain." *Courtesy of http://bookofthrees.com*

Survival: The Brain Stem ("Reptilian" Brain)

Developmentally first in the brain's wiring sequence, the lowest, "reptilian" part of the brain automatically operates all of the functions we need to stay alive physically. The brain stem functions outside of our conscious thought process and serves as our "automatic pilot." Think of Godzilla, who stomps around Tokyo, not because he is angry with the citizens but because he is feeling threatened and thus the need to fight for survival. The more stimulation he gets from hearing planes, guns, and voices over the loudspeakers, the more afraid he feels and the more rageful he becomes. However, the *whole* of Godzilla's brain functions like our brain stem—the lowest, reptilian part of our brain; therefore, he is *always* on autopilot.

Our brain stem serves as a relay station through which the signals from most of our senses pass between our body and our brain. Taste, touch, vision, and the sense of our position in space all pass through the reptilian brain. Independent from our will, our reptilian brain prompts us to react reflexively to threat with thrashing, distress, and primitive alertness, like Godzilla. This part of the brain regulates the level of our general resting state, our sleep, our body's temperature, our bodily sensations, and our most primitive arousal systems.

The brain stem's internal sensors give us information about our body's response to gravity, balance, and movement and tell us where we are in space. The proprioceptive (perception) system sends us signals about our body via our muscles, ligaments, and joints and registers the depth of touch or compression we receive (e.g., swaddling and holding a baby closely to soothe him). The tactile sense conveys information about the "flavor" of the physical contact we experience by way of our largest organ, the skin. This tactile sense "turns on" in utero and continues to mature with caregiver touch. All three parts of the brain are turned on via stimulation of the baby's senses, first by the baby's caregiver, then by the independent movements of the child himself. Coordination amongst these parts is crucial and develops as the child's physical abilities unfold developmentally through play.

The reptilian brain responds automatically to stimuli and cannot mediate the nature of the stimulation it receives. For example, it cannot shut out negative stimuli and let in only positive. In order to produce a calm state of equilibrium in our bodies, the reptilian brain requires a stable, controlled environment. Ideally, the person who engineers the baby's environment is an attuned primary caregiver who is consistently present to modify the baby's temperature, exposure to noise, stimuli, hunger, thirst, and arousal as necessary to return the baby to a calm resting state. Think about how we soothe infants: we reduce stimulation, we rock them, we touch them, we give them deep pressure at times through swaddling. Through this patterned, repetitive stimulation, the lower, primitive center becomes regulated and the infant experiences calm as his normal resting state.

However, if the caregiver is inconsistent in her response and if the infant is exposed to chaos or shouting, left in the cold or ignored, or is shaken, his little nervous system stays on alert and never reaches the calm state. Sleep is disrupted, arousal is high, proprioception is off, and touch is experienced as dangerous. Moreover, the infant's stress response inhibits brain development. Like Marco, the neglected or abused infant experiences a primitive, on-alert bodily reaction to his environment, which he comes to interpret as stress or danger.

The early experience the baby has with his primary caregiver—positive or negative—sets the stage for the quality of life he will have. Information

---

Since it cannot discriminate on its own, the reptilian brain needs an external monitor to judge and provide the exact experiences necessary for its growth and proper function, and that monitor is mother

we glean from observation and testing can give us specific information about a child's reptilian brain development that can guide us in his healing. The prospect of you, your child's primary caregiver, presently providing just the right environment, stimulation, and experiences that will allow your child's reptilian brain to develop fully, is one we will explore as we learn more about our capacity to modify a child's difficult behaviors by changing his brain.

Potential Problems and Solutions: The "Reptilian" Brain

Stress caused by any of the aforementioned circumstances bathes the infant's impressionable developing neurocircuitry in cortisol, the stress hormone that signals, "Stop! Alert!"—suspending normal functioning and growth. Prolonged stress turns on the flow of cortisol and does not turn it off. The absence of the infant's birth mother arouses the most profound stress because at this developmental moment his sense of self is completely merged with that of his mother. The baby senses that death is imminent when he is separated for a significant time from his birth mother. However, because he is still alive, the infant's only option is to disavow this devastating emotional state. Thus, the infant learns to dissociate from his pain, which alters neural pathways for pain perception. Later in childhood, this child may have an atypical or absent response to his own pain and not recognize pain that he may be inflicting on others.

The traumatized child's malfunctioning stress response prevents him from discerning what is truly threatening from what is not. This child may seem to be oblivious to danger, taking inappropriate risks and behaving recklessly. A distorted recognition of threat shows up in other ways, such as superficial engagement with unknown others (followed later by promiscuity); perception of a harmless object, event, or person as dangerous; incidents of rage or mute isolation that result from a chronic sense of fear that cannot be verbalized; and the constant need to control that arises from a deep-set fear of the world as dangerous. Generalized, ever-present anxiety takes hold and becomes the child's "resting state," markedly diminishing his tolerance threshold so that the slightest frustration or provocation will set him off.

Developmental disruptions in the lower brain lead to body-system regulation problems. The inability to feel true hunger and satiation causes gorging, excessive focus on food and eating, hoarding, and eating disorders.

Appropriate and timely signals for elimination can be distorted or nearly absent, yielding to diurnal accidents and age-inappropriate bed-wetting. Night terrors erupt and disturbed sleep patterns persist when the regulatory system for sleep is developed based on trauma. The child may have difficulty getting to sleep and staying asleep, which disrupts not only his restorative rest but also that of his parents. The child may seem clumsy, unaware of where his body is in space. Likewise, sensitivity to touch may be altered, and he may be insensitive to pain or hypersensitive to touch.

Key interventions involve those that regulate this lower system. Regulation of the child and his environment through his parents' abundant and timely interventions provides the most crucial experience the child needs to build new neural pathways in his lower brain. Parent-assisted formal occupational therapy interventions are often helpful for these children. Large muscle movement and vestibular interventions such as swinging, walking, rocking, or sitting on a ball—an action that requires constant body adjustment—can improve self-regulation. Experiencing body pressure through wearing weighted vests or through self- or parent-squeezing exercises can help. Soothing music set at the tempo of a resting heart (sixty to seventy beats per minute) can assist in the child's acquisition of self-regulation. Massage and brushing interventions can help the child learn more accurate sensitivity to touch.

Emotions: The Limbic System ("Mammalian" Brain)

Built upon the reptilian brain and named for responses and behaviors we have in common with other warm-blooded creatures, the "mammalian brain" is the center that drives our emotions and provides a sense of self-as-connected and responsive to others' emotions. Think of your dog: "Fido" looks into your eyes and comes to understand from your physical disposition and your emotional state what his behavior should be. He can respond to your soothing tone of voice and to your tension or anger, and he is oriented to what is meaningful to *you*. Just as your emotions determine what is meaningful for your pet mammal, a mother's emotions determine what is meaningful for her infant.

This mammalian part of the human brain—the limbic system—is the seat of our drive for attachment, which is essential for our survival as individuals and as a species. For all warm-blooded animals, living in groups provides the protection and the opportunity to provide the nurturing that

Within the mammalian brain lie the neural pathways that hold the predominant emotional disposition of the infant and the infant's basic sense of self as good or bad

is necessary for raising our young to maturity. The bonding instinct (nature) impels us toward others, while the *quality* of the caregiver's response (nurture) determines whether we develop the social abilities needed to be a part of the group. The use of reparative nurturing—giving your child in the present those relational experiences he missed early on—is what this handbook is all about. Using this approach can influence where a child of early trauma and neglect ends up—inside or outside the bars of prison.

The mammalian brain is the seat of and arousal agent for our primary feelings—joy, anger, fear, sadness, and shame; it enables us to recognize those emotions in others. Once again, the child's relational experience drives the production of neural connections in this part of the brain. The child's primary caregiver serves as an interface between the child and his experience of the world, "coloring" how external stimuli imprint in her child's brain. Her actions, reactions, narration, interpretations, and creation of the meaning of events become the child's actions, interpretations, and understanding. If the child's primary caregiver is optimistic, if she sees the good in her life and her place in the world, and if she regulates her feelings well, her child will begin to see himself as good, worthy, and acceptable. He will learn to interpret and react to his experiences in a like manner and perceive the world as a safe place.

On the other hand, if the caregiver is depressed or absent, or is pessimistic or aggressive—seeing primarily the wrongs in the world and interpreting those wrongs as personal vendettas—the child will learn that the world is unsafe, unwelcoming, and perhaps even dangerous. In this case, the child comes to believe that he is "bad," alone, and unacceptable and perceives that the world and relationships are frightening, antagonistic, and dismissing. This basic sense of self, whether oriented toward delight, pleasure, and goodness or toward anger, depression, and hostility, is formed by about nine months of age (Zero to Three, 2003).

You may have had, or will have, the experience of being with a child whose basic sense of self is negative. No matter how many positive experiences he has had, he does not believe that he is any good. He insists that *you* are angry with him when *he* has had a bad day and he hears you as yelling when you are just slightly raising your voice. He sees and he hears you based on what he sees through his frightened eyes and hears with ears tuned into the negative—rejection, his own unworthiness, and his unacceptability. Changing this stance cannot happen through verbal reassurance, any more than altering the personality of a whipped dog will change through words. It changes only with your consistent emotional response, with your recognition of and soothing response to his fear, and through the patterned, *repetitive* response of acceptance, emotional regulation, and interpretation of events as meaningful in a positive way.

Potential Problems and Solutions: The "Mammalian" Brain

Disruption of limbic system (mammalian brain) development underlies problems with the child's emotional responses and interpretation of others' emotions. The inability to readily focus awareness externally gives rise to lack of empathy, emotional outbursts, hypersensitivity to rejection, depression, anxiety, over-interpretation of anger, rage at perceived interpersonal slights, an internal experience of shame, unwillingness to try new activities, sensitivity to criticism, and the perception that others are intentionally harming him. As the child focuses on internal emotions at the cost of external realities, he can also be distracted, experience difficulty shifting attention and tracking, and display low frustration tolerance.

Key interventions are those that may reduce the child's sense of perceived threat. Adults can change their tone of voice and their level of eye contact to reduce the threat. Understanding and attuning with the child's emotional responses (e.g., "I wonder if you're feeling pretty anxious right now"), apologizing when you have inadvertently hurt the child, and exaggerating positive emotional expression may help in the moment. Helping the child interpret events and emotions differently and encouraging his attempts at trying new activities (without trying to talk him out of his fatalistic sense of doom) may eventually amend his sense of worthlessness.

Higher-Order Thinking: The Neocortex ("Human" Brain)

The top of the brain is the neocortex, or what we refer to as the "human brain" because its highest functions are unique to our species—homo sapiens—setting us apart from other mammals. The human brain is the highest and most evolved center in the brain in terms of both position and capability. While this part of the brain continues to grow and change throughout life as we engage in new experiences and learn to do new tasks, it has two experience-sensitive growth periods—eighteen to thirty-six months and adolescence.

The neocortex is responsible for the way that we, as adults, respond when we are not in crisis and enables us to regulate ourselves to function successfully in a crisis. Self-awareness, explicit memory, inhibition of impulses, solving problems, and calming ourselves down are capacities of the neocortex that allow us to be our best, rational self. A particular part of the neocortex that is in physical proximity to the limbic system (the midbrain) and has reciprocal connections to the limbic system and smooth muscles develops in response to infant need and maternal response to those needs (Schore, 1994). This area, the right prefrontal cortex, houses connections formed by the infant experiencing his mother's response to his needs. If a mother is attentive and regulates her infant's distress, this part of the cortex becomes an internalized "Mother Teresa" that sends soothing signals down to the activated limbic system and/or brain stem, essentially communicating, "It's okay—mother will take care of your needs." If a mother's emotional response to her infant's needs is angry, overwhelming, not in sync, or absent, the distress signals from the infant's lower brain become heightened, arousing distressed emotions in his mammalian brain. When the infant is experiencing this unmet need for connection, his stomach and intestinal system react, his eyes expect anger, and he feels shame. The infant's body is on high alert: "I am alone and little in a dangerous world!"

We all tend to parent as we were parented, whether we have had the experience of being soothed or criticized. The right prefrontal cortex houses the experientially-based template for how we will parent when we are adults. The good news is that this part of the brain remains plastic throughout life and is capable of changing in response to new, patterned, repetitive experiences with caregivers and later with spouses. We can become better parents than our parents were and become better partners if

---

Neural connections in the right prefrontal cortex develop based on the infant's experience of his mother's response to his needs

we have new experiences of being soothed, of having our emotions mirrored and our needs met, and of feeling meaningful connection.

The prefrontal cortex of children who have been abused and neglected is altered in its ability to regulate arousal levels coming from the mammalian or reptilian brain. For these children, an internal or external soothing presence cannot override impulsive behavior. Greatly fluctuating emotions thwart any attempt at bringing thought to the fore to gain control. Therefore, a child behaves impulsively and unhealthily, not because of how he thinks but because of how he feels. Emotions such as fear and pain are so strong that there is no way for a child to cope rationally. Parental attunement is crucial not only to helping the child to reregulate but also in helping him, after he is regulated, come to understand what has been going on inside him. Teaching the child to label his feelings and to form a narrative about his internal world reengages the child's capacity for thought and reestablishes the primacy of the cortex.

Potential Problems and Solutions: The Neocortex ("Human" Brain)

The "conductor" of overall body-mind coordination, the neocortex, can fall victim to developmental disorders not only in itself but also in those of the mid- and lower brain as it attempts to coordinate the disarray of neural connections. This can result in a host of functional challenges including difficulty with cause-and-effect thinking, inability to regulate emotions based on a caregiver's response, and inadequate conscience development (i.e., "If I want it, I'll just take it!").

Key interventions are those in which relationships play the major role. As caregivers, the better able we are to understand and reflect the child's world to him, just as a mother would do for her one-year-old infant, the better able the child will be to understand himself and others. Providing consistent structure and following through with consequences helps the child learn cause and effect without harming his view of himself. We need to understand the child's experience of feeling alone and be present for him, knowing that it will take innumerable patterned, repetitive experiences of us being there for him before he believes that we can make a difference.

Using the Brain Map

This survey of the potential results of developmental interruption in each part of the brain gives us defined neighborhoods to look at as we begin sorting out the puzzle of the hurt child. Any one child will not have all of the difficulties presented; rather, he will have an array of symptoms particular to him. Each child is one of a kind, and each child's experiences are unique to him. We cannot create a one-size-fits-all formula for healing traumatized and neglected children. However, in treating any hurt child, we must begin at the beginning and formulate our approach from the bottom up.

The three-part structure of the brain gives us a viable map we can use to create a healing plan tailored to your unique child. Carefully reviewing the child's early history, combined with observing his interactions with others—especially with his primary caregiver—along with examining the results of available physical and neurocognitive testing, give us some "knowns" that we can superimpose upon a map of a developmentally sound brain to more closely pinpoint the child's developmental gaps. Although we need to create an initial treatment plan, it is only the starting point of a process and journey that will unfold at the child's pace and in the child's way.

We know that Marco's brain was wired for survival on the streets of Brazil and that now he is safe, though he does not feel safe. What can help him? Marco's parents enrolled him in occupational therapy to give his body the patterned experiences he missed so that parts of his brain could develop more fully. They played rhythmic music before he went to bed and had a regular ritual of rocking him, even as he got older. By about age twelve, Marco began to participate in track and swimming, and the patterned, repetitive muscle movements of running and swimming helped him to feel more competent, to reduce his fear, and to feel bodily regulation. Marco's parents understood that certain events like him being exposed to their stress, having a bad day at school, or the weather turning to rain triggered his survival responses, and they began to help him be aware of those triggers. They responded by providing him with extra after-school snacks and fruit while they chatted about the day and by talking about his fear in their regular family meetings. They truly began to see the world through Marco's frightened eyes, and as a result he felt less alone, more connected with his parents, and safer in the world.

Key Points for Chapter 3

1. Your emotionally distressed child's behavior may seem irrational and confusing at times. If you understand what he is "seeing," you may be able to respond in a way that comforts his deepest fears instead of confirming them.

2. As the brain grows, the child's experiences "become flesh" as the repetition of experiences with his caregiver stimulates neural growth and connection.

3. Our early experiences have a disproportionate impact on brain development because they are the means by which the brain will grow from 30 percent of adult brain weight at birth, to 70 percent by age two, to 90 percent by age six (Berk, 2004).

4. Discovering the part of the brain fundamentally responsible for the particular difficulty the child is having allows us to choose the nurturing interventions he needs to heal.

5. The reptilian brain (brain stem) contains connections that determine the arousal level of the infant based on caregiver's response. Later, this part of the brain may respond to environmental conditions that trigger a sense of danger.

6. The mammalian brain (limbic system) contains connections that determine the predominant emotional tone for the infant and the infant's basic sense of self-as-good or -bad. Later, this part of the brain may respond to relational and emotional conditions that trigger feelings of safety, security, and goodness or of danger, anxiety, and badness.

7. The right, prefrontal cortex contains connections that reflect the mother's response to the infant's needs. Later, this part of the brain responds to attachment security within relationships either by initiating soothing responses or by signaling a sense of danger and loss.

4.
Thinking Like a Five-Year-Old
What Happened and When Impacts
Your Child's View of Relationships

There is in every child at every stage a new miracle of vigorous unfolding,
which constitutes a new hope and a new responsibility for all.

ERIK ERIKSON

~ FIVE-YEAR-OLD PATRICIA was angry when her mother told her to stop
playing magic castle and to come to dinner, so she told her mother, "Go
away!" Patricia, used to getting her way, continued to play, not noticing
that her mother had slipped out the door. A little later, Patricia went to
the kitchen and ate the dinner her mother laid out. After she finished, she
called out for her mom, and when she got no answer, she went to the neighbor's, where her mom would frequently go for coffee.

The neighbor, who knew Patricia's mom had an alcohol problem, told
Patricia to stay put and wait for her mom, who would be back soon. At bedtime, Patricia's mom still hadn't returned, and the neighbor told Patricia
that "her mom said" for her to sleep overnight. Patricia's mom still was not
back when Patricia awoke at the neighbor's house the next morning, and
her mom stayed away so many days thereafter that the neighbor had to call
Children's Services. As a result, when Patricia was placed in a foster home,
she came to believe that her mom never came back because she had told
her to go away that evening she disappeared.

Time and Development Changes Everything

A child who is five years old understands the world in a fundamentally
different way than he does at thirteen. At five, he has different cognitive
and physical abilities, different social and emotional needs, different sexual awareness, and different moral understanding than he does when he
is thirteen. For example, at five, the child may not understand that ghosts
are not real, nor can he pole vault, handle frustration on his own, or be
without his parents for lengthy periods of time. As parents, we naturally
tend to our child's needs according to his chronological age because we are
assuming his chronological and developmental ages are the same. However, for children who have had problematic early years, chronological

and developmental ages are not the same. Aspects of development may be skewed and irregular, with some aspects remaining "stuck" and some progressing at a regular chronological clip. For example, when Patricia in the story above was ten years old, she remained fearful, as if she were still five, that her anger would cause people to disappear, so her anger came out "sideways" in destruction of property and rages at being told "no." Although she looked like a ten-year-old physically, her emotional responses were "stuck" at a five-year-old level. This is why we need to understand child developmental stages across all domains—to be able to identify and meet the child's need at the *expressed* developmental age instead of responding to the child at his chronological age.

Within the field of child development, human maturation has been dissected into stages in order to describe how and why we develop the way we do. A child cannot achieve developmental milestones on his own: healthy child development at every stage and across all developmental domains occurs *within relationship*, beginning at conception and continuing through childhood to adulthood. From conception through toddlerhood, that crucial relationship is the one the child has with his primary caregiver. Therefore, we draw aspects from child developmental theory that are grounded in a *relational* perspective to inform our work of healing children. This chapter and the next will guide you through the process of identifying your child's expressed developmental age in order to meet him there so you can begin to heal him.

Developmental Domains

When looking at child development, we see it as a whole divided into seven domains: relational, psychosocial, emotional, physical, cognitive, sexual, and moral. Children develop and learn in all domains at once to varying degrees within each domain. The amount of growth that occurs during any given stage of development will vary by domain. Development in each domain is dependent upon the changes that have occurred and

---

Development within each domain is affected by a unique combination of biology and relationship, and changes in one domain impact changes in other domains

are occurring within the other domains. At any particular age there may be phenomenal growth in some domains while there may be little to none in others. Activity or lack thereof in one domain at a certain age can affect development in other domains. Delays in the development of one domain will negatively affect growth within other domains.

Within each domain, processes are complex and rarely occur in isolation. Rather, domains overlap and their functions become integrated, resulting in the development of the child as a whole. Ideally, in the context of adequate nurturing, development follows a relatively orderly progression and takes place over time. Growth rate varies with each unique child, affected by the individual's genetic and environmental influences. Additionally, environmental factors such as inadequate nurturing can alter the unfolding of overall development, leaving gaps in some domains that negatively influence growth in others. The work of healing a hurt child is to identify those gaps and their influence on his general development, then to repair the gaps by giving the child the relational and environmental experiences he has missed.

As you foster the development of your child as a whole, you need to have a keen awareness of the basic domains wherein your child will assimilate his developmental and developmentally reparative experiences. The following are the domains and their particulars.

Developmental Domains
➤ Relational: one-to-one interaction and interdependency. The earliest and most essential interpersonal task is forming an attachment to the primary caregiver, as this relationship becomes the template for all relationships in the future.
➤ Psychosocial: interactions with others, groups, and communities. The assumption of social roles, familial and group membership, individual and cultural identity, and religious or spiritual orientation are social developmental tasks grounded in childhood experiences.
➤ Emotional: anything related to one's emotions, temperament, personal traits and characteristics, personality and identity, self-esteem, and mood and affect regulation as appropriate for age and situation.
➤ Physical: anything relating to the physical body structure, including bones and cartilage, muscles and ligaments, skin, organs and the circulatory system, and neurons and their networks. Motor,

sensory, and nervous system development and the coordination amongst systems are considered within this domain.

➤ Cognitive: anything related to the intellect or to mental processes, including abstract and concrete thought, perception, memory, reasoning, concept development, and problem solving. Language, in its requirements for symbolization, memory, and creation of meaning, is the most complex of the developing cognitive activities.

➤ Sexual: the domain encompassing physical, cognitive, psychosocial, emotional, and moral domains. Growth in the sexual domain is ongoing through all developmental stages beginning in utero. Motivating connection with others, the sexual drive includes touch for affiliation, bonding, soothing, pleasure, and procreation.

➤ Moral: conceptualization and internalization of social rules and mores, shared values, and principles that are protected and organized around a higher order taught via parental modeling, indoctrination, values clarification, and developmentally appropriate education.

The Nature of Developmental Stages

Within each developmental domain and across the spectrum of domains, there are specific and fixed developmental stages that mark human growth. These stages share several defining attributes, as follows.

Stages are Progressive

Individual differentiation, or becoming independent, along with the accumulation and refinement of skills reveal the progressive nature of stages of development. Developmental stages build upon one another, as in the example of mobility, where crawling leads to walking, which develops into the ability to run and jump. Over time, skills become refined; for example, in the development of fine motor skills, the child begins by grasping small objects with the thumb and forefinger and gradually develops the ability to hold a crayon and to color. Developmental delays will become amplified across time. Those delays that are reparable require remediation beginning with the earliest instance of developmental interruption.

Stages are Marked by the Completion of a Particular Developmental Task

Change occurs within each individual stage while the sequence in which the stages unfold remains fixed. The completion of each stage is marked by the mastery of its specific developmental task. Within the array of Jean Piaget's developmental stages, for example, a child in the preoperational stage of cognitive development lacks the understanding of conservation of matter. Children who have not mastered this stage do not know that the amount or volume of an object does not change when its shape changes. For instance, if there were two identically sized pieces of clay, one rolled up in the shape of a ball, the other rolled into a snake, in front of a child who is working through the preoperational stage, he would say that compared with the ball, the snake piece is bigger because of its length. A child moves into the concrete operational stage when he can discern that, in fact, the two pieces of clay are of the same volume and two whole cookies are more than two half cookies.

Some Stages Appear without Seeming to Have Developed from an Obvious Precursor

A new ability or cognitive capacity that marks the beginning of a new stage may appear to have no precursor. In an infant, stranger anxiety seemingly develops instantaneously at around eight months. The infant's newfound cognitive capacity to differentiate between his primary caregiver and others, which occurs at this time, results in clear and recognizable anxiety upon separation from his caregiver. The infant has achieved the developmental stage of attachment marked by the understanding that he and his caregiver are not one and the same entity.

Successive Stages Evolve from the Simple to the Complex

Stages occur in a regular sequence that is biologically driven, and they generally occur in the same way across cultures. For example, in the domain of cognitive development, the sensorimotor stage, wherein a child learns about himself and his environment through motor and reflex actions, is followed by the preoperational stage, wherein a child begins to use symbols to represent objects. The unfolding of development across all domains is predictable, and successive developmental stages progress toward increasing complexity.

Child Development by Domain

Widely accepted developmental theories exist for several of the seven do-mains, while there is no standard theory that is widely relied upon for others. Here we outline normative developmental stages in the relational, psychosocial, emotional, physical, cognitive, sexual, and moral domains. We are including this information to provide a general reference for de-velopmental stages in each domain that will help you in the assessment of your unique child and his needs. Memorizing any of the levels and stages is unnecessary. What is important to remember is that in every domain there is an age-related way of behaving and of understanding and seeing relationships, cause and effect, and the world that is qualitatively different from a previous or succeeding way of seeing. Understanding the stages helps you not only understand how your child sees the world cur-rently, but how he understood what happened to him before he came into your care.

Relational Development

We begin by looking at the relational domain because of the broad and comprehensive effects the child/primary caregiver relationship has on development. John Bowlby, a British psychiatrist in the first half of the twentieth century whose interest in child development led to his pioneer-ing work in attachment theory, believed that there are four distinguishing characteristics of attachment (Bowlby, 1982).

Bowlby's Characteristics of Attachment
1. Proximity Maintenance—the desire to be near the people to whom we are attached
2. Safe Haven—returning to the attachment figure for comfort and safety when the child needs it and/or in the face of a fear or threat
3. Secure Base—the attachment figure acts as a base of security from which the child can explore the surrounding environment
4. Separation Distress—anxiety that occurs in the absence of the at-tachment figure

The concept that not only the child's attachment to the primary care-giver but the *quality* of that attachment determined psychological well-ness ran contrary to the accepted theories of the time. Bowlby's own

Through relationship with the primary caregiver initially, and then with the secondary caregiver and others, the child incorporates his earliest experience into his view of himself and the world

childhood experience of maternal deprivation, due to the belief that too much maternal attention would spoil a child, provided him with the deep emotional insight that underlies his theory. Today, it is widely accepted that maternal-infant bonding is vital to normal child development. In fact, we now measure a child's wellness based on the *quality of his early relationship with his primary caregiver* because research confirms that it *directly influences* development of all aspects of the whole self—relational, psychosocial, emotional, physical, cognitive, sexual, and moral.

Invariably, emotionally distressed children have experienced a break in their relationship with their primary caregiver early on (conception to three years of age), whether due to neglect, abuse, abandonment, or removal. We must examine the nature of the child's primal relationship to understand why a child is the way he is, what his relational deficits are, and what remedial relational interventions we need to carry out to heal him.

The primary caregiver's 24/7 role begins at conception and lasts to age three, when the child is ready to begin to depend upon dad as well as mom. At age three, while still relying on mom for a secure base, the child's relational circle gradually expands to include dad as half the parent team, siblings, and extended family. At age five, the child branches out to include relationships with friends, teachers, and community members with these external-to-the-family interactions gradually increasing through emancipation.

As you look back at your child's early development, you will be examining his relational unfolding beginning with conception, if you have that information. Concentration will be on your child's experiences with a primary caregiver through age three because of the indispensable and 24/7 nature of her presence. We need to know as much as possible about this period of time in your child's life so we can more thoroughly understand

The most fundamental relational experience occurs in these early years, and deficits in this experience are at the core of the distressed child's difficulties

Relational Development Progression

Conception to 9 Months—
Relational Entity: "MomMe"
- infant and mother are one; the infant does not experience a separateness
- mom's feelings are infant's feelings
- wholly dependent upon one consistent, ever-present primary caregiver for all needs
- primary caregiver's interventions to regulate the infant are essential
- continuous physical and emotional proximity vital

9 to 12 Months—
Relational Entity: "Mom/Me"
- infant begins to "hatch," i.e., psychologically separate from his primary caregiver
- protests this separation when primary caregiver is absent
- begins to understand that primary caregiver still exists if she is not present so protests to get her to return
- continuous proximity and regulation still essential

12 to 18 Months—
Relational Entity: "Mom & Me"
- infant experiences herself separate from primary caregiver, but still fully needs her to be present as a safe base
- fear of strangers
- very upset when separated from mother or when can't accomplish a task
- resentment of new baby (nothing must come between Mom & Me)
- proximity with caregiver as safe haven essential

18 Months to 3 Years—
Relational Entity: "Mom & Me & Other Parent"
- three people are present in the child's inner world
- copies parents' actions
- dependent, clinging, possessive
- parallel play with others
- resists parental demands
- active bids for autonomy (challenges parents' "nos")
- proximity to primary caregiver as secure base from which to explore and to which to return essential

3 to 4 Years—
Relational Entity: "Mom & Me & Dad & Siblings"
- jealousy of same-sex parent; "romantic" attachment to parent of opposite sex (3–5 years)
- beginning of identification with same-sex parent: in play, practices sex-role activities
- imitates parents
- cooperatively plays with others
- imaginary friend (continues through age 6 or so)
- still needs parents as omnipresent secure base

4 to 5 Years—
Relational Entity: "Mom & Me & Dad & Siblings & Friends & Extended Family"
- starts to show responsibility and express guilt
- prefers to play with other children
- becomes competitive
- prefers sex-appropriate activities
- still needs secure base in parents, but can tolerate short periods of separateness

5 to 12 Years—
Relational Entity: "Mom & Me & Dad & Siblings & Extended Family & Peers & Teachers & Community"
- interested in others, what others are doing
- social engagement in school milieu
- needs parental proximity and affirmation, and parents as secure base non-school hours

12 to 18 Years—
Relational Entity: "ME & Peers & (Mom—Dad—Siblings—Extended Family—Teachers—Community)"
- self-absorbed
- wants to be with peer group more than family
- needs parental availability, support, and guidance for security, affirmation, and safety

(Child Development Institute, 2015; Horner, 1989; Mahler, et al., 1975; Kohlstaedt, 2005; Berger, 2014)

the gaps in his relational development, which essentially means the gaps in his relationship with his primary caregiver. *The most fundamental relational experience occurs in these early years, and deficits in this experience are at the core of the distressed child's difficulties.*

Psychosocial Development

In the 1950s, based on his extensive psychotherapy work with children and adolescents from all socioeconomic backgrounds, psychiatrist Erik Erikson developed an eight-stage model for human psychosocial development (Erikson, 1993). He considered each stage to be defined by an age-specific "psychosocial crisis" that must be satisfactorily resolved before the next stage would be sufficiently negotiated. Each of the eight stages presents a relational dilemma that must be settled positively in order for the child or adolescent to be capable of reaching social, emotional, and relational maturity.

It is through Erikson's psychosocial developmental lens that we see the world from the point of view of the growing infant, child, and adolescent. Our intention is to understand where along a child's developmental path there may have been a developmental deficit or break so that we can address that break with reparative parenting. Notice (in the table on page 65) that stages one through four require consistent, active parental (the agent) input, while in stages five and above the agent role shifts to the self. Thus, it is through the child's relational development as outlined on page 63 that his basic sense of identity is formed.

The successful resolution of each dilemma—that is, being able to answer "yes" to the questions in the following descriptions—is essential for the child to be able to experience the feeling of well-being, not just momentarily, but deeply in his core self. The achievement of "I'm worthy, I trust others and the world," "I'm capable," "I'm patient and respect authority," "I'm competent," and "I'm me" is necessary to become fully adult. Children who do not resolve each of these five foundational dilemmas experience great difficulties in relationships, in their social and emotional lives, and in finding their way in the world. Failing to resolve the first dilemma creates a domino effect that thwarts the child's capacity to resolve all others. Successful resolve of the first dilemma but failure to resolve the second thwarts the resolve of each subsequent dilemma, and so on. The chart shows Erikson's stages of psychosocial development. For our

Erikson's Eight Stages of Psychosocial Development

STAGE	THEME	DILEMMA	AGE
1	Hope	**Trust vs. Mistrust** *Does my caregiver sufficiently meet my needs so that I trust others, feel worthy, and trust that the world is okay?*	**Infants, Birth to 12 to 18 months**
2	Will	**Autonomy vs. Shame and Doubt** *Am I supported by my parents in my bid for autonomy while I am given appropriate limits that keep me safe so that I learn "I can" while trusting/ respecting authority?*	**Toddlers, 18 months to 3 years**
3	Purpose	**Initiative vs. Guilt** *Am I encouraged by my parents to pursue my desires and goals such that I learn to take initiative while managing my frustration so I can feel like a "good kid"?*	**Preschool, 3 to 6 years**
4	Competence	**Industry vs. Inferiority** *Am I encouraged and supported by my parents in being successfully industrious such that I come to feel competent?*	**Childhood, 6 to 12 years**
5	Fidelity	**Identity vs. Role Confusion** *Who am I, what do I believe, and can I be myself and still be accepted by peers and family?*	**Adolescence, 12 to 18 years**
6	Love	**Intimacy vs. Isolation**	**Young Adults, 19 to 40 years**
7	Care	**Generativity vs. Stagnation**	**Middle Adulthood, 40 to 65 years**
8	Wisdom	**Ego Integrity vs. Despair**	**Seniors, 65 years onward**

purposes of understanding child development, we provide descriptions only for ages birth to eighteen years old.

Accurately identifying your child's psychosocial resolution status is the crucial first step in helping him heal. Due to neglect and abuse that occurs from conception through the first eighteen months, the majority of the highly distressed children we are working with have not resolved the first dilemma, "I'm worthy, and I trust others and the world." The implications of this fact are profound: *A child cannot resolve this foundational dilemma without being in relationship with a primary caregiver who is committed for the long run.* Thus, the most important work you, as a parent, will be doing with your distressed child is re-creating his primal experience, this time with the abundance of care, attention, and presence he missed.

Accomplishing this with an older child can seem like an overwhelming proposition; however, it really is as "simple" as replicating a baby's experience with a loving, ever-present primary caregiver—the investment of 24/7 care for your child until his "cup is full." Once you and your child resolve his first dilemma, then you will move on to address and resolve each subsequent dilemma. Time is relative in this whole process. What

The first four of Erikson's psychosocial crises (through age twelve) are resolved within the child's relationship with his parent. Can you see where the break was with the child whom you are parenting?

naturally unfolds at each age and stage when a child is adequately cared for from the start may not and (except for the first stage) likely will not take as long in your reparenting work as it would have had you raised your child from the beginning.

Emotional Development

The unfolding of the emotional spectrum begins before birth and expands rapidly such that the child can express the five major emotions—glad, sad, mad, scared, guilt/shame—usually by the age of about three years (Child Development Institute, 2015). Tension-release gives way to distress-relief at two months, and as it does, happiness emerges. Fear/anger then comes on board around eight months, followed by guilt/shame as early as age two. Sadness arrives as the child's language and cognitive development allows. Notice (in the table on page 67) that the child must have a clear sense of the importance of his primary attachment figure before he begins to feel guilt and shame. Look to the relationship, then, if your ten-year-old does not seem to experience appropriate guilt. Does he have a relationship with you that allows him to feel bad about hurting you without feeling like he will lose you?

Unfortunately, the rapid natural unfolding of human emotion is not always accompanied by vital parental mirroring—a process wherein the parent naturally reflects back her child's emotions in words and nonverbal cues—which enables the child to understand what he is feeling and why. Thus, the distressed child, who has experienced a break with his primary caregiver in the first three years, will not be able to accurately label/understand his emotions or match them to internal sensations. This phenomenon becomes extremely important as we develop an understanding of a child's remedial needs. The "reparenting" necessary to fill the child's

Developing the range and subtlety of emotions requires brain growth and accurate and timely reflection from the parent

Emotional Development

In utero to 1 month ➤ generalized tension release	**1½ to 2 years** ➤ temper tantrums (1–3 years) ➤ resentment of new baby ➤ does opposite of what he is told (18 months–3 years)
2 to 3 months ➤ distress relief ➤ some smiles	
4 to 6 months ➤ distress relief ➤ enjoys being cuddled, played with ➤ social smile in response to another	**2 to 3 years** ➤ fear of separation ➤ negativistic ➤ violent emotions, anger ➤ dependent, clinging
7 to 9 months ➤ protests separation from mother ➤ enjoyment of interpersonal games like "peek-a-boo"	**3 to 4 years** ➤ affectionate toward parents ➤ jealousy of same-sex parent ➤ imaginary fears of dark, injury, etc. (3–5 years) ➤ expressions of sadness
10 to 12 months ➤ can give affection ➤ fear of strangers	
1 to 1½ years ➤ very upset when separated from mother ➤ fear of bath	**4 to 5 years** ➤ responsibility and guilt ➤ feels pride in accomplishment

developmental gaps must include parental mirroring of emotion and exploration of the relationship between emotion and internal sensation.

Physical Development

Although physical development is a domain that may be more familiar than others, it is important to review the unfolding of a child's physical capacity to make sure all stages have been successfully negotiated. Distressed children, especially those who were physically neglected, often have developmental gaps in their physical growth. Early physical stimulation is essential not only for building the capacity for motor skills, but also for the expansion of neural networks throughout the brain that affect all domains of functioning. Outward, visible signs, which are a reflection of brain growth, can give us much of the information we need to assess lapses in growth. Remedial physical and occupational therapy, neurofeedback, and neurological reorganization approaches can address the deficits in the growth of the entire brain. Healing a child's physical deficits greatly enhances his capacity for relationship due to the comprehensive effect of physical development on brain development.

Physical Development: The First Year through the Fifth Year

Birth to 3 months
Babies begin learning the basics of self-movement and begin to master the skills needed for hand-to-mouth coordination and holding objects. They develop vestibular, proprioceptive, and skin sensorial abilities through physical movement and exploration, which are foundational for all later learning. They make basic distinctions in vision, hearing, smelling, tasting, touch, temperature, and perception of pain.

3 to 6 months
Babies are quickly becoming stronger and more agile and can pull themselves up on a crib. They can make discoveries with objects (for example, a rattle makes noise when it is moved) and localize sounds.

6 to 9 months
"Child-proofing" becomes important as babies get more mobile. During this time, most begin to control trunk and hands, sit without support, and crawl about; they can reach and grab objects.

9 to 12 months
By this time, most babies can stand unaided and walk with aid. They can respond to simple commands.

1 to 2 years
Walking and self-initiated movement become easier, balance improves, and eye-hand coordination becomes more precise. Toddlers can control bowel and bladder, turn knobs, and walk up and down stairs with aid.

2 to 3 years
Children become more comfortable with motion, increasing speed and coordination. They can manipulate small objects with increased control. They can run, kick a ball, and ride a tricycle.

3 to 4 years
Movement and balance improve. Most children can stand on one leg, use a slide, throw and catch a ball, and draw crosses and circles. Children develop the ability to cross the midline, or move one hand, foot, or eye into the space of the other hand, foot, or eye. This is a crucial skill for writing, reading, and putting on shoes and socks.

4 to 5 years
Children are now more confident, and most are able to master mature motor control: they can skip, broad jump, dress themselves. They develop fine motor skills that allow them to write, use safety scissors, and cut a continuous line.

(http://www.pbs.org/wholechild/abc/physical.html)

Close observation of a child reveals the spectrum of physical abilities he has and does not have at a given chronological age, this being our measure of his developmental maturity. Often overlooked in terms of relational capacity, complete physical development provides the neural foundation for capacities in all domains. Notice also that the development of the infant's physical ability to separate from his mother corresponds to psychological separation. We'll see that the child's cognitive development

Understanding physical development can help you see what your child may have missed. Can he use both sides of his body, is he hypersensitive or insensitive to touch, does he lose coordination when stressed?

goes right along with physical development in his capacity to separate. But as is the theme in this book, it is only through the child's secure relationship with his attachment figure that physical and psychological separation and identity development can happen effectively.

Cognitive Development

In the 1920s, child psychologist Jean Piaget formulated his theory of cognitive development (Piaget, 1992). Piaget described four stages of cognitive development, each relating to a person's ability to understand and assimilate new information. What is important to know about cognitive development is that it unfolds more as a continuum than as set-in-stone ages and stages. We want to look for the place in the continuum where the child is cognitively, no matter his chronological age. Understanding how the child conceptualizes the world will allow you to relate to him within *his* view, instead of yours. The ability to see the world from the *child's* point of view is crucial if you are to build a relationship with the *real child*, as opposed to who you think he is or should be. Notice (on page 70) how cognitive development parallels physical development and how they both set the stage for development of relationship and eventually identity.

It is also important when reviewing a child's early experience to note how old he was when events happened and how he most likely understood those events given his relational, emotional, and cognitive development. For instance, in the story of Patricia, she was removed from her biological mother at age four. Because of her age, she most likely saw that removal as her fault. She was at the stage of magical thinking where saying it makes it so. Her interpretation of this experience in turn may impact her willingness to assert her anger, and it may come out in indirect ways that don't threaten to make someone else "disappear."

One of the most common places along the cognitive continuum for a distressed child to become stuck is in the area of concrete thinking. For example, the child may only understand those things he can tangibly see, hear, or experience—"the now"—instead of being able to think in abstract terms—"the not-now"—about possibilities, ideas, and what-ifs. This can be frustrating for parents because the only timeframe in which they can work with this child is the now. Relying on the child to imagine his present actions in context of the future as leverage for change does not work.

Piaget's Four Stages of Cognitive Development

STAGE	AGE	TASK
Sensorimotor	**Birth to 2**	➤ The infant learns about himself and his environment through his senses, motor, and reflex actions ➤ Establishes habits, hand-eye coordination, object permanence (things continue to exist even when no longer present to the senses) ➤ Experimentation/creativity/trial and error experiments; "little scientists" ➤ Differentiates self from objects ➤ Recognizes self as agent of action and begins to act intentionally, e.g., shaking a rattle to make a noise ➤ Learning takes place via assimilation—absorbing new information and creating new schemas (a set idea about what something is)—and accommodation—modifying an existing schema to include new information
Preoperational	**2 to 6**	➤ The child begins to use symbols to represent objects ➤ Develops the ability to imagine, but thinking makes it so (magical thinking) ➤ Reasons more intuitively than logically ➤ Thinking is egocentric: has difficulty taking the viewpoint of others, has difficulty appreciating future time ➤ Classifies objects by a single feature, for example groups all blue blocks together regardless of shape
Concrete	**7 to 14**	➤ Makes rational judgments, thinks logically about objects and events (it is what it is), gradually moving toward thinking/understanding abstractly ➤ Understands conservation (the number, mass, and weight remains the same no matter the organization) ➤ Classifies/sorts objects according to several features and can order them in series along a single dimension such as size
Formal Operations	**14 and up**	➤ Capable of hypothetical and deductive reasoning (hypothesize, test, reevaluate) ➤ Understands abstract concepts ➤ Engages in formal, systematic thinking ➤ Becomes concerned with the hypothetical, the future, and ideological problems

Therefore, parents are limited to the present mode in providing motivation for the child, while their own ability to think beyond the present pulls them out of the moment and out of the child's world.

Sexual Development

Distressed children often display sexualized behavior that is inappropriate for the situation, and/or does not match the norm for their chronological age. As uncomfortable as these behaviors may be for parents, they

Identifying how your child thinks about the world—his cognitive level of development—can help you intervene in ways that are successful. Are you talking about "what-ifs" or the future to your *concrete-thinking* child?

need to be addressed proactively. The origin of inappropriate sexualized behavior must be understood, as it is typically connected with exposure, abuse, or trauma the child has experienced. Parents who are uncomfortable dealing with this aspect of their child's behavior can instead focus on the behavior as an expression of the child's need to heal from abuse or trauma. Merely forbidding a particular behavior will not meet the child's need for resolution, which can be thoroughly addressed only within his relationship with his primary caregiver.

Toni Cavanagh Johnson, PhD, child sexual behavior specialist, states that there is no standard for normal sexual behaviors in children (Johnson, 2014, 2015). This is due to differences in developmental age, exposure, family and societal values, and living conditions. Although each of us has our own sense of what seems *not normal* in terms of childhood sexual behavior, there are some distinctions about what is within a normal range that are useful for us in helping emotionally distressed children. Johnson has divided the continuum of childhood sexual behaviors into four groups. In this chapter, we discuss only the first group. In Chapter 12, we will discuss the other three.

Johnson's Continuum of Childhood Sexual Behaviors
1. Natural and Healthy Childhood Sexual Behaviors
2. Sexually Reactive Children
3. Mutually Engage in Full Range of Adult Sexual Behaviors
4. Children Who Molest Other Children

Understanding that a child naturally becomes a sexual being while still in utero may give parents a foundation upon which they can establish their sense of what is normal behavior. An infant experiences an involuntary reflexive sexual response—erection or lubrication—which has occurred in ninety-minute cycles since his fetal state. After birth, the infant gradually becomes more actively interested in exploring his own body, at first proceeding randomly and indiscriminately, then more thoroughly but without giving preferential treatment to his genitals. An infant experiences his mouth (oral gratification) as being the most important source of sensual pleasure.

Johnson describes the unfolding of sexual behavior as the infant becomes a child, breaking down this development by ages within her four divisions of the continuum as follows.

Johnson's Stages of Sexual Development

Most children ages 0 through 3 will
➤ be curious and explore their own bodies
➤ watch or poke at others' bodies
➤ randomly touch their genitals for pleasure
➤ talk openly about their bodies
➤ be able to say and understand, when taught, the appropriate names for body parts (head, nose, stomach, penis, vagina, etc.)
➤ experience an erection or vaginal lubrication

Most children ages 4 and 5 will
➤ experience vaginal lubrication or erection
➤ randomly touch their genitals for pleasure
➤ feel curiosity about everything, including bathroom functions and where babies come from
➤ play games like "doctor"
➤ have the ability to recognize males and females
➤ begin to recognize traditional male and female gender roles and to distinguish these gender roles
➤ be conscious of one's own body, how it appears to others as well as how it functions

Most children ages 6 through 8 will
➤ prefer to socialize with their own gender almost exclusively and maintain a rigid separation between males and females
➤ recognize the social stigmas and taboos surrounding sexuality (especially if parents are nervous about the subject)
➤ understand more complex ideas with regard to sexuality and begin to understand intercourse apart from making a baby
➤ look to peers, media, and other sources for information about sex
➤ mimic or practice kissing/dating
➤ possibly engage in same-gender sexual exploration
➤ have a stronger self-concept in terms of gender and body image

Most children ages 9 through 12 will
➤ have an emerging sense of self as a young adult
➤ feel conscious of their sexuality and how they choose to express it
➤ understand jokes with sexual content
➤ feel concerns about whether they are normal (i.e., is it normal to masturbate, have wet dreams, etc.)
➤ feel anxious about puberty, when it will happen, how it will occur, how to be prepared, etc.
➤ feel shy about asking questions of caregivers, especially regarding sexuality, and may act like they already know all the answers
➤ value privacy highly

Most children ages 13 through 17 will
➤ understand that they are sexual and understand the options and consequences of sexual expression
➤ choose to express their sexuality in ways that may or may not include sexual intercourse
➤ recognize the components of healthy and unhealthy relationships
➤ have a clear understanding of the possible consequences of sexual intercourse
➤ have the ability to make reasoned choices about sex based on knowledge
➤ recognize the role media plays in spreading views about sex
➤ have the capacity to learn about intimate, loving, long-term relationships
➤ have an understanding of their own sexual orientation, which is different from sexual behavior

Most adolescents ages 18 and over will
➤ enter into intimate sexual and emotional relationships
➤ understand their own sexual orientation, although they may still experiment
➤ understand sexuality as connected to commitment and planning for the future
➤ shift their emphasis from self to others
➤ experience more intense sexuality

Important, but not included here by Johnson in her summary, is the child's interest in his own urine and feces, which develops naturally during the period of eighteen months to three and a half years as he

Children naturally explore their bodies. Their sexual interest in themselves and others develops in line with other age-related relational, social, emotional, cognitive, and physical changes.

becomes potty-trained. In this period, the child can develop an anal focus in exploration of his sexuality. Normatively, this may be a passing stage some children traverse on their way through their sexual maturation. Unless the child gets stuck in this stage, preferring things anal over things genital, parents need not maintain concern.

Moral Development

When we consider what it takes to have a moral center—a conscience—we can see that at its core, conscience requires adequate relational, psychosocial, cognitive, and emotional development. For a child to care about others, he has to have had the infant experience of being cared for adequately enough by his primary caregiver to develop relational security and trust. When a child comes to trust his caregiver, he feels bonded to her and thus unequivocally values his relationship with her. When the child displeases his caregiver and she gets upset with him, he worries his relationship with her may be at risk. The child then begins to think about how his actions might affect the relationship with his caregiver because he does not want to fall out of favor with her. As the child gets older, he generalizes this concern for how he affects relationships and begins to consider his impact on other relationships: he will have developed a conscience. Learning right from wrong originates out of the same trust and value a well-cared-for child comes to feel with and for his primary caregiver. If the child's caregiver tells him that an action is wrong, he will not want to displease her by doing this wrong action. Later in his development, the

Stages of moral development unfold in synchrony with relational, psychosocial, emotional, and cognitive development of the child; the more the child is understood and feels secure in relationships and in the world, the more developed his sense of justice and morality become

child will gain the ability to think abstractly, at which time he will be able to understand right and wrong as ethical principles. A parent who has established a safe and trusting relationship with her child can and does use her relationship with him as leverage in parenting. The child does as the parent requests because he wants to remain in her good graces.

However, if a child has not been cared for adequately, if he has been hurt in response to having a need, then mistrust and hurt are what he knows, and these feelings become the lens through which he sees the world. He has not developed relational security and trust; thus he feels alone in the world, just trying to survive. Since this hurt child does not trust anyone to take care of him, he does whatever he needs to do, including stealing, lying, and hurting others, in order to meet his needs. Lacking the ability to think abstractly, this child is unable to take another's point of view. He cannot see that another person might feel differently than he feels, nor does he care about others or his impact on them. Additionally, if his emotions remain undifferentiated because he did not have anyone to notice and reflect his anger, fear, happiness, sadness, and shame as distinct states, he cannot read his own feelings, let alone those of others.

Moral sensibility naturally develops in childhood if a child is appropriately cared for and nurtured. There are particular behaviors we see in children who have not been adequately cared for in their early years: an enduring lack of conscience, undue focus on self-interest past the age of six, persistent disrespect for authority continuing after the toddler years, and relentless "con-artist" behavior are all indications a child has not developed a reliance on adults in his early years. While these behaviors are understandably unpleasant, frustrating, and very concerning for parents, they are behaviors through which a child can mature over time if parents provide him with a consistent and attuned relationship.

Lawrence Kohlberg created a theory regarding the stages of moral development (Kohlberg, 1974) that came from Piaget's theories of cognitive development. Many distressed children remain in the pre-conventional stage of moral development due to relational insecurity borne out of inadequate caregiving in infancy (see page 76).

Kohlberg's Stages of Moral Development

LEVEL	STAGE/AGE	DESCRIPTION
1	**Pre-Conventional/2–6 years**	1. Obedience/punishment orientation: "How can I avoid punishment?" 2. Self-interest orientation: "What's in it for me?" paying for a benefit
2	**Conventional/7–14 years**	3. Interpersonal accord and conformity orientation: social norms/good boy–good girl attitude 4. Authority/social order–maintaining orientation: law and order morality
3	**Post-Conventional**	5. Social contract orientation: principled conscience 6. Universal ethical principles

Key Points for Chapter 4

1. Development within each domain is affected by a unique combination of biology and relationship, and changes in one domain impact changes in other domains.

2. The seven domains are: relational, psychosocial, emotional, physical, cognitive, sexual, and moral.

3. Stages are progressive, some stages appear without seeming to have developed from an obvious precursor, and successive stages evolve from the simple to the complex.

4. Bowlby's four precepts of attachment are proximity maintenance, safe haven, secure base, and separation distress.

5. Through relationship with the primary caregiver initially, and then with the secondary caregiver and others, the child incorporates his earliest experience into his view of himself and the world.

6. The most fundamental relational experience occurs in the first years, and deficits in this experience are at the core of the distressed child's difficulties.

7. A child's identity and the way he consistently responds to others and to society involve the resolution of Erikson's eight psychosocial crises, the first four of which are resolved within the child's relationship with his parents.

8. Stages of moral development unfold in synchrony with relational, psychosocial, emotional, and cognitive development of the child.

5.
One Moment He's Two, the Next Moment He's Fifteen

Understanding Your Child's Developmental Skews

The hunger for love is much more difficult to remove than the hunger for bread.

MOTHER TERESA, ROMAN CATHOLIC NUN

〜 I WALKED INTO the family's living room for my weekly visit and was surprised to see Marsha, a very large thirteen-year-old girl, sitting on the lap of her foster mother, Anne, a thirty-year-old, very small woman. I noticed Marsha's behavior, which was not that of a thirteen-year-old, immediately. She was tracing Anne's face much like a two-year-old might trace her mother's face. She was looking deeply into Anne's eyes, seeing the delight that most nine-month-old infants find in their mother's eyes. Marsha's overall behavior seemed to me to be that of a one-year-old, and I saw she was getting the nurturing that I knew she'd missed when she was abandoned in infancy. When I later asked Marsha about her time with Anne, she replied, "I was getting my 'mommy time'! Anne says I missed out on being mommied when I was a baby and so she is giving me lots of mommy time."

The Developmental Need Beneath the Behavior

As we have seen, developmental stages occur and can be tracked both within the child himself across the relational, psychosocial, emotional, physical, cognitive, sexual, and moral domains and within the relationship between the child and his primary caregiver. In the previous chapters, you studied child development from both age and domain perspectives, prefaced with the premise that each child is unique. Our sole purpose in teaching you child development is this: you must be able to recognize your child's need at the development level he is expressing it. This is the task you will learn in this chapter of the child development portion of the book. Be assured that in the intervention chapters we will focus on teaching you *how to meet and parent* your child at his identified developmental level, whether the child is momentarily regressed or stuck in a developmental stage.

Seeing your child "as he is" will be essential to you understanding what he needs from *you* to complete his development in any given domain

Learning to identify your child's expressed developmental level accurately so that you can respond to his need takes practice and patience. Most parents need to refer to the preceding sections of the developmental section quite often in order to match up the behavior they are seeing in their child to its correct developmental age. We presented the material in both age and domain formats to make this process as smooth and straightforward as possible. It is time for you to put this wealth of information to use to get to know your child thoroughly and on the deepest level possible so you can do the work of healing him. We will help you "get into your child's head" by seeing the world through his eyes and his needs, because "We don't see things as *they* are; we see things as *we* are."

Chronological Development versus Developmental Age

A child's developmental age is not necessarily the same as his chronological age. If a child experienced chronic neglect, abuse, or trauma, his linear development in any or all domains may have been disrupted. Thus, this child's developmental profile will be skewed in relation to his chronological age because his development was arrested by his unfortunate experiences. If the child's parent does not recognize or accept his developmental age and instead responds to him at his chronological age, she will be unsuccessful and her child's need will go unmet.

For example, let us say your five-year-old is throwing a grand tantrum in response to you saying "no" to his request for a cookie. If developmentally on track, your five-year-old child would not have had a tantrum. He might have complained about your denial of his want and let it go, or he might *seem* to let it go and later sneak a cookie behind your back. However, in this case, the child's tantruming behavior belies his chronological age. Therefore, it would be fruitless and frustrating to respond to his behavior with an explanation as you might with a developmentally normal

Understanding the developmental age of your child's behavior is vital so that you can meet his need successfully

Troubled children may get "stuck" at certain stages of development or regress to earlier stages in times of distress

five-year-old, as this would not curtail his tantrum—in fact, it would probably exacerbate it.

For that reason, you would need to respond to the tantruming behavior at this child's present *developmental age of two* by pulling him into your lap and soothing him. It is the developmental task of a two-year-old to learn to self-regulate, which he learns to do within the relationship with his primary caregiver. This response, then, would be appropriate and helpful because the tantrum is telling you that the child *cannot self-regulate* in the moment and needs you to do it for him, which is the way he will learn to regulate himself.

Although the potential to move smoothly through developmental stages is there, how the child masters each stage depends on the level of relational safety he experiences with his primary caregiver. A child moves through or gets stuck at certain stages in development based on *the level of safety he feels and the nature of his relationship with his primary caregiver.* Troubled children may get "stuck" at certain stages or go back to those stages in times of distress, whether that stress is real or perceived. The five-year-old in our example is showing us that either he has momentarily regressed or he has not yet completed this two-year-old developmental stage. In either case, he needs you to help him negotiate his frustration in the now. Discerning whether the behavior signifies a momentary regression or represents an incomplete stage takes a longitudinal view of the child's developmental status. Accumulating a series of domain charts for your child, like the one on page 80, over time provides the information needed to make the assessment.

The Developmental Domain Chart

Jim FitzGerald, CEO of Intermountain, developed this domain chart to help understand a child's developmental skews (FitzGerald, 2001). Using a chart like the one below, you will be mapping your child's *developmental status* at any point in time across domains. Notice that the child's chronological age is only stated in the chart's header, while the rest of the chart reflects the child's developmental age.

My child's present chronological age is __5__ **years** __2__ **months. Date** 01-27-2010

Developmental Age	Domains						
	RELATIONAL	PSYCHOSOCIAL	EMOTIONAL	PHYSICAL	COGNITIVE	SEXUAL	MORAL
16							
15							
14							
13							
12							
11							
10							
9							
8							
7							
6							
5	X	X	X	X	X	X	X
4							
3							
2							
1							
0							

This chart reflects a child who is developmentally five years old across all domains. This child has not experienced relational trauma, abuse, or neglect. Notice that the lines connecting the Xs, which mark the child's developmental age, form a straight line.

Using the Domain Chart

We will give you several examples to help you understand how to use the domain chart in working with your child. We will start with considering the five-year-old who is throwing a grand tantrum in response to you saying "no" to his request for a cookie. Let us add to his history the fact that the child pushes you away, refusing to let you intervene in his behavior or to soothe him because he is not yet able to allow himself to be soothed by his primary caregiver. Due to neglect, this child has learned to handle life on his own, independent of caregivers, so he feels he does not need

In responding to your child's need, find the youngest developmental age he is expressing amongst the domains and intervene accordingly

anyone. Even in his display of the tantruming behavior that matches an age three years lower than his chronological age, the child is not accessible for caregiver intervention because of his lack of trust.

In assessing a child's developmental level across the domains, the most important and sometimes the most difficult thing to do is to *set aside* his chronological age to look at the actual behavior itself. In this case, part of the child's behavior can be described as a two-year-old's on-the-floor-beating-fists tantrum. The other part of the behavior is the rejection of adult comfort—the behavior of a child who feels more independent than expected for his chronological age. Confusing and contradictory as these behaviors are when taken together, they nevertheless give us the

My child's present chronological age is __5__ years __2__ months.

Developmental Age	RELATIONAL	PSYCHOSOCIAL	EMOTIONAL	PHYSICAL	COGNITIVE	SEXUAL	MORAL
16							
15							
14							
13							
12							
11							
10							
9							
8		X					
7							
6							
5				X		X	
4							
3							
2			X		X		X
1							
0	X						

information we need to map the child's development across the seven domains and thus to determine his current need.

At this moment, the child in our example is five years old chronologically but eight years old developmentally in the social domain due to his premature independence, which is attachment deficit–related. In the relational domain, because he never learned to trust and depend upon a primary caregiver, this child remains infantile. Cognitively, "later" does not exist for him in terms of getting his cookie; "now" is all he knows due to his concrete thinking level. He is five years old developmentally in the physical and sexual domains, while he is two years old developmentally in the emotional domain (having a tantrum) and in the moral domain (Me, me, me!).

The chart on page 81 reflects a child who is *not* developmentally five years old across all domains. This child has experienced relational trauma, abuse, or neglect. Notice that the lines connecting the Xs, which mark the child's developmental age, form a *skewed* line. The map of this child's current developmental status would display a skewed profile rather than a level one. In responding to this child's needs, we would look to find *the youngest developmental age he is expressing* and respond accordingly. Therefore, the care this child needs in the present matches that which we would give an infant: picking him up and holding and rocking him. However, because the child is rejecting adult soothing, the adult would remain in the room speaking calmly to the child, first waiting until he deescalated his behavior, then picking him up to hold and rock him.

The child considered in the chart on page 83 is a teenager who is having significant behavioral dysregulation both at home and at school. This child is often triggered by comments or events that stimulate his shame response. He can become both verbally and physically violent immediately when he *interprets* his present experience as a condemnation of himself.

The origin of the child's core shame is severe abuse, which started in the womb, and profound neglect, which he experienced from the moment of his birth. He did not have his needs met very often by his primary caregiver; thus, early on he became self-reliant. His behavioral models were his birth parents, with his mother displaying dissociation and depression, and his father displaying high reactivity and unpredictable rages, which often became physically violent.

Again, this chart reflects the development of a child who is much younger across most domains than his chronological age; thus the chart

My child's present chronological age is __15__ **years** __1__ **months.**

Developmental Age	Domains						
	RELATIONAL	PSYCHOSOCIAL	EMOTIONAL	PHYSICAL	COGNITIVE	SEXUAL	MORAL
16				X+			
15							
14							
13							
12							
11							
10							
9							
8							
7							
6							
5						X	
4					X		
3							
2		X	X				X
1							
0	X						

is skewed. In this child's relational, psychosocial, emotional, and moral developmental domains, his capacities are primal and preverbal due to the abuse and neglect he suffered. Although chronologically he is fifteen, this child operates mostly from unconscious defensive impulses that have all along served to keep him safe in a world he cannot cognitively understand with any more sophistication than a five-year-old. Yet, he is in a fifteen-year-old body with the physical capacity of at least a sixteen-year-old adolescent, which renders him a danger to himself and others when he is volatile. In order for parents and teachers to relate to him in a way that does not trigger his primal rage, they must use an approach not unlike that which is used with a baby: soft voice, minimal expectations, attending to physical needs such as hunger, thirst, elimination, rest, and climate control.

If adults were to approach this child with expectations that are fitting for a teenager—maintaining personal grooming, keeping his room clean, treating his belongings with respect, doing algebra homework, having give-and-take relationships with peers, and so on—this child would certainly become highly dysregulated on a regular basis. He does not have the ability to accomplish these chronologically age-appropriate tasks, nor can he control his primal emotions; thus, when he is expected to perform, he easily and rapidly becomes highly dysregulated. Adults, if they are not attuned to the child's infantile developmental needs, can become very intolerant of a fifteen-year-old who is as self-absorbed as an infant and who has the capacity to cause major violence and disrupt the status quo on a regular basis.

The next example (page 85) is that of a child who was highly precocious for her age in several domains, while in the relational domain she remained infantile due to a minimally attuned primary relationship with her birth mother. The child was sexually abused from an early age by her mother's boyfriend, a man who did meet her need for food, clothing, and shelter in a somewhat attuned way but who exploited her need for physical contact, instead using her to meet his needs for closeness and sex. Thus, this girl was somewhat able to function in the world of a ten-year-old, but with highly sexualized social, emotional, and physical behaviors. Relationally, this child's development had remained infantile due to her unmet needs for safety, security, and trust in a primary caregiver. She never learned to truly let go and depend upon an adult; instead, she became controlling of adults through her ability to seductively charm them.

This girl behaved socially, emotionally, physically, and sexually like a teenager, and in fact had already entered puberty when she was nine years old, a common occurence for children who have been sexually exploited. However, this behavior was just that—a mimicking of the behavioral traits of a teen over-engrossed in her sexuality. Morally, the girl was no more than a toddler, reflecting the age when the sexual abuse hijacked her development in that domain. Cognitively, this child was a bit younger than her peers because her premature focus on sexuality displaced her ability to concentrate academically. Healing this child's relational wound would become time intensive in that her survival had become entwined with her ability to control adults with her sexualized behavior, rather than being built upon trust and dependency on an adult who could truly see and meet her needs.

My child's present chronological age is __10__ **years** __3__ **months.**

Developmental Age	Domains						
	RELATIONAL	PSYCHOSOCIAL	EMOTIONAL	PHYSICAL	COGNITIVE	SEXUAL	MORAL
16						X	
15							
14		X		X			
13							
12			X				
11							
10							
9							
8					X		
7							
6							
5							
4							
3							
2							X
1							
0	X						

Now we will go back to the vignette of Marsha that began this chapter and look at her developmental chart. We know that she is thirteen, is large for her chronological age, and was sitting on her foster mother's lap, tracing her face. Marsha also craves sweets, and when her mother says that she has to wait for an ice cream until after dinner, she throws a fit. As we find out, when she hears "no" or "later," she thinks "never." We also discover that Marsha at times dresses provocatively and dances around in front of adult males seductively. She takes things she wants from her mother's purse as long as no one is looking. How would you chart Marsha's development across the domains? On page 86, put an "X" in the box that matches Marsha's developmental age in each domain; then connect the Xs with lines to get a sense of her developmental skews.

Marsha's present chronological age is __13__ years __3__ months.

Developmental Age	Domains						
	RELATIONAL	PSYCHOSOCIAL	EMOTIONAL	PHYSICAL	COGNITIVE	SEXUAL	MORAL
16							
15							
14							
13							
12							
11							
10							
9							
8							
7							
6							
5							
4							
3							
2							
1							
0							

As a final exercise, the chart on page 87 is for you to complete for your own child at his present level of development. Making a pictorial representation of your child's expressed developmental age will be useful in both seeing (and accepting!) your child as he is in the present, in identifying his needs, and in choosing effective interventions. The goal of understanding your child's developmental profile at any given moment is to help you provide your child with the structure, support, and nurturance at the level he is expressing his need.

Repeat this exercise at intervals throughout the year. Over time, you will be able to see your child's progress by comparing the series of charts you have accumulated. Having a longitudinal view is valuable for parents who feel discouraged when faced with what they feel in the moment to be yet another behavior indicative of incomplete development.

My child's present chronological age is _____ years _____ months.

Developmental Age	Domains						
	RELATIONAL	PSYCHOSOCIAL	EMOTIONAL	PHYSICAL	COGNITIVE	SEXUAL	MORAL
16							
15							
14							
13							
12							
11							
10							
9							
8							
7							
6							
5							
4							
3							
2							
1							
0							

Key Points for Chapter 5

1. Seeing your child "as he is" will be essential to understanding what he needs from *you* to complete his development in any given domain.

2. Understanding the developmental age of your child's behavior is vital so that you can meet his need successfully.

3. Troubled children may get "stuck" at certain stages of development or regress to earlier stages in times of distress.

4. In responding to your child's need, find the youngest developmental age he is expressing amongst the domains and intervene accordingly.

6.
It Goes Both Ways—Attachment

Creating a Secure "Umbilical Cord" Between Your Child and You

Piglet sidled up to Pooh from behind.

"Pooh?" he whispered.

"Yes, Piglet?"

"Nothing," said Piglet, taking Pooh's hand.

"I just wanted to be sure of you."

A. A. MILNE, *WINNIE-THE-POOH*

∽ STACIE CRAFT WAS FRANTIC. She was at her wits end with Trey, the beautiful five-year-old boy she had adopted. Trey would "accidentally" destroy her favorite possessions, wouldn't go to day care, and even clung to her ankles when she tried to go to the bathroom. At one point, when Stacie was about to leave for a hair appointment, Trey became so rageful that Stacie had to hold him to keep him from hurting himself. In the midst of his rage, Trey cried out, "Mommy, Mommy, why did you leave me?"

Stacie wasn't the one who left Trey—it was his biological mother, from whom he had been removed at nine months of age—but as Trey became attached to Stacie, he feared in the deepest part of himself that his attachment with Stacie would end just as it had with his birth mother, with an incomprehensible loss, aloneness, and fear. He was terrified to venture out because Stacie might not be there when he returned. He didn't *know* he was afraid; he just was overwhelmed with feelings, especially with the terror that he would once more be abandoned. Trey's terror came out as rage at Stacie, and he couldn't express it directly for fear of losing her, so Trey expressed it by destroying things that Stacie held dear. Although Trey was taking it out on Stacie, his birth mother was his true target.

The insecure attachment pattern that Trey had developed during the few months he spent with his birth mother was transferred onto the new relationship he was building with Stacie. It would take Stacie much time and unending patience along with innumerable patterned, repetitive, safe relational experiences for Trey to begin to believe that Stacie would be there for him. Over time, Trey would learn to trust Stacie, and then to trust being away from Stacie—to separate from her but carry inside him a sense of the safety he feels when with her, knowing that he can return to that safety when needed.

Attachment Is the Foundation of All of Our Relational Expectations

In the scenario above, Trey is in the beginning stages of developing a secure attachment with Stacie. In this chapter, we will go into more depth regarding the nature of attachment itself and how the *quality* of a child's attachment to his primary caregiver determines his developmental trajectory.

We talk in terms of "attachment to" and "attachment relationship," but what exactly is "attachment"? Attachment, as we will be referring to it, is actually a *behavior*. When we are looking at a child's abilities to form caring, protective relationships, we are looking at his *behavior* with others, especially his behavior with his primary attachment figure. We evaluate four factors, identified by John Bowlby in his pioneering work in the field of attachment, as we observe how a child relates to his primary attachment figure (Bowlby, 1982; 1988).

Criteria for Assessing Attachment Status
1. Does the child show a desire to be with his primary caregiver?
2. Does the child actively use his primary caregiver as a safe base from which he explores his world?
3. Does the child actively use his primary caregiver as a safe haven to which he returns for comfort and safety?
4. Does the child show distress when his attachment figure is absent?

In Trey's story, we see that although Trey desires to be with Stacie, he cannot tolerate separation from Stacie, and he becomes more than just distressed in her absence; he becomes overwhelmed, distraught, and destructive. Attachment is a two-way interactive *process* between two individuals who each display distinct attachment behaviors. However, these behaviors—though distinct—are not *separate*, but rather entwined. Attachment behavior is bi-directionally causative as well as responsive, meaning both the child and mother initiate and respond to one another in turns. This process can be referred to as "serve and return," like in a game of tennis. *Most of what occurs within the human experience happens within relationship.*

Even experiences that occur when you are alone may take place "in relationship" because the experience still involves two—you and the person "in your head" that helps you feel safe and connected. In the healing process, although we tend to focus on the attachment behaviors of the

The Circle of Security: as the parent, you are the hands (at the left of the diagram) that provide your child with the safety to adventure away from you (top of the circle) and be welcomed back (bottom of the circle) on his return. Copyright © 1999. Used with authorization of Circle of Security International for this publication only.

child in the parent-child dyad, understanding the attachment behavior of the *adult* in the role of the primary caregiver is essential for parents. It is within the parent's side of the dyad that the changes must first occur to shift the child's behaviors. *Your behavior as a parent is the catalyst for your child's healing and for his complete growth and development.*

In most healing paradigms designed for children, a focus on the adult's behavior is rarely put at center stage. However, recent developments in the study and application of interventions that are proven to be effective in healing children do reflect this vital focal shift. At the Marycliff Institute in Spokane, Washington, a group of therapists/researchers has developed a practical application of Bowlby's theory of attachment behavior. The Circle of Security™ project (Hoffman, et al., 2006) has evolved to the point of being a credentialed protocol for the teaching of adequate attachment sensitivity and behaviors in caregivers.

A diagram of the Circle of Security (above) gives us a visual conception

It is *your* behavior as the adult that is the primary tool for change

A child learns to identify and regulate his feelings within his relationship with his primary caregiver via her direct and timely intervention as he expresses himself

of how the child's four attachment behaviors play out within relationship with a caregiver who is lovingly meeting the child's needs.

In this diagram, the adult hands signify the safe base/safe haven provided by the child's primary caregiver, while the call-out box describes the "job" of the primary caregiver in her relationship with the child. Following the child around the attachment cycle, beginning at what is called the "top half" of the circle, we see that the child's need is to go out and explore his world with the *full support, protection, and enjoyment* of his primary caregiver. As the child's *need for exploration* gives way to his *need to be with* his primary caregiver, he returns to her as pictured in the "bottom half" of the circle. In his return to his caregiver, the child needs her to *welcome him back positively and provide for him the necessary sense of safety and comfort.* It is important to note that the caregiver also takes charge of the returning child when necessary by *organizing his feelings.*

The Circle of Security is a concise representation of both what a child does naturally and what he needs from his primary caregiver as he does what he does. *The circle displays the foundational process as seen from the perspective of the child's needs that is essential for parents to learn as they work to heal their distressed child.* We will consistently refer to this diagram throughout the rest of the book to help you determine what your role needs to be as a parent within your growing relationship with your child as you work to identify and meet his needs.

The Circle of Security may seem to be a simple illustration, but it includes not only a summary of the child's fundamental behavior and needs but also a summary of the indispensable primary caregiver attachment behaviors necessary to meet the child's needs.

Adult Attachment-Promoting Behavior Essentials
(Summarized from the Circle of Security)
1. Always be bigger, stronger, wiser, and kind.
2. Support your child's explorations with delight.
3. Happily welcome your child's returning from his explorations.
4. Identify and meet your child's need for safety, comfort, and regulation.

How Attachment Develops

A safe emotional bond, a deep connection with a singular person, is the basic and universal component of our human social structure. The foundation of human attachment lies within the relationship between mother and child, embraced by family and supported by community. The drive for attachment is biological; it is encoded in our genes. Attachment is the link that allows us to survive: we seek care and give care ideally within an organized system of behavior to assure proximity to and accessibility of the person who takes care of us.

The process of attaching builds specific neural pathways in the brains of both giver and receiver. We have borrowed Carla J. Shatz's statement, "cells that fire together wire together" (1992), and expanded it to "brains that fire together wire together" to describe this connection. The attachment process is biologically replicative: neural pathways within our brain are duplicated within the brain of our primary other and vice versa. How often do we catch ourselves thinking the exact same thing as our primary other? This is due to the neural connections that grow in both brains through stimulation by the repetitive, interactive experience with the other person over a significant period of time.

Researchers (Ainsworth, et al., 1978) have documented that attachment behavior is universal and that it occurs along a spectrum from secure to disorganized. Whereas most of us (about 65 percent) have a secure attachment style, about 15 percent of us have an insecure attachment style and about 5 percent of us may have a disorganized style. From early research, this appears to be equally true in Uganda as in the United States. Attachment style does not predict all later problems, but attachment does have a strong influence on how we deal with the vagaries of life and relationship (Sroufe, 1995).

Secure attachment develops over time as the infant experiences the constant presence and timely nurturance of his primary caregiver. Although the "giving" would appear to be one-sided, the infant, indeed, participates equally through his accepting response to his caregiver's actions. When the primary caregiver cuddles and rocks her infant, he feels soothed and expresses this through his trusting "giving in" to the caregiver's body and rhythm. The caregiver feels her infant's receptive response and equally "sinks in" to the experience, which biochemically translates in her as the release of the "love hormone," oxytocin, into her system. This

The infant sees and understands himself and the world through his caregiver's eyes

blissful state is the infant's gift to his caregiver. *This reciprocal interaction is the foundation of the attachment experience that is absolutely necessary for complete human development across all domains.*

The key factor in establishing a secure attachment pattern is the consistent presence of a singular primary caregiver. This does not mean that in establishing secure attachment the child can have a singular primary caregiver for this day, and another for the next. The infant must have *the same caregiver every day* if he is to have the consistent, repetitive relational experience sufficient for him to become securely attached. It is within his relationship with his primary caregiver that the infant learns who he is and what he feels and gains his outlook on life and his understanding of the world.

Through mirroring—the caregiver's verbal and nonverbal streaming narrative to the infant about his ongoing experience across all domains of being—the caregiver reflects to her infant his unique self and his feelings and fosters his comprehension of his experiences. As the caregiver accurately responds to her infant's needs and soothes his distress, she is teaching him how to calm and soothe himself. Via her reactions to her own experience in the present and based on her viewpoint on life formed from her accumulated experiences and knowledge, the caregiver in effect "downloads" her outlook on and her understanding of the world into her infant's brain (Tronick, 2003).

Thus, the infant sees and understands himself and the world through his caregiver's eyes. For example, if the caregiver is attentive to the infant's needs, is positive about life, and mirrors the positives she experiences in her infant, the infant will feel valued, have a good outlook on the world, and think well of himself. On the other hand, if the caregiver is inattentive, is depressed, and expresses annoyance at her infant and his needs, he will feel worthless, have a negative outlook on the world, and think he is bad. Trey's early experience left him with these negative thoughts and feelings about himself and the world, and his birth mother's abandonment traumatized him, leaving him stuck in a state of terror such that he could not let his adoptive mother out of his sight. The implications of this "downloading" phenomenon are profound for the child and for you. Essentially, *your child as you know him today is the product of the quality and nature of the caregiving he experienced before you came into his life.*

Attachment Patterns

The pattern of attachment a child develops is profoundly influenced by how his primary caregiver treats him over time. *The attachment pattern that results from the care a child receives in infancy (the first two years of life) becomes the child's template for all future relationships.* This pattern is fixed and enduring and cannot evolve without a new, long-term reparative relational experience with a *securely attached* primary other. As the infant and his caregiver engage in their relational "dance" over time, a "dance pattern" develops that we can identify in order to understand what help the child and/or the caregiver may need to remedy any attachment problems that may exist.

The adult brings the attachment pattern she developed in her own infancy into her relationship with her infant. The "quality" of the adult caregiver's attachment behavior in the present depends upon the quality of emotional support, nurturance, mirroring, and care she received beginning in infancy, as well as the level of trust she attained within her experience of being cared for as a child. Consequently, the relational pattern ingrained in the caregiver tends to be self-perpetuating: she will treat her child as she was treated, and her child, in turn, will treat his child as he was treated.

Many of us say at one time or another that we will not treat our kids how our parents treated us, and we truly believe that through our resolve we can and will do better. However, because our attachment pattern is actually seated in the neural architecture of our brain, we are destined involuntarily to repeat what we have experienced relationally—good or bad. If we have arrived in adulthood with an insecure or disorganized attachment pattern, this is the pattern we will engage in with our children. There is hope, however. Just as the hurt child who receives reparative

---

The attachment pattern that results from the care a child receives in infancy becomes the child's template for all future relationships

parenting can heal and form a secure attachment with his new caregiver, we, as adults, can also heal if we choose to consciously participate in a reparative relationship with a securely attached other, such as a therapist, spouse, or close friend. In this way, even if we came into adulthood with an insecure or disorganized attachment, over time we can "earn" secure attachment because this process actually changes our brain at the neural level to match that of the securely attached other with whom we have built a trusting relationship.

Secure Attachment

There are three major patterns of attachment that can develop in infancy: secure, insecure-avoidant or ambivalent, and disorganized. As we refer back to the Circle of Security, these patterns will come alive for us in a way that we can understand and remember. We have looked at the behavioral cycle, which when repeated consistently from the time we are born through toddlerhood (and beyond) produces a secure attachment: (1) a child has a secure base from which he can explore with the delight and support of the parent (top half of the circle), and (2) he has a welcoming, safe haven to which to return when he needs his parent's care (bottom half of the circle). This cycle instills within the child a sense of safety, security, and trust in his primary caregiver. The ability to rely on and trust intimately in another develops from this experience, leading to trusting in others and the world, and to being able to carry a secure attachment pattern into adulthood.

Insecure Attachment Patterns

Insecure attachment has two ways of presenting—avoidant and ambivalent—each of which is a result of particular parent/infant behavioral patterns. If we take the Circle of Security and change the bottom half of the circle such that the parent does not want the child to return or

---

**A secure attachment allows the child to carry within him
the knowledge that his caregiver will be there for him when he returns
from exploration, making separation possible**

does not express an attentive welcoming or the child feels uncomfortable returning for some other reason, an insecure-avoidant pattern is established. If we change the top half of the circle such that the *parent* needs the child for her *own* comfort, and thus does not support the child going out to explore or the child feels uncomfortable going out to explore because he is overly concerned with how his mother is doing, an insecure-ambivalent pattern is established.

Both the avoidantly and ambivalently attachment-patterned child have adapted to the needs of the parent as a means of survival. In carefully monitoring what his parent needs in any given moment, the child assures his survival by meeting his parent's needs the best he can so that she will then, he hopes, have what it takes to meet his needs. Unfortunately though, the child's need for his parent's mirroring to understand who he is and what he is feeling, for his parent to regulate his distress so that he learns how to do so for himself, and for his parent to interpret the world such that he gains a realistic, stable perspective is not addressed or is overlooked in lieu of his parent getting her needs met.

A child's insecure attachment pattern typically evolves within a primary relationship in which the caregiver has an insecure attachment pattern herself. However, an insecure attachment pattern can develop even if the child's caregiver is securely attached: a child's particular temperament (e.g., extreme shyness or hyperactivity) or genetic problem (e.g., autistic spectrum disorder or schizoaffective disorder) can interfere with parenting behaviors that lead to a child becoming securely attached. When the child, through no fault of his own, is not receptive or is incapable of adequate reciprocation, parents can become disheartened and feel ineffectual in their parenting role, but this is not the common scenario encountered in working with distressed children.

Disorganized Attachment

The third attachment type, disorganized attachment, is the most serious and difficult to work with and to transform. By its very nature, disorganized attachment cannot be defined by a standardized pattern. On the

**An insecure attachment develops from the child's fear
of leaving or returning to the caregiver**

A disorganized attachment results from highly inconsistent interactions that leave the child in a constant state of fear when he approaches the adult or separates from the adult

Circle of Security, disorganized attachment would be represented by the combination of both insecure-anxious and insecure-ambivalent patterns. In this dynamic, the parent is highly inconsistent in her interactions with her child such that the child remains confused and alone, lingering for the most part out at the opposite side of the circle from what ideally should be the secure base/safe haven. The child longs to be safe and trusting of his parent, but her behaviors are so random and unpredictable toward him that he cannot establish an attachment strategy—or pattern of behaviors—that is effective in consistently drawing his parent to him. At his core, this child is in a constant state of fear, as his natural need for a secure base from which he can explore and a safe haven to which he can return does not get met. A parent who produces a disorganized attachment in her child is one who developed this kind of attachment in her own childhood.

A child who displays a disorganized attachment has had repetitive experiences of inconsistency within his relationship with his primary caregiver that have left him frightened and alone. The parent may be abusive in one moment and briefly loving the next. She may ignore the child and his needs much of the time but then provide for his needs now and again. At those times when her child feels like a bother to her, this parent may send him out to explore regardless of his desire to do so. When she needs him to meet her own needs, this parent will bring her child back to her no matter if he wants to return or needs her at the time. This experience of changeability and inconsistency gives the child no choice but to become untrusting and fearful of caregivers, and of adults in general. The child's attachment behaviors become as inconsistent as those of his "caregiver." He will generally be unregulated, unpredictable, and hypervigilant, as it takes stability, consistency, and caregiver regulation to develop those same capacities in the child.

Although incapable of truly fending for himself and meeting the full array of his needs, the child with a disorganized attachment will insist upon remaining in control. Developing a personal locus of control was the child's only option in the face of the relational chaos he experienced. In not being able to count on his primary caregiver to meet any of his needs consistently, the child learned to take over in any way he could. However, the child does not stop seeking or wanting what he needs from his caregiver. Thus, he will approach her at those times either when he feels overwhelmed with need or when he deems it safe to do so. This establishes a pattern of the child accepting a relationship with an adult or caregiver *on his terms and only when he is in charge.*

The tendency is for us to call a child with this pattern "controlling," meaning that we experience him as oppositional, defiant, and ungovernable. In turn, our automatic response to this behavior then tends to be authoritarian and controlling. However, this parental stance only makes things worse and the child digs in deeper, demanding control at any cost. Authoritarianism activates the child's core terror because his experience has fostered a deep, fundamental distrust of adults. Threats or brandishing consequences drive the child away, only strengthening his will to stay in charge.

The child with a disorganized attachment can even seem at times to be like a feral creature—extremely leery of everything and everyone, constantly on guard. His fighting, affronting exterior is the shell that is keeping his tender, terrified, interior self safe. Though what we want is to get a hold of this child and "tame" him, we need to approach him on his terms. *This frightened child will only feel safe to approach us at those times he truly feels accepted and understood.* When working with this child, it is essential that we first anchor ourselves in the knowledge of how he came to be this way in order that compassion can be our guide. Trey's behavior was characteristic of a disorganized attachment: he was terrified of his mother leaving and angry and disorganized when she returned.

Attachment patterns are like templates: most of the time, a parent with insecure attachment, whether anxious or avoidant, will produce a child with her insecure pattern. Likewise, a parent with a disorganized attachment most of the time will produce a child with a disorganized attachment. Most important for our consideration, however, is the child

---

A child with a disorganized attachment may look rageful, chaotic, angry, and controlling but feels terrified and will feel safe approaching us only when he feels deeply understood and accepted

**It is you, the parent, who is the change agent for your child.
A child can change if a parent changes,
and a child can change alongside a changing parent.**

with a disorganized attachment: he inserts his relational template of terror, aloneness, and inadequacy into his relationship with his idealistic and hopeful adoptive or foster parent. The child's fear and resistance will likely be stronger than the parent's relational style, resulting in the parent experiencing the pain and distress of the child's inner world within their relationship. This is where the miracle of applying therapeutic parenting comes into play. With self-examination, self-regulation, persistence, structure, attunement, empathy, and some of the techniques you will learn in this book, you can bring your child's relational pattern into a calmer, more organized state.

In working with children with less than secure attachment strategies, the same template tenet applies: *for the distressed child to heal, it is optimal that the adult in the healing dyad has attained a secure attachment pattern in childhood or has "earned" one as an adult through relationship with a securely attached adult.* This is optimal, but many of us have insecure attachment styles and can still be a change agent in the life of a child if we continue to look at ourselves and grow. Although a sense of security increases for all maltreated children who are adopted, disorganization persists for maltreated children who are adopted by parents with disorganized attachment patterns.

Identifying Problematic Attachment Behaviors in Your Child

A child may display outward behaviors that indicate he has a problem with attachment, or he may have inward patterns that are not so easily seen. There are several ways you can go about identifying a problematic attachment behavior in your child: (1) key into your own emotional experience in the moment with your child; (2) make use of the Circle of Security to figure out where on the circle your child is in the moment; and (3) consult a therapist specializing in an attachment-focused approach. Although all of these methods can be useful, some guidance is necessary before they can be used accurately.

Tuning in to your own experience with your child can tell you what your child may be feeling in the moment

Keying in to your own emotional experience in any given moment with your child takes guidance and practice, but it can be an effective way of identifying your child's attachment behavior. Within relationship with your child, there is an emotional give and take that ebbs and flows like the ocean onto the shore. If a small wave comes in, a small ebb flows out, whereas if a big, crashing wave comes in, a much larger ebb with a strong undertow flows out. In the same way, a child's behavior "comes in" to his parent's emotional sphere and the parent's linked emotion "flows out" to her child.

A child, in effect, tends to "script" the adult to whom he is emotionally close, imposing his pattern upon her, powerfully eliciting a response that corresponds with his pattern of attachment. In discerning what attachment behavior your child is expressing, you can "check in" with yourself to identify how you are being emotionally "tugged" by your child. You essentially will experience what your child is experiencing, so if you are able to tune in to yourself in the moment, you will be able to identify your child's present experience.

For example, if a parent begins to feel confused and disorganized in the presence of her child, she is feeling the ebb from the flow of her child's confusion and disorganization. If the parent is feeling anxious, she is feeling the backwash from her child's present anxiety. If she is feeling ambivalent, the parent is picking up the wave of her child's present ambivalence. This same process created the child's attachment behavior in the first place: he became "scripted" by his original primary caregiver's behavior, which flowed into him and ebbed back to her.

Let's take Trey's example. Stacie felt emotionally overwhelmed and angry. She felt trapped and was beginning to regret ever having adopted Trey. She felt hopeless and secretly wished that she could just get rid of Trey; life would be so much easier without all of this chaos. When we found out what Trey had gone through and what he was feeling, it was remarkably similar to what Stacie felt. Trey felt angry that Stacie wasn't his "real" mother; he thought that Stacie had stolen him from his "real" mother. Trey felt hopeless about seeing his birth mother again and was terrified of being abandoned again—exactly what Stacie was secretly thinking of doing. When we figured this out, Stacie was able to reflect those feelings back to Trey, saying, "Oh, honey, I can only imagine how terrified you are, how angry you are with me, and how frightened you are that I will abandon you too." With that simple statement, Trey felt understood and his behavior calmed down. Stacie also used the Circle of Security to realize that she needed to do more "welcoming back" after Trey and she had been apart and to provide measured, small moments of separation that Trey could tolerate and thus feel successful negotiating.

The crucial difference between your child's original parent-to-child scripting and your child's attempt to script you in the present is that you, as the parent who is working to heal the child, will not be responding to your child from his script. You will *feel* pulled into your child's script, but instead of responding according to those elicited feelings, you will be responding from the anchored place you have cultivated within yourself. For example, instead of acting on your anxiety, which you absorbed from your child, you consciously choose to remain calm and centered. From this calm place, you then interact with your anxious child, which disrupts the child's attempt to "script" you. It is your disruption of your child's attempt to script you—the result of the cycle of attachment created within his first primary caregiver relationship—that becomes the catalyst for change in his attachment pattern. Your inner experience of your child's high anxiety, rage (terror), low trust, and discomfort with intimacy or emotional withdrawal is a gift, as it is a direct physiological and emotional insight into your child's internal experience, which can inform your responses. Notice here that we are *not* asking for you to list out your child's problematic behaviors. The two-dimensionality of listed behavior limits insight into your child's inner world because it does not include a key factor in the attachment relationship—*you!*

Parents can also make use of the Circle of Security diagram to identify their child's problematic attachment behavior. As a securely attached parent, you become "the hands"—the starting and ending point on the Circle of Security—the child's secure base/safe haven. From that viewpoint, you can observe the behavior of your child in the moment. Is he clingy? Is he anxious when he goes out to explore or does he even go out to explore? Does he go out to explore without seeming to need your attention or protection? Does he clearly need you when he is out exploring, but tries to manage on his own? Is he coming back to you when he is tired or frustrated, or does he remain where he is instead, expressing his need by throwing, breaking, or getting despondent about his toy? In other words, does your child use you as a safe base from which he explores, ask for support in his exploration when he needs it, and return when he needs you as a safe haven, displaying the cycle of secure attachment?

At first, it may seem difficult to identify your child's behavior in terms of the Circle of Security. The key is to use the *circle of secure attachment* as a template. Where on this template is your child's behavior different from that of a securely attached child? Check in to your own feelings in the moment. Do you feel relied upon as a parent by your child? Do you feel smothered by your child? Do you sense that your child is not responding to you but instead is trying to pull you into his relational script: is he prompting you to *react* instead of *respond*? Identifying the relational dynamic your child is trying to re-create with you yields both the problem of and solution to his attachment deficit. Over time, if you interact with your child *as if* he were a securely attached child—that is, embodying his secure base, supporting and delighting in him as he explores, and welcoming him back to you, his safe haven—his relational behavior will eventually morph into that of a securely attached child. Changing one side of the relational equation (your response) necessarily changes the other side (your child's behavior).

In some cases, the option of consulting a therapist may be the only way parents can become objective enough to set aside their own reactivity or issues so they can see their child and his needs clearly. When you feel triggered and cannot calm yourself, when you begin to blame your child for the chaos or disharmony, when you cannot relieve yourself of feeling overwhelmed, it is time to elicit some much-needed support from a specially trained professional. All parents need this support at some point in their parenting journey because it truly does take a village to heal an emotionally dysregulated child. We will be examining the motivation for various behaviors later, and with guidance you will be able to *see the child underneath the behavior*.

On Fostering Positive Attachment Behaviors in Your Child

Although the topic of how to foster secure attachment in your child will be covered in Chapter 10, a few caveats are useful to introduce here. As parents, we tend to see our responsibility in raising or healing children as *doing* things *to and for* our children rather than *being someone* for them. Even using the word "intervention" can be interpreted to imply this. However, by "intervention" we mean *intervening in the child's relational pattern*, rather than running him through a standardized behaviorally oriented program.

Our premise is that "there are no troubled children, only troubled dyads" (FitzGerald, 2015). The core problem as identified in traditional "treatment" protocols is the *child's behavior*, when actually the core problem is one of *adult orientation*. You, as the primary caregiver, must assume the role of "the catalyst" and use your *behavior* as the agent of change in your child's emotional life. As you continue this training and learn more about healing your distressed child, we encourage you to "aspire to know him more than to understand him, to become a deep resource and powerful agent of change" in your child's life.

Parental Attachment Behavior

If you were your child right now, what would you want and what would you need? Would you want a parent who really "gets" you, one who can see and be responsive to your needs (even if you cannot express them in words), and one who accepts you just as you are and is absolutely committed to you? Or would you want a parent who is stressed, frustrated, rushed, and impatient? Of course you would want the caring, available, and attentive parent. The real question is, "How do I become *that parent* for my child, a child whose needs are often hidden under difficult behaviors, who often seems to act younger than his chronological age, and who frequently pushes me away?"

The answer to this question has two parts. First, you have to come to know yourself as the parent you are presently—what aspects of parenting feel natural and easy to you, and what demands of parenting feel challenging and difficult for you. Second, you will need to learn some particular "therapeutic" parenting skills that you may not have acquired yet or learned through your own experience of being parented. Via this training, you have the opportunity to look closely at yourself as well as to learn the *adult attachment behaviors* that are going to be vital to know and use in your parent-child relationship. Again, *your behaviors as a parent are the means by which your child's healing and his complete growth and development will take place.*

Misattunement happens; the question is how to repair and bring your child back into feeling safe in your relationship

Initially, what you may find to be the most difficult yet the most essential thing you will do as a parent is to *regulate your own arousal so that you can be present to regulate your child's arousal.* This means that when you are stressed or when your child's behavior is triggering, you are able to quell your reactivity and become objective enough to *see and meet* your child's presenting need. Optimal parenting is patient, sensitive, accurate, timely, emotionally available, and cooperative (Ainsworth, et al., 1978). However, it is impossible to carry out these parental behaviors every time you interact with your child, and it is unrealistic to expect this of yourself. The goal is to optimize these parental attributes in yourself so you can be as present as possible in your relationship with your child.

It is inevitable that parents are not always present, aware, or attuned to their child; hence, some of the child's needs may go unmet in the moment. However, this misattunement does not constitute a failure on the part of the parent but rather a temporary gap in the parent-child relationship. Relational gaps are to be expected and are an unavoidable part of every relationship. Nonetheless, those gaps, or misattunements, cannot go unattended. Acknowledgment of the relational break or gap on the part of the parent provides the glue that reunites the parent with her child, bringing them back into their synchronous dance. In fact, within a relationship, an act of sincere apology—wherein one fully acknowledges her behavior and its negative impact on the other—actually increases the dyadic bond, making it stronger than it was before the break.

Attachment research has shown that to form a secure attachment with a child, birth parents need only to be accurately attuned to and meet the needs of their child 30 percent of the time. This, at first, seems like a staggeringly low figure. However, that amount of patient, sensitive, accurate, timely, emotionally available, and cooperative adult interaction is sufficient for *a child of securely attached parents* to generalize his sense of security with them and his trust in them.

In contrast, when a parent commits to a permanent relationship with a *distressed child*, the percentage of high-quality parental interaction necessarily must increase. Healing a child requires changing his dysfunctional relational pattern, a transformation that will take countless repetitions of nurturing interactions with a securely attached parent—enough repetitions to allow the child to generalize his experience of the parent as a secure base/safe haven. Each child is unique in his capabilities and in his capacity to attain such a relationship with his parent; therefore, it takes whatever time it takes for any particular child.

To get a sense of the journey a child must embark upon to reach the objective of forming a trusting relationship with a securely attached parent, a visual aid may be helpful. See the numbers below. A child born to and raised by securely attached parents begins at zero and proceeds to experience life in the positive realm to the right of zero. A child born into trauma, neglect, and abandonment begins life somewhere to the left of zero and has to heal from his negative experience before he can begin to live in the positive realm to the right of zero.

NEGATIVE EXPERIENCES   -4   -3   -2   -1   0   +1   +2   +3   +4   **POSITIVE EXPERIENCES**

When a child suffers trauma, neglect, and abandonment *alone*, without the safety, support, and guidance of a nurturing primary caregiver, he "swallows the experience whole" without "digesting" it. The feelings associated with traumatic experience "get stuck" in the child, remain unresolved, and color the child's view of the world as terrifying. Processing and coming to terms with traumatic experience is only possible when a child feels safe and has the insight and support of his primary caregiver. *Healing can occur only in the present within relationship with a secure, safe primary caregiver*, the "safe haven" who was absent in his life during the trauma. Therefore, a significant additional amount of patient, sensitive, accurate, timely, emotionally available, and cooperative time above and beyond the 30 percent must be spent with a distressed child to heal his wounds and create trust and security. This may seem like a tall order for many parents, but the goal is attainable by means of training, through accurate introspection, and with the support of others.

**Remember that the task of meeting your child's needs
is possible because you already have many of the parenting
skills necessary, and you can learn those skills you may be lacking
through training and with the support of others**

In Chapter 1, you completed a self-inventory and an exercise through which you determined your present parenting strengths and weaknesses, as well as the parenting skills you would like to learn. Please review your work now, asking yourself if you need to adjust anything, need to ask any questions, or need to complete your plan for acquiring the skills you wish to have.

A Note about Adult Attachment Status

It is often the case that as parents get deeper into the process of healing their child, they come upon issues in their own lives that are unresolved, whether from childhood or from a time in their adult past. Sometimes these unresolved issues can be addressed within the course of the dyadic, parent-child treatment. Other times, adult issues may need to be attended to in a one-on-one setting with a therapist.

Arriving at adulthood with a secure attachment pattern intact is not as common as it might seem to be. Many adults carry into their parenting roles varying degrees of an insecure attachment pattern—a pattern which theretofore had not come to light. If this is the case for you, do not panic. The issues that led to insecurity can be addressed and resolved with therapeutic guidance within your relationship with your spouse or within a one-on-one relationship you build with a therapist. Remember, within the crucible of a relationship with a securely attached other, an insecurely attached adult can transform her insecure attachment pattern into one of earned security. It is possible for the insecurely attached parent to do her own work while parenting her child because as she heals toward secure attachment, so too can she heal her child.

Key Points for Chapter 6
1. It is *your* behavior that is the primary tool for change in your child's relationship with you.
2. A child learns to identify and regulate his feelings within his relationship with his primary caregiver via her direct and timely intervention as he expresses himself.
3. The attachment pattern that results from the care a child receives in infancy becomes the child's template for all future relationships.
4. A secure attachment allows the child to carry within him the knowledge that his caregiver will be there for him when he returns from exploration. Secure attachment allows separation.

5. An insecure attachment develops from the child's fear of leaving or returning to his caregiver, and his pattern of behavior becomes organized in a way to ensure that the caregiver returns.

6. A disorganized attachment results from highly inconsistent interactions that leave the child in a constant state of fear when he approaches the adult or separates from the adult.

7. A child with a disorganized attachment may look rageful, chaotic, angry, and controlling, but he feels terrified and will feel safe to approach his parent only when he feels deeply understood and accepted.

8. It is you, the parent, who is the change agent for your child. A child can change if a parent changes, and a child can change alongside a changing parent.

9. Tuning in to your own experience with your child can tell you what your child may be feeling in the moment.

10. Misattunement happens, but you can repair it with your child and bring him back into a feeling of safety in your relationship.

7.
Discovering the Meaning
of Your Child's Actions

Making Sense of the Need
Beneath Your Child's Behavior

Behavior is the mirror in which everyone shows his image.

JOHANN WOLFGANG VON GOETHE

~ FOR ABOUT A WEEK, everything had been going really well, and that afternoon, Phillip, age fifteen, had even brought home a good report card for a change and was eager to show it to his parents, who said they would have time to look at it later that evening when they got home. Phillip stormed off to his room and started ripping his posters off the wall and throwing and breaking his things. His parents, just about to set off on their first date night in several months, were dismayed and confused.

The next day, as Phillip's parents sat with Phillip and talked about what had happened, he told them that the place he had lived before he was adopted had too many kids, and if he did well, the adults ignored him and the children teased him about being a nerd and a "brainiac." Phillip had hoped it would be different with his newly adopted mother and father, but when Phillip had arrived home with his report card, his parents had been busy, too focused on their date, and he felt left out, abandoned, and ignored all over again. The feelings this event brought up for him were, "See, no one really does care after all" and "I'm a worthless nerd."

Behavior Is Your Child's Way of Showing Feelings and Needs

The goal of this chapter is to present the "translation" process, which involves looking at your child's behavior, discovering its underlying meaning, and meeting the underlying need. The examples are intended to give parents an introduction to how the complete translation process works—from the parent eliminating her reactivity, to observing the child's behavior, to translating its meaning, to responding in a way that meets the expressed need, and finally to creating a narrative that puts the behavior in the context of the child's past experience. To integrate the art of translating your child's behaviors into your daily routine, you will need to study and practice the specific use of the process in myriad settings and situations. Later, in chapters on intervention, we will explore in greater detail how parents can intervene in a wide range of specific behaviors to meet the needs their child is "voicing" with his actions.

What It Takes To "Read Your Child"

Foster/adoptive parenting involves much more than providing adequate nurturance. To be effective, you must learn to read your child's *behavioral cues*, which represent his *needs*. This task is the cornerstone of parenting a distressed child, yet it is one that is difficult to master. Reading your child's behavior first requires you to set aside your own emotions and reactivity in the face of your child's often-difficult behaviors. The adult in the parent-child relationship must be well versed in emotional self-regulation and be aware of personal triggers. The goal in teaching you the various developmental and genetic underpinnings of behavior and of having you apply these to your child is to help you understand that much of his seemingly incomprehensible behavior is not actually aimed at you. Your child is operating in the world as he sees it through the filter of his early history.

Often parents get frustrated with their adopted child because he may not be fulfilling the image of who they wanted their child to be. Therefore, *parents need to be students of who their child is*, dismissing all expectations and imaginings. The reality of parenting adopted children is that they come to you with a unique set of hereditary factors, personal histories, and divergent world views as we have already learned. These differences must be embraced and understood, rather than targeted for change to accommodate the family's need for comfort and familiarity. Making a conscious effort to understand and embrace your child's uniqueness allows you to affirm him instead of inadvertently labeling him as "off," "wrong," or "bad" and wanting him to change. It is worth repeating that parents must be prepared to commit to their child and his healing *without expecting the child to respond appreciatively or to give back*, especially at first.

Your child's behavior is a cue to his needs, and reading his cues accurately allows you to meet his needs accurately

To accomplish this, first *parents must consciously release their children from meeting their personal needs.* Approaching this resolve with intent solidifies the stance parents need to take when raising a distressed child. Unconditionally accepting your child requires effort, yet doing so is essential to help him reach his potential. *Your ability to fully accept your child just as he is creates the kind of security he needs to be able to grow and change.* This takes understanding, gentle firmness, and flexibility from parents, while not selling out. The most effective parental stance is this: be "bigger, stronger, kinder, and wiser" than your child (Hoffman, et al., 2006). In parenting a distressed child, it is also helpful to step back and recognize the opportunity you have to broaden your perspective of what "normal" is. You may also find that this distinctive type of parenting will change you in profound ways, bringing deeper meaning to your life.

Children "Speak" through Behavior

A child's avoidance, need to control, defiance, and other undesirable behaviors are actually survival skills he developed under the unfortunate conditions of his early life and relationships. In having had an inadequate caregiver early in his life, the child was on his own to manage himself and his world, thus only capable of reacting to his experience (behaving), not of understanding and communicating his experience (using his words). When asked, children who are displaying "out of control" primitive behaviors often say that they feel like there is a monster inside of them. Seeking to understand, parents can get even more frustrated and assume the child is holding back when they ask him why he did something and he responds, "I don't know." Parents must recognize that their child *actually does not know why he does what he does,* nor does he understand why he has such enormous fears and rage inside of him. A child's behavior is the vehicle through which he communicates these overwhelming feelings. Therefore, if parents want to help their child, they must learn to "read" their child's behavioral language.

Translating behavior includes more than parents deciphering the message just for themselves: ultimately, *the child needs to understand himself if he is to change and heal.* It is only through the child's engagement in relationship with his current primary caregiver that he learns how to identify what prompts his behavior. This process unfolds over time via the parent and child's shared exploration of the child's world. As their discovery progresses, both parent and distressed child come to understand the root cause of the child's difficult behaviors. Inevitably, what parent and child will begin to realize is that behaviors such as tantruming, hiding, hyperactivity, or aggressiveness are often triggered by the child's deep, primal fear. At its core, this primal fear or terror is actually the fear of dying, which the child began feeling in infancy due to abandonment and trauma associated with his birth mother, his only known link to survival due to his nine-month-long fetal experience.

Parents are often confounded by the persistence of this core feeling of fear/terror in their child, especially when they are providing more-than-adequate nurturing and safety for him in the here and now. However, even if a child is well nurtured and physically safe in his new home, enduring neural pathways associated with past trauma are easily reactivated—think of Marco, for example, in Chapter 3. In the present, triggers such as hunger, perceived abuse, or felt abandonment can activate the child's core terror, which in turn leads to his out-of-control behavior. Parents might easily confuse fear-based outbursts with willful disobedience, an unfortunate misinterpretation that averts the developing trust between parent and child. In order to begin to trust, the child needs his parent to "get" that his unresolved, deep-rooted fear is fueling his undesirable behaviors.

For parents to get a clearer view of their child's inner emotional world, it often helps for them to get a more visceral sense of the feelings that most commonly trigger difficult behaviors. On page 112 is a sampling of verbal expressions of those feelings your child may only be able to communicate at this time with his behavior. After you read the list, it is helpful to go back and review it while keeping in mind that each statement is actually the child's expression of one of five core feelings.

As you work within your relationship with your child to heal him, it will be up to you to unearth the feelings prompting your child's behavior. This can be a process of trial and error that may take much practice, but if you look through the lens of the five *core feelings stated in child words*— glad, sad, mad, scared, ashamed—you can more quickly identify the source of your child's behavioral reactivity. The majority of the statements on page 112 are rooted in the emotions of fear or shame, while the rest are rooted in the emotions of anger and sadness. Even though fear and shame are the most common feelings fueling a child's difficult behavior, they also can be the most difficult for parents to discern and/or accept. Parents live in a world that feels relatively safe and accepting, so remembering that

Feelings Beneath Misbehavior

Which one of the core feelings—glad, sad, mad, scared, or ashamed—underlies each statement?

1. "I am afraid."

2. "I don't trust you (or anyone else); I only trust myself."

3. "I need to control you and everything (to feel safe)."

4. "I feel powerless—I can't control anything (but I try)."

5. "I (truly do) need your attention (my cup is so empty)."

6. "I need you so much, but it's way too scary to let you know (because my birth mother abandoned me and I'm deeply afraid you might abandon me too.)"

7. "You don't care about me!"

8. "You just don't 'get' me!"

9. "Nobody understands me, nobody really wants me."

10. "I feel unlovable, worthless."

11. "I can't do it (I honestly can't do what you're expecting me to be able to)."

12. "I can't do it (if I try I might fail)."

13. "I'm a nobody, I don't belong, I don't fit in."

14. "I don't deserve it because I'm a bad kid."

15. "I want what I want (I haven't learned "No" yet)!"

16. "I'm grieving, I miss_____."

17. "I'm afraid—what's going to happen next?"

18. "When are you going to get rid of me?"

19. "When I leave home (it's safe there) to go somewhere, I'm afraid I'm never coming back."

20. "When you leave me, I'm afraid you're never coming back." ◆

The five core feelings underneath your child's behavior are
glad
sad
mad
scared
ashamed

their child experiences the world with uncertainty takes conscious effort. Aligning your expectations to the likelihood that the emotion prompting your child's challenging behavior is either fear or shame poises you to "see" your child more readily.

Respond Rather Than React

Accurately calibrating your expectations regarding your child's behavior prepares you to *respond rather than react*. If you can visualize and anticipate your response to your child's range of problematic behaviors, you will have a greater chance of staying nonreactive. Remaining neutral in the face of your child's behaviors allows you to have the objectivity necessary to discern and meet the needs he is expressing with his behavioral language. Every parent will experience at least some specific child behaviors as triggers to their own reactivity, especially if the behavior feels like a personal threat or a challenge to parental authority. We recommend that you study yourself and learn what particular child behaviors are triggers for you. You have already explored these in Chapter 1, but this is a good time to go back and revisit them.

Using the table below, imagine *your child* engaging in each of the described behaviors and rate *your* level of reactivity to each one. Focus on your *immediate gut reaction right now* and not on how you *think you might feel* if your child behaved this way at some point in the future. Some of the listed behaviors may seem repetitive, which is intentional to help you identify your own reactive patterns. This is not a contest to see how wonderful a parent you are, but rather a personal journey into your true self, the self that is actually engaging in the relationship with your child. You must get to know the "you" *your child experiences*—the "you" that comes across to him nonverbally, no matter how you think you are controlling yourself. Therefore, be honest with yourself here: in the long run, this will only help you to become the parent your child needs. Becoming your child's parent is a process, not an event, so allow yourself patience and time.

Parent Triggers Exercise

What are your triggers? Read the following list of challenging behaviors and rate how you immediately feel when you think of each behavior. Trust your first "gut" response. Please note that this is a broad spectrum of possible behaviors, and while certainly no child has them all, most children have some of them.

In rating your reactions to each of the behaviors listed, you have been courageous in looking at yourself more closely. Please do not be alarmed at yourself regarding *any* of your reactions to these challenging behaviors. Each one of us gets triggered by any number of difficult child behaviors. You are not alone! You have just taken the first step toward identifying your personal triggers *in order to learn how to control your reactivity* so you can be present for your child. You are in the process of learning how to stop *reacting* and how to start *responding* to your child. Even if your reactions feel overwhelming right now, it really is possible to learn to manage them, as you will see.

Identifying My Triggers

MY *IMMEDIATE* REACTION IS:	COMPASSIONATE 1	NEUTRAL 2	ANXIOUS 3	ANGERED 4	RAGEFUL 5
What if your child:					
acts impulsively all the time		1	2	3	4	5
acts overly cute and charming when he wants something from you	1	2	3	4	5
acts stiff and/or rejecting when you try to give him hugs	1	2	3	4	5
always delays, stalls, or tantrums when it's time to go or switch activities		1	2	3	4	5
always denies his actions even when you catch him red-handed	1	2	3	4	5
always seems to need your attention when you're doing something else		1	2	3	4	5

	1	2	3	4	5
behaves well with everyone except you	1	2	3	4	5
blames you for his problems	1	2	3	4	5
breaks his toys deliberately even when they're new	1	2	3	4	5
can't make or sustain eye contact with you	1	2	3	4	5
can't seem to learn from his mistakes—shows inability for cause/effect thinking	1	2	3	4	5
chronically lies to you	1	2	3	4	5
chronically uses a baby voice around you	1	2	3	4	5
consistently ruins special events and/or holidays with his behaviors	1	2	3	4	5
constantly argues with you	1	2	3	4	5
constantly mopes around, seems chronically depressed	1	2	3	4	5
dissociates, spaces out when you're talking to him	1	2	3	4	5
does sexually explicit behaviors in front of you or in public	1	2	3	4	5
doesn't trust you	1	2	3	4	5
has prolonged temper tantrums during which he might break things	1	2	3	4	5
is affectionate with "mom substitutes," but not with you	1	2	3	4	5
is blatantly disobedient—does specifically what you have prohibited	1	2	3	4	5
is constantly demanding of you	1	2	3	4	5
is cruel or abusive and hurts animals/other children	1	2	3	4	5
is extremely hyperactive—can't or won't sit still	1	2	3	4	5
is noncompliant with simple house rules	1	2	3	4	5
is only affectionate on his terms	1	2	3	4	5
is oppositional with you	1	2	3	4	5
is sneaky—does things behind your back	1	2	3	4	5
makes you feel afraid around him	1	2	3	4	5
makes you feel exploited and manipulated	1	2	3	4	5
makes you feel like you constantly have to walk on eggshells	1	2	3	4	5
needs your constant, close supervision	1	2	3	4	5
plays the other parent off you—goes behind your back trying to split parents	1	2	3	4	5
pokes you, grabs you, hangs on you	1	2	3	4	5
puts forth minimal or no effort in school	1	2	3	4	5
refuses to bathe, brush hair or teeth	1	2	3	4	5
refuses your help, even if he fails without it	1	2	3	4	5
regresses after you've made substantial progress in your relationship	1	2	3	4	5
seems like he has no self—only a shell	1	2	3	4	5
seems oblivious to your consequences	1	2	3	4	5
seems to lack a conscience	1	2	3	4	5
self-harms: cuts self, bangs head, picks scabs until bloody, pulls hair out, hits self	1	2	3	4	5
takes no responsibility for his actions	1	2	3	4	5
tells others that you are abusing him/being neglectful of him	1	2	3	4	5
tries to control everything you do	1	2	3	4	5
won't go to sleep at bedtime	1	2	3	4	5

Managing Your Triggers

Before parents can see their child and his behavior objectively and clearly as separate from themselves, they must first learn to manage their reactivity to him and his behaviors. To this end, we will return to the inventory you completed above and use your results as the basis of your self-study. Nonjudgmentally, look over the chart and identify which child behaviors elicited an anxious, angry, or fearful reaction in you. Which behaviors brought forth a neutral or compassionate response in you? Now look more closely at those behaviors for which you rated your own reaction as a "4" or "5." Challenge yourself to look at each of these negative reactions with the goal of finding the root cause and accompanying feeling that is fueling your reaction. As you consider which root cause may be driving each reaction, it is also helpful to identify any patterns that may emerge.

For example, is there more than one behavior related to your child's *defiance of your authority* that elicits your anger or rage? If so, ask yourself what this pattern might be about. Maybe you will find that your reactive pattern is rooted in the *fear* that you are an incompetent parent, or you may be feeling *panicked* because you sense you are *losing control* over your child. As you are uncovering the feeling fueling your reactivity, do you find yourself blaming your child for causing your reaction? Reassure yourself that although the reactivity you are experiencing is an *automatic, patterned response*—one that you developed over time to cope with difficult feelings—you can in turn develop a *new patterned response* that will serve in deepening your relationship with your child.

Begin to develop this new patterned response by consciously dropping any blame you are placing on your child or yourself. Instead, decide to focus on self-observation. In our example, you would begin by watching yourself each time you react with anger or rage when your child is defiant toward you. Remind yourself that *you are not actually reacting to your child's behavior* but to your own *feelings of fear or panic of losing control that get triggered inside you*. You are not trying to *accept* your negative reactivity, which will likely continue during this stage of your work. Rather,

---

You must learn to manage your reactivity to your personal triggers so that you can be present for your child to translate his behavior

you are taking the observational first step in the process of *shifting an automatic reaction that is getting in the way of getting closer to your child.* You will need to practice this self-observation over a period of days or weeks until you are able to do it regularly.

After you consistently can observe yourself reacting, the next step is to consciously practice *pausing before you react* so you can begin to have some control over your reactivity. Again, it will take days if not weeks to get used to interrupting your urge to react to your child's triggering behavior. Once you can stop yourself more times than not, your work will turn to discerning what is prompting your child's behavior in the first place. For example, you would begin by asking yourself, "What is my child *saying to me* with his defiant behavior?" Then, you might proceed by identifying the core feeling your child's behavior has aroused *inside of you.* Identifying *your core feeling* also gives you a taste of what *your child is feeling* in the moment.

Let us say you figured out that your child's defiance prompted *your reactivity* because it triggered *your fear* of losing control as a parent. In identifying your own feeling of fear, you are then able to see that your child's defiance is not a comment on your competence as a parent, but rather is an expression of *his fear* that *he* is losing control. Remember, because your child did not have adequate, consistent nurturing early in his life, his only choice was to rely on himself to survive, which put him in the position of being in control of himself. In our example, your child is responding with defiance because your authority is a threat to him being in control. *Seeking control is a survival tactic engraved as a neural pathway in your child's brain that is automatically activated when he perceives there is a present threat.*

For you *and every parent,* is not a matter of *if* you are reactive to your child or his behaviors at times; rather, it is a matter of *what* about your child and his behaviors triggers your reactivity. *Getting to know your triggers and how to manage them is essential if you are to help your child.* Your goal is always to *respond* to your child, not to *react* to him. The following steps summarize the process of managing your own reactivity.

Learning to Manage Your Reactivity
➤ Identify the specific child behavior that is triggering your reaction
➤ Look inside yourself to discover the underlying feeling that is the actual trigger for *your* reaction
➤ Recognize that you may be blaming your child for your reaction

➤ Choose instead to observe yourself over the next few days/weeks when you find yourself reacting to this triggered feeling

➤ When this self-observation begins to come easily, start practicing pausing before you react

➤ After a few days/weeks, as you become capable of pausing instead of reacting, you can then proceed with the steps of translating your child's behavior

As you discovered while taking the triggers inventory, you are not actually triggered by *everything* your child does. Therefore, the good news is you will not constantly have to be working so hard to arrest your reactivity. Yet you have identified *your set* of triggers; thus you can begin practicing to pause when these triggers push your buttons in order to stay objective. From this nonreactive stance, you are actually able to see your child and his needs clearly and as separate from yourself. Now you are ready to proceed with the step-by-step process of translating your child's behavior.

Examining Your Child's Past

To translate your child's behavior accurately, you will need to have a clear, comprehensive view of him that begins with the earliest information available about his history and extends through your present experience with him. There are questions you can ask yourself to help put together the pieces of your child's experience in order to form a clearer picture of your child that will be invaluable in your quest to understand him. The answer to these questions will come from knowing something about your child's genetic inheritance and his temperament; knowing or surmising what some of his past experiences may have been; knowing some basic information about child development; and considering your observations and experiences with your child thus far.

In making sense of this information about your child's life to date, you are generating a context within which you can more clearly see your child and understand his behavior. Just as in imagining, let us say, how circumstances in a pound pup's former life may have contributed to his wariness of people, having a context for your child's behaviors makes all the difference in your gaining an understanding of him that leads to compassion. Additionally, well-surveyed territory is easier to explore than uncharted wilderness. The following questions can help you define the terrain of your child's past experience, which will become the context for your understanding of why your child does what he does. You may not be able to answer all of the questions, which is common.

Questions about Your Child's Past
➤ What genetic factors on both the birth mother's and father's sides are known or suspected?
➤ Did the birth mother use illegal drugs, alcohol, or prescription medications during the pregnancy?
➤ What was the birth mother's life like while she was pregnant with your child?
➤ What were the circumstances of your child's birth experience?
➤ What is your child's temperament?
➤ What was your child's general life experience, including his experience with caregiving, during his first year of life?
➤ What was your child's general experience, including his experience with caregiving, from age one to when he became your child?

To create the defined territory of your child's experience, we recommend that you use the answers to these questions to write an actual *narrative*, or story, about your child's earlier life. Include any pertinent photos of people, homes, and locales available. In developing an actual written narrative of your child's life, you will have a dependable reference that you can employ as you proceed to learn to translate his behavior. You will come to depend on this "his-story" you have created to help you understand what is going on with your child today. As you decipher the meaning of your child's behavioral language within the context of his past, keep in mind that the process always *begins with you controlling your reactivity*.

Translating Your Child's Behavior

In order to translate your child's behavior, you first need to be able to identify the feeling underneath his behavior. This may prove to be easier than you think because the entire range of human feelings can, again, be summed up with five words, which represent the five categories in this closed array. They are, in child-level language: glad, sad, mad, scared, and ashamed. You can take any feeling word there is and categorize it into one of these five feelings.

glad	sad	mad	scared	ashamed
delighted	lonely	irritated	timid	disgusted
happy	sorrowful	enraged	afraid	detestable
cheerful	tearful	aggressive	worried	terrible
serene	anguished	frustrated	terrified	yucky
free	grieved	provoked	frightened	embarrassed
satisfied	desolate	angry	anxious	useless

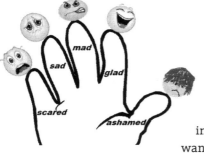

The five basic emotions

Of course, this list represents only a few of the endless number of feeling words that exist in each category, but you can use the main categories as a guide to pinpoint the core feeling that you have or that you are seeing under your child's behavior. Why would you want to categorize your child's feeling so simplistically? The answer is that most children have a relatively limited cognitive capacity to understand feelings in more abstract terms. There is also a need for you to speed up your own cognitive process so that you can begin to gain an immediate understanding of your child and/or yourself in any given moment.

It is easy to teach these categories to a child so that when you sit and talk with him about an incident, he can understand your verbal translation more precisely at his cognitive level. Using a diagram of an open hand, which parents and children can sit together to create, you can label each of the five fingers with one of the five categories of feelings, like the example above. For younger children, parents can trace the child's hand and then draw a face on each finger that represents one of the five feelings. Displaying this diagram in an often-seen location can remind both child and parent of these terms so they are more readily able to verbalize their experience.

One thing to note about children who have a significantly neglectful history, such as those who have spent their first years of life in an overcrowded orphanage, is that they truly may not know what feelings are. Furthermore, many children have not had sufficient mirroring experience with a primary caregiver, so they do not know what feelings mean in terms of matching each to a physiological state in their bodies. Teaching a child what his feelings are in terms of how he experiences each one in his body may be a necessary first step in the process of teaching your child about himself. Then you can use the feeling words as your "language for emotion" in the context of translating behavior, a process that can be broken down into defined tasks—the first one of which you learned in the previous section of this chapter.

The tasks in the process of translating behavior are a guide you can use as you and your child are learning to see him and his behaviors in a new way.

Tasks of Behavioral Translation

1. Become competent in controlling your reactivity to your child's behavioral triggers so that you can remain objective.
2. Name your child's behavior and the feeling driving it.
3. Recognize the need your child is conveying through the behavior.
4. Meet the need!

Later:

5. Find a connection between this emotion and an environmental trigger or event.
6. Determine what your child's behavior means within the context of his history.
7. Create your child's narrative so you will have context in which to view your child and his behavior and he will have a way to come to know who he is.

The tasks summarized above provide only the scaffolding for your inquiry. You will need to ask yourself specific questions to complete each of these tasks. Below are questions you can use to gather the information you will need to work through each behavior translation. By working methodically, you simultaneously gain the information you need to decipher the meaning of the behavior and maintain the objective mind-set necessary to see and meet his need. As you begin to practice translating, you will likely need to answer these questions at a time other than when the behavior is occurring. You will need to take your time in answering the questions accurately, as well as in assembling the resulting information into a cohesive translation. It is helpful at first to actually write down the questions and answers for yourself.

Translation Questions Guide
1. How would I describe the *actual* behavior of my child?
2. At what age would this be a typical behavior?
3. How old is the child, chronologically?
4. Is the behavior occurring inside or outside relationship?
5. What part of the brain do I think the behavior is coming from?
6. What is the brain signaling the child to do?
7. What is the emotion underlying the behavior?
8. What is the current trigger for this emotion?
9. What circumstances in the past may have elicited this emotion in my child?

Successful translation of your child's behavior will include the answers to these specific questions, some of which you may already know. Translating behavior can be an intimidating task for some parents, requiring time, patience, and realistic expectations. Also, you may have to fight the feeling of urgency to want to right the behavior or solve it in the moment it occurs. Reminding yourself that you actually have time, and that you can take your time, relieves the pressure of having to manage your child's behavior immediately. Taking time to calm yourself and breathe deliberately as the behavior is happening often changes the atmosphere enough that the behavior begins to subside on its own. As parents become familiar with the questions and agile in their use over time, the prospect of translating behavior will become much less daunting. Again, it is helpful for parents as they start the translation process to write out both the questions and the answers as a way of helping them see the whole picture.

Be prepared for the possibility that you will be in a practice mode with this process for a while; therefore, do not get discouraged if you cannot instantly make on-the-spot translations. Akin to learning a new language, gaining competence in the process of translating behavior will be a matter of patiently riding out a learning curve. As you feel more confident in using the translation process, you will be able to start using it in the moment, when the behavior is actually occurring. You will also begin to see patterns in your child's behavior; thus you will have ready translations for those behaviors that are repetitive.

To give you a more realistic sense of how these questions are used to reach an understanding of a child's behavior, we have included some examples of the questions in use by a parent who is translating the behavior of her struggling child.

Example: "The Cookie Tantrum"

1. What is the *actual* behavior of my child?
   My child is lying face down on the kitchen floor, beating his fists and the toes of his shoes on the floor while screaming, "Nooooo!"
2. At what age would this be a typical behavior?
   I would guess that this tantruming is a behavior typical of a two-year-old child.
3. How old is the child, chronologically?
   My son is seven and a half tomorrow.
4. Is the behavior occurring inside or outside relationship?
   My feeling is that my child is tantruming because he's trying to get me to give in . . . that would mean the behavior is happening within our relationship.
5. What part of the brain do I think the behavior is coming from?
   Considering that the lower brain would signal an automatic behavior—which this isn't—and the upper brain would think through the situation—which is not happening!—I'd guess it's the middle, reactive brain that's in charge right now.
6. What is the brain signaling the child to do?
   It's not signaling flight or freeze, so it must be signaling fight!
7. What is the emotion underlying the behavior?
   It looks like anger to me, but it's so overblown in relation to the circumstance that I'm going to guess there's some fear under it.
8. What is the current trigger for this emotion?
   I told my child he would have to wait until after dinner to have a cookie.
9. What circumstances in his past may have elicited this emotion in my child?
   Fear of not getting what he needs, like when he was neglected as an infant and not having anyone to help him reregulate.

This example is fairly straightforward in that this child—who is behaviorally a two-year-old—is throwing his tantrum *within relationship* with his primary caregiver. This child is, in effect, tantruming *at* his parent as a way of communicating his anger and fear to her, as a way of trying to leverage getting what he wants so he has a sense of the control he did not have when he was living with his birth mom, who infrequently met his needs. If this tantruming behavior were to occur *outside relationship* with the parent, it would be meaningless and without purpose. If we imagine this child being denied the cookie and then throwing his tantrum when no one is around, we see that the behavior ceases to be *communication*; thus it ceases to have a purpose. Effective communication requires there to be both a demonstrative sender and an attentive receiver. *There is always a meaning, purpose, and/or reason for a child's challenging behavior, which is serving as his form of communication.*

Let us now look at a similar scenario, this time with the child's undesirable behavior occurring *outside relationship* with the primary caregiver. Note that the same questions work equally well in assisting a parent in translating the behavior of her distressed child when the behavior is communicative but not directly observed.

Example: "Stolen Candy"
1. What is the *actual* behavior of my child?
   Yesterday, sometime after he returned from school and before bedtime, my son stole the Halloween candy I had bought for trick-or-treat night without my knowledge, as I discovered today.
2. At what age would this be a typical behavior?
   I'd say that any child around seven years old might normally try stealing sometime or other.
3. How old is the child, chronologically?
   My son just turned ten.
4. Is the behavior occurring inside or outside relationship?
   Definitely outside. . . . It seems almost like he's living in his own little world.
5. What part of the brain do I think the behavior is coming from?
   He would have had to use his thinking brain to figure out where the candy was in the first place, and then to make a plan to steal it when I wouldn't be around to catch him in the act—which must have been when I was out in the garden after dinner. But his thinking brain wouldn't be telling him to steal just for the heck of it. So something else would have had to trigger him. It can't be the lower brain because nobody steals purely automatically, so it must be the middle brain saying, "fight, flight, or freeze."

6. What is the brain signaling the child to do?

    Hmmmm. . . . Well, for some reason, it must have told him to bypass me, or else he would have at least first asked me for the candy before he stole it, so I think it signaled "fight," like he was on his own again, fighting for survival.

7. What is the emotion underlying the behavior?

    Let's see. . . . The five feeling categories are glad, sad, mad, scared, and ashamed. He certainly wasn't glad, he didn't seem sad, and shame would come into the picture probably after he stole the candy, if at all. So he could have been mad at me for some reason and stole the candy to take his anger out on me. But there was the possibility that I wouldn't have discovered that the candy was gone or that I wouldn't have figured out that he was the one who took the candy, so there must have been something else going on. I guess there's only one possibility left . . . that he was scared for some reason . . . but scared of what? Did something happen that I don't know about?

8. What is the current trigger for this emotion?

    That's not so easy. Let me think back. . . . When he came in the door from school yesterday afternoon, my son threw down his backpack, stormed off up to his room, and slammed his door, not even stopping to take off his coat. He's usually hungry for the afternoon snack we always have together, but when I called him to come down for it, he yelled through his door to leave him alone. It felt like he was going to handle whatever it was that happened yesterday at school on his own because he didn't even want the snack when I left it outside his door. I felt like he didn't need me or want me in his life just then. So whatever happened before he got home from school made him fall back into his old driven-by-fear pattern of not relying on anyone, especially me, his parent, even to provide him with food when he was hungry. This is what may have been underneath his stealing the candy.

9. What circumstances in the past may have elicited this emotion in my child?

    That's not hard. . . . Before we adopted our son, he was practically the adult in the home he came from even though he was just five, having to take care of his birth mother when she was drunk, along with his little sister. On top of this, there was commonly little to no food in the home.

A child's past often lends us clues we can use to understand his behavior in the present. The feeling under the child's disarming behavior can be triggered by a current event or circumstance that reminds him—consciously or unconsciously—of something traumatic in his past. Most of the time, your child will not be able to make the connection between past trauma and his present feelings because he did not have an adult early on in his life who helped him connect his feelings with his experience. Therefore, asking your child the question, "Why did you do that?" is not only fruitless, but *it induces shame in the child because he does not know the answer.*

Consequently, it is up to you, your child's parent and best advocate, to figure out what your child is feeling and what sets off his difficult behaviors. Fortunately, you are not being left on your own to struggle with this task. Parents who have come before you have discovered that most children get triggered and that some triggers are fairly universal. For traumatized children in particular, there are some common triggers for difficult behavior that can be predictable or expected. Knowing these will give you a starting place as you work to determine what specifically is prompting your child's feelings and behaviors. Below is a list of potential triggers for challenging behavior.

Potential Triggers for Your Child's Difficult Behaviors

➤ Feeling fear (almost always connected in some way to difficult behavior)

➤ Feeling shame or being shamed—even if it is just the child's perception he is being shamed

➤ Physical dysregulation: being hungry, needing sleep, needing to be warmer or cooler or hydrated, sensory overload or lack of sufficient sensory input

➤ Being overstimulated by an activity or event

➤ Not understanding something

➤ Having to try to do something beyond his abilities

➤ Being caught by expectations that are too high (either yours or your child's)

➤ Leaving home (even if it's just for mundane errands)

➤ Mom or dad leaving, or the child having to separate from mom and dad even for a short time

➤ Changes in routine, transitions—including shifting from one activity to another

➤ People arguing, yelling, threatening, fighting
➤ Time of the year sparking a memory of trauma or stirring the unconscious memory
➤ Certain places, lighting, smells, tastes, sounds, sights, touch
➤ New experiences/new people
➤ School starting, ending, or breaking for holiday
➤ Birthdays (stirs up thoughts or feelings about child's birth mother or birth family)
➤ Times of grief or loss, or exposure to themes of loss
➤ Holidays (especially Mother's and Father's Days, Thanksgiving, Christmas)
➤ Illness, medical appointment, or a crisis for either the child or the parent
➤ Developmental change or reaching developmental milestones

Making a list of triggers specific to your own child, whether you have recognized them in the list above or in the course of your work with your child, gives you a ready reference that can be useful, especially when emotions are running high. Recognizing that your child has a fairly definable set of challenging behaviors and triggers can actually be a relief. Anytime you can corral information about your child, you feel more in control as a parent, and thus more competent. Building an information arsenal that includes your child's narrative, your experience with your child, your translations of his behavior, your familiarity with your child's triggers, and your knowledge of basic child development gives you the knowledge and the confidence you need to make sense of why your child does what he does.

Focus on Understanding Behavior, Not on Changing Behavior

In addition to having the benefit of other parents' experience (the list above) in defining your child's triggers, you also have access to the combined knowledge of professionals who have done the research and have worked with innumerable families struggling with the same issues your family has. While focusing on changing behavior has long been an approach therapists have used in attempting to help their clients get better, in the realm of working with distressed children, focusing on *changing behavior* has proven to be ineffective. Relatively recently, we have discovered that *understanding a child's behavior* is actually the key to healing his distress.

In the process of focusing on understanding distressed children's behavior, you will find that your child has core themes that underlie many of his behaviors and arise from the unique circumstances of his genetics and early life. In identifying these core themes, we are able to add yet another layer of knowledge to the bank of information parents can draw from that will allow them to more readily translate their child's behavior, and thus more quickly identify and meet their child's needs. We will look at translations of needs in context of the specific behaviors that children use to convey them.

On page 129 are a few items from the list of child behaviors you worked with earlier to better understand yourself and your reactivity. This time, you will be looking at this list to better understand the *message and need your child is conveying* with each behavior. The child's behavior is described in the left column, the reason for it is in the middle column, and the origin or one possible translation of its message is in the right column. Since a behavior may translate in more than one way, the translation we offer may not necessarily be "the" right one or "the" one that your child may be expressing with the given behavior. Nonetheless, we are suggesting a likely translation for each behavior to help you to begin to think in terms of the *purpose and meaning* of your child's behavior. Our goal is to help you develop an *empathic* mind-set so that empathy eventually becomes your automatic response when your child is dysregulated.

While any list of challenging child behaviors can be quite extensive, the reasons for those behaviors are actually relatively few, as you can see in the middle column. These nine reasons could be applied to the entire list you reviewed at the beginning of this chapter to determine what your particular triggers are when it comes to challenging child behaviors. This is because a distressed child's relational deficits occurred during his earliest years, when his core developmental tasks included gaining a sense of trust and safety in care, developing the capacity for self-regulation, and establishing a sense of self-worth. Mastering these foundational tasks requires that the child be in relationship with a singular, attuned, present, and committed caregiver. When a child does not have this relationship, his basic needs for trust, safety, regulation, and self-worth remain unmet. Thus, the distressed child's challenging behaviors stem from this deficit that is at the core of his being.

Child Behaviors with *Suggested* Translations

YOUR CHILD'S BEHAVIOR	REASON FOR BEHAVIOR	ORIGIN OR MEANING OF BEHAVIOR
Always delays, stalls, or tantrums when it's time to go or switch activities	to control transitions	When things change, I'm afraid I'll be abandoned.
Behaves well with everyone except you	to preserve emotional distance	You're getting too close and I am afraid you'll leave me.
Can't understand others' feelings—lacks empathy toward you/others	underdeveloped brain	Lacked adequate primary caregiving relationship
Constantly mopes around, seems chronically depressed	needs to be nurtured	I'm alone and don't belong.
Makes you feel afraid around him	to feel powerful	This is how I learned to get what I need.
Puts forth minimal or no effort in school	to avoid shame	If I try I might fail.
Regresses after an accomplishment	to prove "I'm bad"	I need you to see me how I see me.
Self-harms: cuts self, bangs head, picks scabs until bloody, pulls hair out, hits self	to ease anxiety	I need to take control of my inner pain.
Tries to control everything you do	to maintain control; to feel safe	If I control you, you won't hurt or leave me.

As you work with your own child in discovering the meaning of his actions, it will become clear to you that there actually is a limited number of messages that he could be conveying, even if he is displaying a broad range of behaviors. If you can keep this observation in mind, it will bolster your sense of competence as a parent. Having a defined set of possible meanings for your child's undesirable behavior (revisit the nine meanings in the middle column of the translations chart above) will help you more readily identify what your child is trying to say to you. Accordingly, your quest to ultimately uncover your child's *core need* will be much more straightforward than you might have thought.

What Your Child Needs from You

Having determined what your child's behavior *means* allows you then to decipher the *need* he is expressing in any given moment. In general and above all, *what your child craves and needs most is your acceptance.* He needs you to accept the reasons he behaves as he does, the feelings that drive his behavior, and the needs he is expressing underneath his behavior. Your child needs *your compassion.* He needs *your empathy* and *your understanding* of him within the context of his life experiences. Your child needs *your patience* as you build a relationship with him and support him in his growth. He needs to experience your *joy and playfulness* as he struggles to know he is safe. Your child needs *your reassurance* that the two of you are on this journey *together* and that *you are committed to him no matter what.*

Due to insufficient nurturing in his past, your child did not experience the relational interactions he needed with a primary caregiver to learn how to manage his physical and emotional needs. Therefore, your child also needs for you to *regulate* him when he cannot regulate himself. He needs for you to *mirror* him so that he can come to know himself. No one before you has helped him to connect his actions with his feelings and motives. Your child needs *your time* so he can learn about the world from within your relationship. In order to make sense of his experiences, your child relies upon you to interpret all that is and all that happens. Your child needs your *attention* so that he can grow to know that he is worthy and valuable. In the past, your child was not someone's priority, so he was not able to know he is precious. Your child needs your *respect* so he can learn that he belongs. Before being with you, your child did not have the security to feel like he fit in, to know he was a part of a family.

To help you grasp what meeting each of these core needs looks like in terms of parenting, at right is a summary of a child's core needs as described above, along with definitions of the generalized actions you would take as a parent to meet those needs.

Naming the need the child is expressing through his behavior can sometimes be difficult for parents because the need is often one of a much

What your child needs most is your acceptance, empathy, compassion, patience, and reassurance

Child's Core Needs/Essential Parent Actions

WHAT YOUR CHILD NEEDS	ESSENTIAL PARENT ACTIONS
your acceptance	embracing your whole, unique child—who he is, what he does, and what he feels
your compassion	understanding the "whys" of your child's behavior in context of his history
your empathy	"seeing into" your child to understand his feelings, thoughts, and behavior
your patience	identifying and following your child's pace
your joy and playfulness	setting the emotional tone that supports your child in feeling safe
your reassurance	showing and telling your child that you're there for him no matter what
your commitment	letting your child know through words and actions that you'll never give up on him
your regulation	using your parent-self (movement, breath, soothing) to alleviate your child's dysregulation
your mirroring	naming and connecting your child's feelings and behaviors to his needs
your time	reorganizing your life to make your child a priority
your attention	focusing on and interacting with your child throughout each day
your perspective	interpreting the world and your child's experiences for him through your eyes
your respect	admiring your child and having confidence that your child "can do"

younger child due to the lack of adequate nurturing he experienced early in his life. Reorienting yourself to the tendency for *your child's behavioral age to be younger than his chronological age* takes time and practice. As you become more able to set aside your child's chronological age in order to see his behavioral age, identifying his need will come more easily. You can refer back to Chapters 4 and 5 as often as you need to in order to refresh those concepts.

Parents also can flounder in *meeting* their child's needs if their distress is aroused by a challenging behavior because that feeling prompts them to move too quickly to "fix" the problem their child is having. Therefore, it is essential that parents slow down and take the time to *name the child's need* under the behavior, lest they jump to an intervention out of *their own need* to ease *their own discomfort or anxiety*. When parents get sidetracked by their own distress, their child's needs can remain unaddressed and thus destined to resurface again and again until they are met.

Identifying the core need your child is expressing with each separate behavior is the first step toward choosing the appropriate intervention to meet the need. In our example "The Cookie Tantrum"—wherein the seven-and-a-half-year-old child was tantruming because his mother would not allow him to have his cookie before dinner—the parent concluded that her child's tantruming behavior was akin to that of a two-year-old and indicative of his dysregulation. She translated this behavior as being an expression of her child's underlying *fear and core need for parent regulation*, which called for the parent to use herself in ways that would shift her child's *unregulated state* to match her own *regulated state*.

The parent could accomplish this by calmly sitting down in a chair near her child, breathing deeply while waiting patiently as her child resolved his tantruming. Another action she could take is to use her voice in a soothing manner to say, "I know this is hard for you," as she awaited his resolve. Alternatively, if the parent knew that her child was responsive to touch, she might have gently touched him or pulled him into her lap to rock him, which would have directly regulated him physically in accordance with her own regulated state.

A child may be displaying more than one core need with his behavior. In our second example, "Stolen Candy"—in which the ten-year-old child stole the Halloween candy—the parent translated her child's behavior as meaning that he felt he could not rely upon her to meet his needs. The parent reminded herself that her child's tendency was to rely on himself—especially when he was under stress—because in the past this child learned that caregivers were not trustworthy to meet even the most basic of his needs, like providing him with food. In this example, the child experienced an upsetting event outside the home, then went into self-care mode as soon as he arrived home instead of seeking out his parent for comfort and understanding. The child even rejected his parent's attempt to reach out to him, as evidenced by his ignoring the snack she placed outside his door. Then he clearly communicated that he did not need anyone by trying to handle his feelings and needs on his own by stealing the candy.

This child's parent concluded that one of her child's *core needs* was for her to *accept* him just as he is, including his need for control and

**Once you've *identified* the need and the *age* of the need,
you must take the time to *name* the need with the child
to help him understand why he does what he does**

self-reliance in the moment. Next, the parent saw her child's need for *empathy*, the need for her to accurately "see into him" to understand his current feelings, thoughts, and behavior. Finally, the parent recognized she needed to *mirror* her child by reflecting how he was feeling and summarizing why he did what he did based on his past. The parent accomplished this as she sat calmly with her child the next day, gently expressing her acceptance, empathy, and understanding of him through her voice as she provided context and meaning for his behavior.

Parent Response: "Stolen Candy"

[Parent goes over to her son, who is slouching on the couch, and sits near him.]

Parent: Wow, it seems like you had *such* a hard day yesterday . . .

Child: What*ev-er*!

Parent: I really want you to know that I care about you, and I want you to know that you're not going to get in trouble about the candy. . . . I just want us to sit here together and talk.
Okay with you?

Child: Hmmmfff . . .

Parent: It seemed you were ticked off about something when you came home from school yesterday. . .

Child: Hmmf . . .

Parent: . . . like maybe something happened at school or on the bus . . .

Child: . . . yeah . . . I guess . . .

Parent: I'm sorry you've had a tough time . . .

Child: . . . yeah, that idiot, Chris, kicked me really hard when I got off the bus . . .

Parent: Ohh, ouch.

Child: . . . and for no reason!

Parent: I'm *so* sorry.

Child: Yeah, I wanna *punch him* in the face . . .

Parent: You're so mad at him.

Child: Uh-huh . . .

Parent: And when you came in the door, you were steaming mad.

Child: Ya *think?*

[Parent purposefully ignores the child's sarcasm.]

Parent: And you went right to your room and slammed the door, like, "There, take *that*."

Child: Mmm.

Parent: And you didn't even want a snack . . .

Child: Nope . . . just wanted to be alone.

Parent: Yeah.
It's been *so hard* for you for so long . . .
It's like you feel all alone . . .

Child: Uh-huh. . .

Parent: Like you don't ever think *any*one can do *any*thing.

Child: They *can't.*

Parent: And you feel like if anything does get done, you'll have to do it yourself . . .

Child: . . . always do . . .

Parent: Like even parents are lame . . .

Child: Uh . . . *Yah-ah!*

Parent: Like, "I don't need their stupid snack. I'll get my own."

Child: Yep!

Parent: It's so hard to believe that you can depend on anyone, especially parents.

Child: Well, I *can't.*

Parent: Like before you lived here, you had to do *everything.*

Child: Mmm.

Parent: Life's not been fun or easy or anything . . .

Child: Nope.

Parent: And why should you think it could be any different anywhere else . . .

Child: 'Cuz it's not . . .

Parent: So hard to feel there's no hope . . .
So hard . . .

Child: Mmm.

Parent: Ya know what?

Child: . . . huh . . .

Parent: I'm glad we can sit like this together.
Thanks for talkin' about everything . . .

Child: Mmm.

Parent: Can you give me a hand in the kitchen? Seems like you're the only one who knows how to tell when the pizza's done just right . . . and not burnt.

Child: . . . yeah . . . all right . . .

Parent: Great!

[Parent gives child quick side hug and they get up and go to the kitchen.]

The parent in this example proceeded to meet the three identified core needs of her child—acceptance, empathy, and mirroring—by skipping consequences for now—for his stealing behavior and for his attitude in this talk with his parent—to move directly into mirroring. Levying consequences right away would have only further alienated this child and increased his resolve to remain self-reliant, leaving his needs unmet. This mirroring approach gives the child the opportunity to develop trust in his caregiver, to feel safe, and to learn about himself—the exact, nurturing parenting experience he needs for his growth and healing. *It is only through a parent's mirroring of her child's inner world that he will come to understand himself and thus eventually be able to verbalize his feelings on his own instead of acting them out.*

Yet parents are often baffled by the idea that *talking with a child is an intervention,* let alone an effective one. Used to doling out consequences to a child who steals, some parents balk at the suggestion that there is an effective intervention that does not include punishment. Such parents are convinced that a child steals because he has not yet learned right from wrong, and believe they must teach him this distinction via consequences. The reality is, though, *the child who steals knows perfectly well that stealing is wrong, so punishing him in order to teach him this lesson is not only useless, it fails to address the actual need the child is conveying with his actions.* Moreover, a punishment approach would only be effective as a deterrent if used *within relationship* because for it to work, a child needs to be invested in *wanting his parent's approval.* For a child who is operating

---

Talking and listening are active interventions.
Doling out a consequence before understanding the behavior
fails to meet the need beneath the behavior and is ineffective.

independently, thus *outside relationship* with his parent, desiring parental approval holds no sway, so consequences would not leverage acceptable behavior.

Key Points for Chapter 7

1. Your child's behavior is a cue to his needs, and reading those cues accurately allows you to meet his needs accurately.

2. You must learn to manage your reactivity to your personal triggers so that you can be present for your child.

3. Teaching your child the five words for emotion—glad, sad, mad, scared, and ashamed—is the first step in helping him understand his need that lies beneath his behavior.

4. Once you've identified the need, and the age of the need, you must take the time to name the need with the child to help him understand why he does what he does.

5. Talking and listening are active interventions. Doling out a consequence before understanding the behavior fails to meet the need beneath the behavior and is ineffective.

8.
Creating an Emotional Connection with Your Child

How to "Tune In" to What Your Child Is Feeling and "Get" Him

For "full" emotional communication, one person needs to allow his state of mind to be influenced by that of the other.

DANIEL J. SIEGEL, MD

✎ A VERY LOUD AND DETERMINED fourteen-year-old Mikayla stomped around the waiting room, disturbing others. This was her last day in the treatment center. Dr. Sanjah, who knew her only slightly, entered the room and told her in a stern voice to sit down and be quiet. Mikayla started moving toward him with a resounding "No!" A nearby staff member, Kyle, who knew Mikayla well, came by her side and quietly asked her to come with him. Mikayla had come to trust Kyle over the eighteen months she had been in treatment, and so she turned to go with him. As they walked together down the hall, Kyle wondered aloud if Mikayla was trying to show how strong she was and how she could handle things on her own; he guessed that inside, she was pretty frightened about leaving. At Kyle's words, Mikayla stopped in the hall and started crying, acknowledging her anxiety about returning home and to public school. Kyle "got" Mikayla, and Mikayla felt understood. Kyle's ability to accurately attune to Mikayla's true feelings and to her need to be understood at this scary time of transitioning back home calmed her. She was now able to return to the waiting room, take a seat, and quietly wait for her appointment. When Dr. Sanjah came out and called her name, Mikayla stood and apologized to him as they walked into his office.

What Is Attunement?

Attunement is the vehicle through which parents develop an emotional connection with their child, and it is the foundational mechanism through which attachment develops. With the goal of creating a harmonious and responsive relationship, parents attune to their child and translate his behavioral language into the needs he is expressing. A child's behavior serves as a door to his inner world—a door that parents need to gently open with their patience and understanding. The process of attunement does not include responding to a child's behavior with interrogation, correction, or consequences. Attunement is the art of *listening to and communicating with the child inside,* while *exploring and reflecting* his thoughts, feelings, and needs. Parents enter their child's internal world to bring out what is inside of him to help the child see and understand himself. The attunement process provides order and gives meaning to all that a child experiences. As the child comes to understand himself through his parents' attunement, he attains the ability to begin to attune to others.

The natural unfolding of attunement begins in utero as the mother feels and responds to her baby's movements. Through verbal and tactile feedback, the mother narrates her experience of her baby as he grows within her womb. As she massages her belly while her baby kicks, the mother might reflect aloud, "Oh, there you are! You're kicking up a storm. I wonder what you're trying to tell me." When the baby is born, the mother continues reflecting her infant's experience in the world as she narrates while holding him as he fusses: "I wonder what's wrong. You seem so upset. Let's figure it out and help you feel better." As the mother meets her infant's need, she narrates what she has discovered about his discomfort: "Oh, you're wet and you hate to be wet. Let's change you." Through his mother's words and action, the infant calms, returning to a more comfortable state. The baby feels safe, loved, and understood, while his mother experiences the relief, satisfaction, and pleasure of having eased her baby into contentment. This dance repeats itself throughout infancy and childhood, and the child learns he can trust in his mother and her care.

Each age and developmental stage has its unique set of rhythms, and as the child grows, his needs change. Parents follow along, attuning to the newness of their child and his needs as he progresses through his development. Parents attune to their toddler's need for independence, their middle school child's need for downtime after school, and their teenager's need for differentiation. Parents meet and greet all aspects of their child's self and inner world, including his coping defenses, which can show up as frantic behaviors or in the silence of withdrawal. Attunement provides structure for the emotional experience that parent and child share, which over time creates an irresistible draw that brings the child gently into relationship and trust. Then the relationship seems to unfold on its own as together parent and child discover whom the child is, inside and out.

This gentle unfolding of relationship through attunement is a foreign experience for an emotionally distressed child, whose complex and troubled history disrupted any chance for him to develop a meaningful bond with a caregiver. The failed attachment process has damaged this child's foundational development across all domains, and the only remedy is to provide him with a successful attachment experience in the present. The distressed child needs a primary caregiver who is committed for the long run to provide the level of care and nurturance that is required to revisit and provide his missing developmental experiences. This process does not, however, resemble the gentle unfolding of relationship that marks the experience of a child raised lovingly by his birth mother. While the distressed child's forever parent is ready and motivated to create connection, the child harbors a profound ambivalence toward coming into relationship. This child's simultaneous wish for and fear of getting close to a primary caregiver holds him in a web of confusion and distrust. Makeshift or random attempts by the hurt child's present parent to get along with him, to elicit compliant behavior, and to connect emotionally inevitably lead to frustration, disappointment, and failure.

Therefore, a forever parent needs to employ *therapeutic attunement* and use it as an *intentional tool* to provide the distressed child with the innumerable nurturing experiences he missed early on. *Intuitive attunement*—that which is biologically driven and implemented by a birth mother following her maternal instinct—flows naturally from the mother's hormonal and neurochemical states, which impel her to be highly focused upon and exquisitely responsive to her infant's mood, expressions, and needs such as hunger, discomfort, and playfulness. *Therapeutic attunement*—that which needs to be consciously applied to re-create the early developmental experiences the child missed—must be studied, learned, and practiced. Questions about how to proceed with this remedial intervention can be answered by referring to the fundamental developmental model of intuitive attunement—the process carried forth by a capable birth mother.

Although much more difficult to sustain and apply, therapeutic attunement does eventually facilitate the child's ability to trust, relate to

---

**Attunement is the art of listening to and communicating with
the "child inside" that allows the child to "feel felt"**

Therapeutic attunement is like learning the foreign language
of your child's inner world. It takes time and practice.

others, and develop a secure, cohesive sense of self. While neither the hurt child nor the therapeutic parent are immersed in a neurochemical bath that could drive them to connect biologically, therapeutic attunement can be used to emulate the more instinctual patterns associated with the development of a trusting relationship. Breaches in the original intuitive attunement experiences of the child can, in fact, be remedied through the consistent application of therapeutic attunement by a capable forever caregiver. Implementation of this intervention does not rely upon the child's assistance: therapeutic attunement requires only that the child be physically present. It is up to the parents to facilitate the creation of an emotional connection with their child. Investment in the process will develop over time for the child as he gains the ability to understand his experience, identify his feelings, and voice his needs.

Necessary Conditions for Therapeutic Attunement

In order to really listen to your child, you must be in a physical, emotional, and interpersonal environment that supports safety for your child. None of us can talk about what we are really feeling if we don't feel valued or listened to. You probably wouldn't want to use therapeutic attunement in the middle of watching a baseball game or in your child's classroom. If you are stressed about work or angry, you may not be in a position to accurately hear what your child is saying. The goal of attunement is to understand the inner workings of your child—it is much like listening to a baby's cries and differentiating the cry that signifies hunger or a wet diaper. It doesn't have to happen all of the time or only when the child is upset. It happens within the structure of your family, a structure that allows time for closeness and listening.

A Safe, Non-Distracting Holding Environment
The first condition that is necessary for therapeutic attunement to occur is having *a safe, non-distracting, one-on-one holding environment*. On the one hand, "holding environment" refers to physical surroundings, structure,

and time factors that are conducive to working with a distressed child. On the other hand, "holding environment" refers to the parent's mind-set, state of composure, and inner reserves. Children who come from backgrounds of loss and trauma often have developed chaotic internal worlds, so an organized, psychologically safe, and predictable external world helps them feel safe, prepares them for transitions, and gives them a matrix within which they can learn to regulate their internal processes. The goal of structuring the holding environment is regulation of the child's internal world.

A setting that conveys a sense of safety for the child may include a simple, uncluttered room, incandescent lighting, comfy furniture like an overstuffed rocking chair, relative quiet, no electronics, no people distractions, and perhaps subtly healing scents, softly flowing music, and cuddly blankets. This same type of setting may also be soothing for and supportive of the parent who needs such environs to maintain a calm demeanor for the healing work. Structuring time is essential for creating a sense of security for the child, and can be prepared by setting and following a schedule that embraces predictability and simplicity, that limits excursions, and that downplays or eliminates extracurricular activities. Parents can start with more structure than they think they may need and decrease it as the child's sense of security deepens. Setting a unhurried pace, along with assuring there are few deadlines, are ways of ensuring that time does not put pressure on the process. Children, especially children with early losses and traumas, need predictability and structure in their lives. The distressed child needs more structure than most—much like the structure needed by a two- and three-year-old.

You may need to adjust the holding environment based on your child's emotions at the time. Is this a time for the parent to stay in close proximity to the child, or would it be more beneficial for the child to remain within the parent's line of sight but not too close? If close proximity is appropriate in the moment, does the parent sit face to face or side by side with the child? Parents use proximity consciously to stay near the edge of their child's level of tolerance for intimacy without intruding into the child's personal/emotional space. Likewise, parents gauge the level of control

---

A *holding environment* refers to the quiet internal *psychological* space of the parent as well as a quiet *physical* space

and containment the child needs presently in the holding environment, staying near the child's growing edge without being overbearing.

If you came from an adequately nurturing environment, can you remember what it was like? Remember the weekday pattern: getting up, going to school, coming home, playing and doing homework, having dinner, and being tucked in bed? Remember the comfort of knowing that someone would be there to ask you how your day was when you got home? Remember how the loosened structure of the weekend felt so different, and that once your chores were done you could go play? Remember the weekend family outing, going to church and then brunch? Conversely, if you had an inadequately nurturing environment that was not structured, do you recall your feelings of anxiety, loneliness, and fear that came with absent or abusive parents, no enforced rules, no family schedule, and not knowing what would happen next? The latter is what the distressed child's world may have been like, and he has brought his feelings of anxiety, loneliness, and fear with him into your home and family. Re-creating his lack of structure would not be healing for the child; he needs the kind of structure described in the former, nurturing scenario to complete his developmental growth.

Adults who care for distressed children need this structure as well. Making organized and regular times to sit down with your child after school, having regular family mealtimes and habitual quiet time before bed, and scheduling a weekly night out with your spouse lends an adult rhythm to your day that is independent from that of your child. Making time for coffee with a friend, time for a phone call with your own parent, and time to commune with your spouse after work instills structure that creates the space necessary to grow and maintain adult relationships. Preserving even a few minutes to be alone each day gives you some time to relax and recoup the energy it takes to respond rather than react.

The holding environment also includes embodying qualities that enable you, the parent, to gently contain your child so you can focus on the development of your relationship with him. These qualities allow you to maintain a therapeutic attitude that is portable and can be carried with you as you negotiate your child's needs, no matter what the location or circumstance. This mind-set poises you to relax and enjoy your child rather than promotes controlling his behaviors. Dan Hughes, PhD, has captured the nature of the holding environment embodied by the parent beautifully with the acronym PLACE, which stands for playfulness, love, acceptance, curiosity, and empathy (Hughes, 2004). Hughes likens the attitude that PLACE instills in the parent to that of a parent enjoying interacting with a toddler. Acceptance and curiosity allow parents to convey approval of the unique person their child is, while valuing the child and being open to learning more about him. Playfulness and love reduce cortisol levels and help parents respond to their child in a way he can more easily understand and absorb. Empathy allows parents to convey their understanding of their child's feelings, thoughts, and wants to him in a way so he knows they "get him."

Putting "Yourself on the Shelf"

The next condition necessary for employing therapeutic attunement is *the parent's suspension of her own needs*. This means that the parent stays in an objective mode in the face of the child's behaviors to avoid taking the behaviors personally. Suspension of self includes being able to put aside personal fears, as well as the need for immediate gratification and loving, grateful reciprocity from the child. Containment of self includes holding onto personal needs and feelings that are not beneficial to the child's healing in the immediate situation, assuring the self that these needs and feelings are important and will be addressed at an appropriate time. As parents suspend and contain themselves, they continue "watching" themselves as they interact with their child and respond to the child's behaviorally expressed needs. This self-observation is essential if the parent is to remain objective while working with the child. Sometimes parents attempt to parent distressed children while holding onto a belief that they can help themselves by helping their child. The reality is, however, that personal issues that have not been mastered are guaranteed to intensify in the process of parenting a hurt child.

In the work of healing a distressed child, the parent must play dual roles, one as a participant and the other as the observer. Instead of standing on the shore coaching the child how to swim, the parent goes to the depths with the child emotionally while keeping one foot on solid emotional ground, lest in drowning, the child pulls the parent under with him. Being the observer enables the parent to see and read the child accurately, while being the participant allows that parent to resonate and be with the child emotionally. This dualistic stance is not always easy for parents to maintain, and some days it may not be possible for parents to sustain. Therefore, knowing "when to hold 'em and when to fold 'em" can be as

To attune accurately, you will have to put your needs for being appreciated and gratified "on a shelf," much as you would when parenting an infant

important as striving to maintain the participant/observer parenting dichotomy. On the days when playing both roles is too much, parents need to "fold 'em" and take time out to regroup and revitalize their energy. As much as they are capable of doing so, parents work to carry out their dual role to create the corrective emotional experience their child needs by maintaining emotional connection without losing judgment.

The Attunement Process

The process of attunement includes four elements: *reading* the child's communication, *resonating* emotionally with the child, *reflecting* what your child is communicating and feeling, and *repairing* to reestablish the connection when it is missed or broken.

Read your child's communication. Your child's communication comes in many more forms than only words. Listen to your child's spoken or implied words in the context of his body language, his emotion, the tone, cadence, and volume of his voice, and the congruence of presentation with meaning. Broad awareness along with active curiosity will allow you to meet your child where he is and gain insight into his internal world.

> Parent: You're saying "I don't care" with your words, but you have a mad face and a loud voice, so I wonder if maybe you do really feel more strongly about it.

Resonate with your child's emotion. Join your child in the feeling he is expressing by imagining what the experience might feel like for him.

> Parent: I wonder if you're really wanting to say, "I'm so mad at you I could break down this house and smash it to bits!"

If your resonation with your child's underlying affect is inaccurate or "off" in scale and he lets you know by getting tenser, you may need to try again.

> Parent: Or maybe you're just plain mad.

As you see your child relax just a bit with this more accurate resonation, you know you are aligning more closely with his internal state.

Reflect about the meaning of your child's expression. Mirror your child's experience of his world in the moment, starting from the outer layer and working inward.

> Parent: When I said I had to work so I couldn't come to your soccer game this afternoon and you said you didn't care, your face seemed to tell me something else.
>
> [Child is crossing his arms and scowling.]
>
> Parent: Maybe you really do care and really wanted me to be there, and you're mad at me because I wasn't there.
>
> [Child is still crossing his arms and scowling, but now he shrugs.]
>
> Parent: Maybe you think I don't care about you because I didn't come to your game, and that makes you really mad, but you also feel like, "What's the use?"
>
> [Child shrugs again, slightly.]
>
> Parent: Because you feel like no one's *ever* cared about you, so why bother to get mad now: it won't make a difference.

Note how the parent in this example started the reflection by stating the precipitating event—not coming to the child's game—and followed this by noticing her child's countenance during his reaction, about which she made a guess at identifying his underlying feeling in the present, and finished with a theory tying the present feeling to the child's history. Knowing through her experience with her child that his nonreactions meant, "Go on," and his shrugs meant, "Yes, you've got it," the parent proceeded, going deeper each time.

Repair when you miss connecting or miss a cue. You are not going to always "get it," and sometimes you will even miss seeing there is something to get. What matters is that you go back and narrate your mistake, right the situation, then proceed from there.

> Parent: I'm sorry that when I said I was not coming to your game yesterday I thought you were too mad to talk about it. I'm thinking now that you actually did want us to talk about it right then because of the way you stood there with your arms folded and a mad look on your face as I went off to the kitchen. I'm sorry I missed "getting you" yesterday. I really do want to know what you were feeling. Let's figure it out.

The maintenance of an empathic, observant state is essential to your growing relationship with your child. The more confusing the behavior, the more important is your ability to actively attune. On the other hand, the frequency of use of *active attunement*—fully processing your empathic observations with your child—depends upon your child's temperament, his place in building his relationship with you, and his present receptivity. Active attunement probably should not be used in more than 10 percent of the day's interactions. Can you imagine how intrusive it would feel for someone to constantly observe, name, and be curious about your behaviors? Too much attunement may push the child away instead of draw him closer. Other children may be ready for, or thrive on, receiving much more active attunement throughout the day. Sensitivity to your child's present state will give you the information you need to determine if it is a time that would be beneficial to talk.

Attunement Specifics

In addition to the crucial four "Rs," *reading (the need underneath the behavior), resonating, reflecting, and repairing,* engaging your child through attunement involves using a variety of actions that help personalize the connective experience for you and your child. Although it is helpful for parents to become familiar with these ways of enhancing connection, they need not memorize them all. A regular review of the following aspects of attunement will help parents integrate them into their work with their child a few at a time. It is important for parents to remember that using therapeutic attunement takes practice and that following a reasonably paced learning curve makes acquiring the skills involved less daunting.

Therapeutic Attunement "How-Tos"
CONCENTRATE ON NONVERBALS. They are far more important than words. Attachment occurs through voice tone, register, pace, volume; through facial expressions via the eyes, mouth, jaw, brow, color, and tilt of the head; and through body posture via position of shoulders, arms, and legs, rapidity

of movement, and straightness of the spine. The parent reads her child's nonverbals, modulates her own nonverbals (a distressed child is exquisitely sensitive to his caregiver's body language), and gauges her level of interaction based on her child's present level of interactive tolerance.

MIRROR FEELINGS. A child is not always aware when he is experiencing a feeling, nor does he always know what that feeling *is*. Mirroring can feel intrusive to a child, but only minimally so if the parents do not force a discussion about what is being mirrored. If they are careful in this way, parents can make frequent use of mirroring to help their child learn who he is. Mirroring is active attunement that takes place in the present; therefore, observations need to be made in the present tense. "You look so sad right now. Your eyes look like they want to cry." Left alone, an observation like this made without an agenda allows connection to take place and also provides an opportunity for further discussion if the child is receptive in the moment.

USE PHYSICAL SUPPORT WHEN POSSIBLE. A gentle hand on the back, an arm around the shoulders, sitting close, holding, and rocking are all desirable ways to support your connection with your child. Although touch can be a positive way to connect, its use must be intentional, appropriate, and measured by the child's level of comfort in the moment. Traumatized children can be anxious about being near or touching others, especially adults in charge. Extra care and sensitivity around touch on the part of the parent can increase trust.

ENCOURAGE EYE CONTACT AND GAZE. Hearts connect through the meeting of eyes, and using the power of eye contact can enhance your relationship with your child. However, there are a couple of important considerations for parents to keep in mind. For the emotionally distressed child, making eye contact can be one of the most difficult things for him to do, as he anticipates anger and rejection. Don't demand, but do notice how eye contact naturally grows as trust develops. In addition, even infants naturally look away to gain some important interpersonal space at times, so some looking away is natural. Have you ever spoken with someone whose eye contact is too intense? Sometimes it is helpful for parents to make working on the transition from no eye contact to open gaze a playful experience for the child. "Hey, Bert, let's play the looking game for a minute or two. Let's see who looks away or cracks up first. I bet it's gonna be me. Ready . . . go!" Constantly making a big deal out of eye contact or requiring it of your child stresses him and decreases his trust in you. Your child can only assimilate the experience of connecting at the heart level at his own pace. Your respect and sensitivity to where your child is in the present with eye contact will make his experiential learning feel safe as he progresses. A little bit of eye contact every day goes a long way.

RECOGNIZE DEFENSES. To survive early relational trauma, distressed children develop psychological defenses that allow them to feel some sense of control. Some of these defenses are anger, joking, silliness, distraction, changing the subject, blaming others, denial, arguing, oppositionality, and many, many more. Within an unpredictable, violent, or neglectful living situation, a child's feelings of helplessness and hopelessness would overwhelm him if he could not claim some measure of control. Acquired defenses become a part of the child's sense of self and travel with him into new environments and relationships. We all have defenses, but for the distressed child, the defense may be getting in the way of what he actually needs from you—closeness and care.

NOTICE INCONGRUITIES. When the meaning of a child's words does not match his body language and nonverbal expression, his feelings are out of sync with his demeanor. Often, this incongruity signals the rise of defensiveness on the child's part. For example, if a child's posture indicates he is withdrawn and depressed, responding with "I'm fine" when his parent asks him how he is doing conflicts with the meaning conveyed by his body. This child's response can be a defensive statement employed to keep his parent at an emotional distance. If the parent lets the incongruity go, and proceeds according to just the child's words, a disconnect emerges that will continue or widen unless the parent makes a repair. "Hey, I think I missed something a little while ago when I asked you how you were doing. Seems like your words might have been saying something different than your body. I wonder if this might be a good time to figure this out together." Noticing and carefully working with incongruities is using active attunement to help the child step out from behind his defensive wall so he can connect. Mirroring the child's incongruent behavior with gentle words helps him become aware of himself.

ELIMINATE QUESTIONS. Children who have been abused, neglected, or removed from their birth homes tend to be highly defended against anyone entering their world. To these children, questions feel like heat-seeking missiles targeting their core shame at worst and like accusations that they are bad at best. Since the child does not yet have self-reflective ability, he does not know the answers to questions posed by his parents, which envelops him in shame. Questions generate an implicit partition between parent and child that positions the parent as one up and the child as one down. When a parent questions a child, the child immediately feels bad and/or guilty. An adult's "Why did you . . ." immediately traps the child in an interrogation room where our hostility fills the space between parent and child, evaporating any potential for connection. Feeling accused, the child has no choice but to iterate automatically, "I don't know," which only knocks him into shame and frustrates the adult.

TAP THE POWER OF THE PRESENT. Connection happens in the immediacy of the now, which is more comfortable for a distressed child to step out of than remain within. An attuned parent remains aware of this tendency and gently corrals her child to stay in the present, carefully watching for signs of the child becoming overwhelmed. Relating in the present stirs anxiety and vulnerability in the child because memories of his unresolved trauma persist in the present. The child cannot separate intrusive anxiety linked to the past from his present experience. Saying "It's not happening now" is of no comfort to a distressed child, who may not even be consciously aware of the memories triggering his fear. As you work with your child, knowing and remembering that his present reality is laced with unregulated fear and terror rooted in his past allows you to be extra-sensitive to even the most minute nonverbal indication your interaction is stirring angst in your child.

RECOGNIZE ALL EMOTIONS, STAYING ABREAST OF CHANGES. A child may have many different feelings at once or feelings that are overlapping, layered, or interconnected. Consonant emotions may be connected with those that are discordant and negative meta emotions (feelings about having feelings, e.g., feeling ashamed about feeling angry) may overlay them both. Anger or giddiness may be a mask for fear or terror. A child may avoid emotions, prevent them from surfacing, or struggle with their expression. Parents can easily fall back to assuming that their child recognizes his emotions and can put words to them. The question, "How are you feeling?" can slip out before the parent catches it, and a sense of shame is triggered because the child does not know the answer. Curiosity about an emotion works to connect parent and child as well as to build the child's emotional vocabulary: "I wonder if you're feeling frustrated right now because the Legos won't go together."

REMEMBER, PARENTS HAVE FEELINGS TOO. Self-disclosure by parents can have a place in working with a distressed child if predetermined that it is helpful in terms of fostering the connection with the child. The extent to which a parent's disclosure will enhance connection depends upon the child's progress in treatment. Early on, children are unable to self-reflect, to see others objectively, and to experience others as separate from themselves. For these children, a parent's use of self-disclosure needs to be limited to the expression of genuine emotion in the moment. When you allow yourself to tear up at an appropriate time—let's say when Bambi's mother dies in the movie—you arouse your child's curiosity, which may prompt him to tear up too. This emotional moment becomes a teaching tool you can use to model the expression of sadness though tears, to connect the feeling to its antecedent, and to pave the way for your child to feel his sadness. As treatment progresses, parents can use an emotional moment to link their own feeling about an event from the child's past to help him process experiences that are unresolved.

MONITOR THE CHILD'S LEVEL OF ANXIETY. The point where the anxious child begins to shift into overload is his point of "critical anxiety." Working at or near this edge with a child is desirable because complacency offers no motivation for a child to grow. As the parent engages with the child, his level of anxiety will fluctuate. When the child begins to feel too vulnerable and nears the point of critical anxiety, he will begin to use his defenses to protect himself. At this point, the parent steps in with either neutral or compassionate acceptance and uses curiosity to give gentle recognition to the defense itself. "Let's take a breather, because I'm wondering if the fidgeting means you're feeling that this is getting to be all too much right now." By stepping in when the child is nearing the edge of his critical anxiety, the parent is providing the regulation the child needs to return to equilibrium. As the parent works with her child, this process gets repeated over and over, eventually becoming internalized by the child, and he attains the capacity for self-regulation.

MAINTAIN CLEAR PSYCHOLOGICAL AND EMOTIONAL BOUNDARIES. Since emotionally distressed children tend to have very poor boundaries due to insufficient parenting in the past, it is necessary for parents to establish, model, and maintain healthy boundaries within the present relationship. Boundaries are essential for making clear which motives, issues, and responsibilities belong to the child and which belong to the parent. Boundaries separate the parent's feelings from the child's, establishing the me-you relational dynamic—the essential construct in all healthy relationships.

INTERRUPT WHEN IT IS THERAPEUTIC. Interrupting a child's chronic behavior pattern rather than stopping it or letting it play itself out can be much more helpful to him in the long run. When you see that your child is once again heading down a dead-end street or is about to fall into the same hole with his behavior, consider catching his attention while he is in the process so he has the opportunity to practice intervening for himself. He is more likely to listen to you when you use curiosity as the interrupter than if you tell him he is heading for a crash. "I wonder where you'll end up if you continue to carry this forward" works better than "You better stop that behavior or you'll end up paying for it." When you give a child who does not yet fully trust you an ultimatum like this, he has no choice but to buck your authority, take control, and do it his way, even if it is not in his best interest. However, if you interrupt an ingrained behavioral pattern, you change its automatic trajectory by creating a window for your child to make a conscious decision about where he wants things to go. When you remove the overlay of your directive and value judgment, your child gets a chance to exercise his ability to reason, to see he has a choice about his behavior, and to discover his own power.

PREDICT THE CHILD'S RESPONSES. From your objective point of view, you are always "watching the action" and are in a position to see ahead. For instance, let's say you're aware what is likely to happen when you let your child know there are five minutes left until it's time to get ready for bed. At these times, using prediction can help your child step off his behavioral gerbil wheel and get into his thinking brain so he has an opportunity to choose a different direction. "I know that this is the time of the day that can be the most difficult for you because you don't want to stop having fun. Bedtime sometimes makes you so mad that you feel like you can't stop yelling and throwing things. I wonder how we can work together to make bedtime less frustrating for you. Let's talk about it."

USE YOUR SELF TO CONNECT. Your "self" means the entirety of you as a person: your temperament, personality, facial expressions, memories, the quality of your voice, the characteristics of your body movements, your view of the world, beliefs, opinions, intuition, emotions, psychological blind spots, and challenges. All of these parts of you come together to support you in meeting the joys and challenges of life. You have lived your life through the lens of your unique body and brain, and thus your self has become "tuned up" and readied over time to tackle whatever may come. In realizing and using the wide scope of abilities you have, you can help your child reach the firm ground upon which you stand.

USE SILENCE THERAPEUTICALLY. In allowing silence to fertilize the moment, parents can capitalize on the opportunity for growth that time offers to both themselves and their child. Anything ranging from a short pause to a few minutes of quiet can give the brain the time it needs to assimilate new information, make connections, and retrieve learning experiences. Lack of incoming stimulus permits fight or flight reactivity to fade, rendering the child more available for connection. Silence can assist the parent and child to focus on the nonverbal aspect of their communication, which can lead to a deeper, more solid connection between them. Sometimes what is left unsaid can ring much truer and more poignantly than that which is talked to death. Since the distressed child infrequently operates out of his "thinking brain," action in silence can speak more clearly and understandably than can words that need to be processed.

CONNECT WITH CORE EMOTIONS. There can be a lot of static that interferes with a parent attuning with her child. Environmental distractions, defensive lures, red herrings, and disruptive behavior all serve to protect a child from the most vulnerable of his emotions—shame/rage, abandonment/shame, fear/dissociation, ambivalence, fear of annihilation/intense pain, and conflicted feelings about feelings. Relying upon her own experience of her child, her gut sense (her child's affect felt within), and her intuition, a parent can tap vital information and sear through the interference to connect with her child's core feelings. Keeping this laser vision operative can assist parents in cutting to the chase where their child's emotional issues are concerned, bypassing delays and preventing derailing of the connection. The more both parent and child practice quickly clearing the way to get to the nucleus of the matter, the fewer negative experiences they'll rack up and have to work through later. Not recognizing and moving through these barriers to connection is one of the most frequent and repetitive errors parents make in working toward healing with their child. It is well worth parents' time to pay special attention to this dynamic, as it can be the biggest source of frustration and felt incompetence they will encounter.

When parents begin to use therapeutic attunement with their child, they will invariably encounter the many layers of defenses within their child. Defenses are generally reflexive and unconscious in nature; therefore, the child has no ability to regulate their emergence. Once functional as fierce guardians of the child's authentic self, defenses can arise in the present

Psychological defenses have protected the child from others and must be approached with respect and care

when the child experiences actual, perceived, or implied threats to his physical, emotional, and psychological well-being. Even when there is no actual threat, the child's defenses can be triggered if *he* perceives there is a threat. The defensive child is living "out of time" with his present circumstances, which causes relational difficulties due to the wall of unnecessary protection the child erects between him and his parents, who are often frustrated by the repetitive nature of this dynamic. Unless this unconscious, defensive process is consciously dismantled, it remains quite durable and persistent.

How parents approach their child when his defenses are triggered determines his willingness to become more vulnerable. If parents get impatient or dismissive with their child regarding his defenses, he will feel shame and rejection because these protective behaviors have grown to be an integral part of how he sees himself. Wishing that your child would *just trust you*, or trying with words to convince your child that he *can trust you* will only frustrate you and elicit feelings of failure in him because, right now, *he cannot trust you or anyone else.* This reality can be difficult for parents to embrace because they see themselves as trustworthy and safe for their child.

Attuning to a defensive child begins with parents compassionately recognizing the emergence of their child's self-protective behavior, which is being fueled by his underlying fears. This recognition is accompanied by parents accepting and valuing their child's defenses for the protection they provided before he came to live with them. By assuming a curious, connecting, nonreactive demeanor, parents poise themselves to address their child's defenses in a way that allows their child to feel safe: "Wow. It seems like I must have said something that upset you. I wonder what it was that made you turn away." Remaining grounded in acceptance, parents can gently explore their child's defenses with him. Using this careful approach as they enter their child's world, parents can help their child move forward in the process of dissolving his defenses. *Entering the child's world, especially where his defenses are concerned, is one of the most essential and powerful aspects of attunement parents can employ.*

In donning an attuned, curious demeanor, the parent prevents divisiveness and stifles the assumption that there is a "right answer." Mothers attuning to infants do not ask "why" or "what" questions: they attend to their infant's discomforts with concern, empathy, and a desire to help. By emulating this approach, parents create a *corrective emotional experience for their distressed child as they join him in his struggles.* A child will experience a world of difference between a parent launching questions of "what" and "why" across a void and a curious, connective parent who wonders openly about what may be going on inside her child. While the parent does not ask questions of the *child*, she does internally ask *herself* the question before she proceeds. For example, first the parent asks herself, "What is my child feeling?" Then attuning to her child, the parent says aloud, "I wonder what's going on behind those eyebrows that look so mad right now." This puts the parent where she belongs—in the same world as her child—and her reflective statement invites her child to participate in the discovery process, even if her reflection initially misses the mark.

Parents can be anxious about reflecting their child's feelings because if they are guessing, they do not want to get it wrong. Parents need not worry, however, because in being curious, they've already engaged their child in the process. A wrong guess will be corrected either by the child or by an adult repair, which can be just as powerful as getting it right initially. Additionally, it is difficult to be anxious and curious simultaneously, so if parents begin by voicing the phrases, "I wonder if" or "I'm curious about," they are actively stepping out of their anxiety and into relationship. For both parent and child, stepping into a relationship of mutual curiosity can feel like climbing out of rough seas onto the deck of a safe ship.

Both verbal and nonverbal warning signs that indicate a child's discomfort is rising can come in many forms: conversation slipping into the past or future tenses, waning eye contact, the child leaning, pulling, or stepping away from you, the child "spacing out," shifting the focus tangentially, fidgeting, and suddenly bursting into anger. These defenses appear automatically in the child as his anxiety is triggered by being in or drawn back to the present. Parents use their awareness of emerging

Try to avoid questions; they can feel like interrogation to a child

defenses to gauge their child's emotional limits, backing off before "the point of no return," wherein the child's dysregulated state takes charge. Stopping the action and giving voice to the dynamics in play in the moment can help your child refocus and come back from the edge when he is becoming overwhelmed.

Parent: Whoa, pardner. I think we were headin' for a cliff over yonder.

[Child quickly shifts his focus to the parent, who's suddenly being playful in the present.]

Parent: But I think we headed that one off at the pass.

[Child looks at his parent with bewilderment.]

Parent: Oh, I was just wondering how we got off track.
Child: What?
Parent: As we were talking just now, it seemed like you got uncomfortable. I was just curious about it, that's all.
Child: Oh.
Parent: I was wondering if you felt uneasy when we snuck a peek into each other's eyes. . . . At least that's when I noticed a shift.

[Child shrugs, looks down.]

Parent: And you know what?

[Child looks up at parent.]

Parent: It's all okay and I'm glad we caught it, because I don't want to do anything to make you pull away. Thanks for letting me know it was too much. Are you wanting to get back to our game? I'm ready if you are!

Here, the parent stopped action in a playful way to set the child more at ease, then narrated the child's experience, reflectively connecting the dots for him as an intervention both to arrest the mounting dysregulation and to teach the child something about himself. To finish up, the parent turned over the control about what was to happen next to the child, so he could safely come back to the present and into relationship with his parent.

A parent may recognize a feeling in her child that she thinks is critical to talk about but that would be too overwhelming to frankly name, so she substitutes a lesser laden phrase, such as "kind of scared" for "terrified." "To me you look ~~terrified~~ kind of scared right now; I wonder what that's about." Parents also steer clear of outright correcting their child if he mislabels his feeling by repeating his words and offering an alternative in a curious way: "So you're saying you're feeling happy right now. Is that an 'everything's okay' happy or a 'jump up and down' happy?" This softer approach prevents what can potentially become a conflict between parent and child from arising. When in doubt, either refrain from making comments about the child's emotions or use curiosity to explore them.

Care should be taken to keep the parent's own unresolved experiences separate from an emotional moment that is used to help the child. Using our example, the parent would not begin to talk about the losses through death she has experienced, or let herself stray into her own unfinished emotional business. Keeping the focus in the now, parents can connect with their child using their present genuine feelings to interact with him at his current developmental age: "I feel so sad right now as I'm remembering what happened to you long ago."

When the parent's own anxiety grows out of a fear she cannot handle containing her child's rising anxiety, she backs off, which renders a dull experience that fails to produce a meaningful connection. On the other hand, surpassing the upper threshold of the child's critical anxiety does not necessarily generate failure; this experience can help the parent know the child's limits, which will increase as the relationship deepens and the child gains the capacity to handle the stress of intimacy. While parents should not actively be testing a child's limits, if they do happen to tip the child over his edge, they can make a repair with him and bring the relationship back to its center.

However, this boundary arrangement can feel threatening to an emotionally distressed child, who often feels safer when feeling the same as the adult. Much like a person with Stockholm syndrome—aligning with the perpetrator to feel safe—when the child sees himself as united with his parent, he no longer feels separate and like a target for his parent's wrath. This defense against vulnerability becomes visible, for example, when a child tries to control his parent by being passive-aggressive, for instance by intentionally ignoring instructions or doing exactly the opposite of what is requested. For the unaware parent, this can result in the parent taking on and discharging the child's anger. This turnabout and blurring of boundaries occurs more frequently than parents might realize, so it is important that you remain alert and nip it in the bud when it happens.

Conversely, at times you may dismiss your portion of the responsibility for the relationship by viewing the child as the problem. This is also a boundary issue. In putting all of the blame on the child ("if only he didn't . . .") you are actually giving away your power and ability to facilitate change. You may succumb to being the parent you don't want to be: the authoritarian who puts the child in a psychological box and expects him to behave and conform and then punishes him when he doesn't. This breakdown in the parent-child connection can have its roots in feelings of being overwhelmed, which arise when you come to think of yourself as powerless to deal effectively with your child's behaviors. Therefore, it is essential that you maintain an observant self who can alert you when your energy begins to wane and your boundaries are slipping. When you start to become the person you don't like, don't blame the child, look within—something has triggered you.

The power of being *just who you are* is the fuel that runs the engine of healing. You observe your child and help him move from a dysregulated state to equilibrium with *your* energy and *your* personality. You use your inimitable self to guide your child through the crucible of emotional morphing, teaching him how to metabolize his own emotions by doing it for him in your way at first. A parent's ability to consciously use aspects of the self to develop the parent-child relationship requires that the parent have a strong, grounded, stable yet flexible foundation she consciously can draw upon to recognize, attune to, and meet the needs that rise out of her child's fears, shame, rage, and ambivalence. This is no small task, yet if parents can stay anchored in an expanded mind-set while focusing on the needs of the moment, they retain access to all of the unique gifts they possess to connect with and heal their child.

Problems in Attunement

Therapeutic attunement is modeled on the natural connection between mothers and infants that unfolds across all developmental domains as the child grows. Using therapeutic attunement and meeting the child where he is emotionally instead of chronologically, parents revisit and repair breaches in the child's developmental attachment process. Determining whether it is an appropriate time to use therapeutic attunement hinges upon the parent's present capacity for maintaining an objective state of mind and emotional stability, not upon the fickle status of the child's connection with his parents. When parents are attuned to their child, they are *actively being with their child,* rather than performing some technique aimed at achieving specific changes in their child or solving his problems. Providing accurate attunement requires parents simultaneously to hold awareness of their and their child's internal worlds and to understand how those internal worlds interconnect, all while regulating their own triggers and anxiety—a grand act of multitasking that makes it imperative that parents do their own work.

When parents experience problems attuning, the first stop on the trail to understanding the "why" is for parents to look at how their own issues might be interfering with making a connection with their child and his experience. Internally, a parent might be fighting against using this empathic paradigm of parenting because her own childhood experience offered so little emotional nurturance. Resentful that she has to give nurturance she did not get, this parent may proceed to replicate how her parents treated her, whether that treatment tended to be laissez-faire or authoritarian. Another parent might resist engaging in the attunement process because she is used to having immediate gratification, a reward that is not possible to attain in the process of healing a distressed child. Still another parent may be suffering from depression and have neither the energy for nor the interest in getting close to her child.

Sometimes problems with attunement are rooted in the parent's own need or desire to avoid her child's pain and rage. This parent's avoidance might be based in her fear of being with someone who rages because her experience tells her that she gets hurt in these situations. A parent might feel she needs to avoid her child's pain because it resonates too deeply with her own internal pain she has avoided and has not resolved. On the other hand, a parent might believe that a child in pain needs to "buck up" and get on with life, just like she, the parent, had to do in her childhood. Yet still another parent might get triggered by her child's rage, get dysregulated herself, and fly off the handle in response.

Problems with attunement can stem from parents having difficulty connecting with experiences they have not had themselves. This is especially true for parents whose child has been traumatized by being a

Are your issues getting in the way of attuning with your child?

witness to or victim of violence, abuse, or neglect. Attuning to the feelings of a child who watched her birth mother get beaten to death by her birth father, or the feelings of a child who was beaten by his birth mother, who broke his leg and arm in the process, is very difficult for a parent whose background includes receiving the nurture and love of parents who never even spanked. Attuning to the feelings and experience of a child who was repeatedly raped by his birth father from the time he was two until he was removed from the birth home at age four can feel impossible and overwhelming to a parent who has always felt safe around her own birth father and safe in the presence of men in general.

Few, if any, parents can escape wrestling with their own reactivity, difficult feelings, or lack of understanding when it comes to being attuned to their child. Each parent, therefore, must become intimately aware of her own internal responses to her child's feelings, needs, and past experiences. She must work through any reactivity that emerges in the course of her healing work with her child so she can clear the way to remain present and attuned. Deep, unresolved negative patterns can and must be identified and worked through outside the relationship with the child.

Key Points for Chapter 8

1. Attunement is the art of listening to and communicating with the child inside. It allows the child to "feel felt."
2. Therapeutic attunement is like learning the foreign language of your child's inner world. It takes time and practice.
3. To attune accurately, you need a *holding environment*, which is the quiet internal *psychological* space of the parent as well as the quiet *physical* space created by the parent.
4. To attune accurately, you will have to put your needs for being appreciated and gratified "on a shelf," much as you would when parenting an infant.
5. The four "Rs" of attunement are reading, resonating, reflecting, and repairing.
6. Tools for the four Rs include concentrating on nonverbals, being a mirror for the child, keeping in the present, use of physical closeness, and encouraging eye contact.
7. Other tools are recognizing all emotions, monitoring your child's anxiety, maintaining boundaries, interrupting negative directions,

predicting behaviors, using silence, and using your own responses to help you read your child's responses.

8. Recognizing psychological defenses is important, but treat them respectfully, as they have kept your child safe. Listen; don't interrogate.

9. Asking "why," trying to talk children out of their feelings, or offering premature reassurance may get in the way of accurate attunement.

9.
Speaking the Language of Hope
Saying What You Want Your Child to Hear

Just as despair can come to one only from other human beings, hope, too, can be given to one only by other human beings.

ELIE WIESEL

PATRICK'S MOTHER HAD ASKED HIM to clean up his room before going out to play with a new friend. Patrick usually followed this instruction, if not perfectly, at least adequately for a ten-year-old boy. But this time, Patrick stormed off into his room and, instead of cleaning it, began to throw things everywhere. He shouted that his mom was unfair and she didn't want him to have friends. He cried and wailed. His mother approached him as his rage began to subside. "My goodness," she said, "something is really bothering you. Let's you and I try to figure this out together. I don't think it's about cleaning your room, but I wonder if it's about your friend. I know you're lonely and you really want friends. I just wonder if you might be worried that this friend won't like you, so you're sort of scared. Let's think about what we can do to ease that worry. In the meantime, let me help you clean your room and we can figure this out together. It won't always be this tough." Patrick calmed as they worked together and told his mom that this was one of the "cool kids" and that he was worried that if he made any mistakes the boy would make fun of him.

Being Particular about Language

The intervention above could have happened a number of ways. Mom could have stood her ground and said, "No playing without room clean up, period!" She could have raised her voice at Patrick, which she probably felt like doing. She could have punished him. What she did and what worked was that she noticed that this was unusual behavior for him and that it was signaling a need. She used very specific language that you will learn in this chapter to be close to him, name the need, work together on a solution, and project hope in the future. She met the underlying need of "I'm scared; please help me figure this out" by being present with him, not by forcing him.

No doubt you will be challenged at times by your child's behavior. The

Traditional approaches like punishment or an authoritarian stance evoke fear, frustration, and shame in the distressed child

question is how to be the best parent you can be in this situation to bring this child back into hope and out of despair. Your child's behavior is his means of communication, and the goal of this chapter is to help you translate tantrums, oppositionality, avoidance, and all other behaviors into his expression of need. Remembering that a child's behavior always means "I need you" is the first step in intervention. After identifying the actual anger, fear, sadness, or loneliness underneath your child's behavior, you can use deduction or active curiosity, as discussed in the previous chapters, to make sense of the need the feeling is conveying.

You may be confused to learn that meeting your child's need can, indeed, suffice as a complete intervention for a challenging behavior. Parents typically want to know when they should carry out the "real intervention"—giving the child a punishment for his unruly behavior—to teach him he must behave differently. However, this traditional approach to intervening in behavior *does not work with distressed children*. Being authoritative and punishing with a traumatized child evokes his fear and distrust, steering the parent-child relationship in the wrong direction. Moreover, *a child cannot behave differently until he understands for himself that behavior is the way he expresses his feelings and needs*—an understanding that comes only through repetitions of accurate attunement by his parents. In this chapter, we will be introducing the "Language of Supportive Control" (Fahlberg, 1990)—the language of hope—as the gold standard for intervention instead of punishment. Healing a distressed child can only take place within a safe, predictable, and attuned relationship with his parent or primary caregiver. Remember, it is not what you do to a child that makes the difference: *it is who you are for the child.*

All Harm Done through Relationship Can Be Healed through Relationship

It is only through patterned, repetitive, safe, relational responses from his primary caregiver that a child can develop the capacity to grow into that healing relationship. Telling your child that you care, or that he is safe, or that you will not leave him does not mean anything to him: he needs to *experience* your care and control to believe it. You must show him through your nonverbal behavior and consistent interactions that you care, that he is safe, and that you will not leave him. This demonstrative approach to establishing trust is especially necessary when you are intervening in challenging behavior. The risks of inducing shame and alienating your child are great if you are out of touch with your child's need for "care-full" intervention. Yet even if it is the hundredth time you have demonstrated how trustworthy you are by consciously parenting with care and empathy, your child may continue to respond with primitive, fearful behavior. Depending on the depth of your child's trauma, it may take a hundred more interactions that are trustworthy until he begins to feel safe enough to relax.

Recovery can be lengthy because a child's difficult early experiences have a disproportionate impact on brain development. If the lower centers in the brain "wire up," or develop, in an environment of trauma and loss in the first few years of life, it takes time to alter automatic primitive responses, and it is literally impossible to alter them with words alone. However, because the brain remains malleable throughout life, even distressed children can change. The brain is an organ of adaptation that builds its structures through interaction (healthy or not) with others. New "wiring" develops based on patterned, repetitive stimulation, and it is through this process that experience actually becomes flesh. In dedicating yourself to engaging in a healthy relationship with your traumatized child, you will eventually help him gain the capacity to trust and depend upon you. Someday, your child will be able to generalize his relational capacity and learn to trust and depend upon others as well.

What do we do, once we understand? In a nutshell, *intervention with the use of Language of Supportive Control means interpreting the accurate developmental level of your child's behavior, identifying his underlying need, naming the need so that he can understand it, and meeting the need within your relationship with him.* However, without the context of a bigger

---

**Language of Supportive Control identifies and names;
keeps the relationship as the medium of repair; weaves the past,
present, and future together into the child's story;
and puts hope into even the most dire of situations**

The Healing Continuum

CHILD'S PRESENT BEHAVIORAL STATUS ⟶	⟶ ULTIMATE BEHAVIORAL GOAL FOR CHILD
acting out	using words; connecting behavior with underlying feelings
inability to self-regulate	being able to self-regulate to return self to equilibrium
stuck in negative/distorted thoughts	recognize and challenge negative/distorted thoughts
uncomfortable with and rejecting of closeness	accept, tolerate, and become comfortable being close to caregiver
not reliant on caregiver	seek comfort and assistance from caregiver—rely upon caregiver
impulsive, needs immediate gratification	impulse control and ability to delay gratification
self-reliant	accept caregiver limits/rules/consequences; develop trust in care and control
others are extension of self	see others as separate from self and be able to empathize with others
inability to reflect upon self	capacity for accurate self-reflection
blames others	take responsibility for actions and effect of self/actions on others
inability to achieve	develop goals and organize toward achievement
reactive to past trauma	triggers disappear, trauma is resolved

picture, intervention can feel like a never-ending and ultimately purpose-less endeavor. Not only must parents identify the problem behavior in context of its developmental level, but they also must see the behavior in terms of a continuum that includes a *target behavior*. Keeping your "eyes on the prize" helps you develop interventions that are effective and make sense in the long run. Remaining cognizant of the overarching goal of in-tervening in your child's challenging behavior gives meaning, direction, and purpose to your actions. Your relationship with your child is the me-dium through which you help your child move along the developmental continuum between where he is today and where he needs to go.

Healing trauma requires there to be a shift from the inadequate re-lational dynamic that existed at the time of the trauma to one that is adequately supportive and reliable. Without this crucial support at the time of its occurrence, trauma gets stuck in an unprocessed state, and until that support becomes available, trauma stays stuck. Trauma eventually can become a non-triggering memory from the past if a child experiences the nurturance and caring of his primary caregiver in the healing process.

Language of Supportive Control

If we are setting aside the traditional, authoritarian approach to parenting and intervention, what are parents to do? Intermountain's signature approach to parenting distressed children relies upon the use of "Language of Supportive Control." LSC is a strategy to help you as the adult stay regulated and to provide a nurturing, secure, and attuned relational environment for the child. LSC is strongly grounded in the foundation of *joining with the child* through the use of both verbals and nonverbals. "Supportive control" means using structure, words, and body language to redirect the child's maladaptive behaviors, modulate his response to overstimulation, and create an empathic relational experience with him—the medium through which he will heal. It helps the child name and understand his feelings, understand his world, and feel that you understand and are by his side. It serves to mediate between an emotionally distressed child's internal world and the external world he does not understand and cannot cope with on his own.

Language of Supportive Control is also a teaching tool, one that instructs through the use of modeling, repetition, and encouragement. By enhancing efficacy, problem-solving abilities, and the capacity for self-control, LSC helps a child gradually increase the number of "I can do it!" moments he experiences, giving him the essential ingredient of efficacy that builds his sense of self-worth. Feeling valuable and worthy are endowments every child has earned by just being alive. The distressed child, however, has never felt these things and, in fact, has always felt that he is bad and a "nothing" that deserves only to be thrown away. Over time, your constant presence will help convey to your child that you think he is worthy. It will take your reliable presence in addition to countless

---

***Supportive control* means structure, words, and body language that help the child name and understand his feelings**

deliberate interactions on your part to provide your child with the number of repetitions of a positive relational experience he will need to change his mind about himself.

In the use of Language of Supportive Control, behaviors are not seen as good or bad, but rather as helpful or not helpful to a child who is learning how to enhance his life positively. In the milieu of LSC, *the child is acceptable and lovable even when his behavior is not.* Parents convey this to their child by focusing upon his *expressed need,* much as they would do for a young infant, rather than on the child's behavior. Focusing on a child's needs communicates to him that you are interested in and committed to relieving his discomfort despite his behavior, and it conveys your unconditional positive regard for him. LSC protocol helps prevent your child's behavior from creating distance between you and him. By focusing upon sustaining your relationship with your child, you prevent yourself from becoming distracted by his behaviors, which once enabled him to survive but now are becoming unnecessary as he grows to trust in your care. Difficult behavior and trust in care and control have an inverse relationship: when a child's difficult behavior increases, his trust in care and control decreases. Likewise, when trust in care and control increases, difficult behaviors decrease. The latter is your ultimate goal in using Language of Supportive Control as the medium through which you heal your child.

Whose problem is it? Your child's aversion to feeling shame propels him to blame anyone other than himself when he does something wrong. *Recognize that you did not cause the behavior and let go of responsibility and any sense of failure or guilt.* If you are not paying close attention, you may inadvertently take on responsibility for a problem that your child needs to work through in order to learn something essential. Focusing on yourself and what you did or may not have done not only makes the behavior worse, it deprives the child of your presence and wisdom when he needs you most.

By taking a step back and using a non-blaming approach with your child *and with yourself,* you can create a calm atmosphere that is essential to resolve a pressing situation. Once you are in a calm place, you need to realize that if anything is going to change, *your child must want to solve the*

Your child's problem is an opportunity
for your child to grow within your relationship

problem at hand. If you can hold in your mind the concept that *a problem is an opportunity for your child to learn and grow*, your thinking brain can activate and get curious about what that opportunity might be. If your child does not want to work toward resolution of a particular problem in the moment, then he is letting you know that his immediate need may be for something else, perhaps comfort and assurance.

If you go on to solve the problem *for* your child, you exclude your child's involvement and take away an opportunity for him to gain sensitivity about the impact his behavior has on you and your relationship. *Using LSC, you affect your child's behavior by being present with him to help him make better choices.* Since it is used as a learning tool, *behavior is never punished* in the realm of LSC. If traditional authoritative parenting and punishment were effective in raising a distressed child, he would not need help and you would not be reading this book. In the end, supportive control is a language and attitude that say to the child, "I am here with you to share in joy, to be with you in difficult times, and to work together to help you grow."

In using Language of Supportive Control, you are accomplishing the following (FitzGerald, 2015):

Elements of Language of Supportive Control

JOINING, that is, announcing that you are a *partner* in your child's experiences: "You and I are struggling," rather than "You have a problem."

SEEKING TO FORM AN ALLIANCE with your child instead of trying to gain compliance: "If we do this together, we'll both feel like we accomplished something," instead of "You better do it."

ADDRESSING THE CURRENT NEED, not making a judgment about the child: "We need to work on this because I know you're lonely and you want friends," instead of "No wonder you are lonely and have no friends."

ATTUNING VIA PHYSICAL AND EMOTIONAL PROXIMITY—staying close to the child and the child's experience: "I'm right here with you because I can see how hard things have been for you," rather than distancing and saying nothing.

REMAINING THE ADULT, THE ONE IN CONTROL—using "I" statements instead of "you" statements: "I feel angry when you don't listen to me," instead of "You make me angry."

HOPING FORWARD—confidently putting in a word for the future: "Someday this will be easier for you and me," instead of staying stuck: "I give up."

REFRAMING—changing how you and the child see the need/feeling beneath his behavior: "Sometimes when you have lots of feelings about what I'm saying, you get overwhelmed and stop listening. Let's start again," versus "I am sick and tired of you just ignoring what I tell you."

CONVEYING YOUR STRENGTH AND COMPETENCE AS A PARENT even if that means admitting temporary defeat: "I don't know what to do right now, but I know that you and I will figure this out," instead of "Nothing I do seems to help."

STAYING NEEDS-FOCUSED, using a teaching approach: "I know that you want my attention and feel like you'll disappear without it, but it's hard for me to listen when you're screaming. Let's find another way to say it so I can hear you better," rather than "Quit your screaming!"

SEEING YOUR CHILD AS SOMEONE CAPABLE OF LEARNING AND GROWING: "Someday you'll be ready to do this without a fight," instead of "You'll never be able to do this if you keep fighting."

DECREASING FAILURE by emphasizing your role as a resource for your child: "We are going to work hard on this together because I know you want to _____ and I'm here to help you get there."

COMMUNICATING RIGHT BRAIN TO RIGHT BRAIN: demonstrating you are open and available by showing your palms instead of saying that you are open and available as you stand there with your arms crossed.

ORIENTING TOWARD PREPAREDNESS and learning by building capacity, rather than shaming by highlighting deficits: "Let's try it another way because you're learning so well how to say 'no' respectfully," rather than "Yelling 'no' will get you nowhere."

ASKING YOURSELF IN EVERYTHING YOU DO WITH YOUR CHILD, *"Does this build rather than harm our relationship?"*: building a trusting relationship is the central goal of parenting your emotionally distressed child.

The importance of joining and forming an alliance with your child as you use Language of Supportive Control cannot be overstated. The reason your child is so deeply distressed is that he did not have a safe, consistently present caregiver to help him navigate the difficult experiences of his earliest years. Your child's life was not built upon the foundation of *trust in care and control,* which takes innumerable repetitions of attuned, positive caregiver interaction to establish. You are at the beginning of that journey toward an alliance with your child that will instill in him the *trust in care and control* he did not develop early on but that he has needed all along. Setting your expectations accurately as you and your child reach for this goal is essential. Your child will need you to hang in there with him for a long time . . . as long as it takes.

To help you gain a clearer picture of using the foundational components of Language of Supportive Control—joining and building an alliance—we will look in as Darryl's dad helps him navigate toward resolution of a particularly shameful pattern of behavior.

Darryl's Story

To Darryl's parents, it seemed like their son's undesirable behavior had been going on forever. Darryl, who is now eight but was adopted at almost four, had been "missing the target" when he went into the bathroom. Recently, Darryl's behavior had been the central focus of his parents' concerns, and they had tried everything in their standard toolbox they could think of to help him get control of himself: nagging; placing Cheerios targets in the bowl; using star charts; levying consequences like cleaning the bathroom and withholding privileges; putting brighter lights in the bathroom; cross-examining Darryl trying to find some motive for his haste (e.g., maybe he was wanting to quickly get back to his Game Boy); visiting the pediatrician; setting a timer to slow Darryl down while he was using the toilet; and—the worst—threatening the use of pull-ups. Darryl's parents were exasperated, and Darryl had sunk into the depths of shame, no longer wanting to come out of his room even for pizza and movie night with the family.

At the end of their resources, Darryl's parents decided to do some research. The issue up for discussion on the foster/adoptive parents' forum that day was toileting. One parent was at her wits' end because her five-year-old foster daughter was peeing on the carpet beneath the philodendron in the hall. Some parents had written in with suggestions for interventions similar to those Darryl's mom and dad had tried to no avail. It was all Darryl's mom could do to stop herself from chiming in about the uselessness of these approaches. However, she willed herself to read on, and she came upon a story another parent had shared that lit up a sudden connection in her brain between Darryl's current behavior and something his foster mom had said: "We think it's that Darryl's not ready to be done with potty training, and he'll grow out of his fear of the 'real toilet' in the bathroom if you just let him go at his own pace."

On the forum, this mom was discussing her foster son's potty problems and how together with his social worker they had figured out what was going on. The problem was that the boy was deathly afraid to use the bathroom toilet in the foster home, even though he was five and had easily adapted instead to using a child's portable potty. Before coming into care, this boy had been living in a dilapidated trailer with his alcoholic birth mom. In the winter, snakes would come up through a hole in the rotted floor of the trailer's only bathroom to find refuge near the warmth of the water heater, which sat next to the toilet. Darryl's mom had an "aha" moment and now could hear Darryl's foster mom's words— "his fear in the bathroom"—loud and clear as if she had said them only a minute ago.

Practically the minute Darryl's dad arrived home from work, Darryl's mom shared her "aha" with him about what might be the reason for Darryl's bathroom problem. Darryl's dad agreed that early on, something must have happened to Darryl with regard to the bathroom that made him unable to stand still to pee. Although they still did not know exactly what had happened to make Darryl afraid of the bathroom, Darryl's mom and dad decided upon a new approach to helping their son based on their theory. To start off, they planned for Darryl's dad to be the one who initially would sit down with their son to begin to work it through. Then, Mom would join them as the process unfolded.

Dad: It seems like it has taken your mom and me forever, but son, we think we now know what might be going on and how to help you with the pee problem.

Darryl: I never want to talk about that AGAIN!

Dad: I hear you.

Darryl: So don't even start. Anyway, it's *my* pee problem.

Dad: What if I was to say that it's been my fault . . . not yours, but mine.

Darryl: Yeah, right.

Dad: I'd really like it if we could solve this once and for all, and I know we can. . . . I'm 99.9 percent sure.

Darryl: Riiiight . . . nothing's never, *ever* 100 percent, *never.*

Dad: You know how Mom and I have always tried to make you be the one who has to fix this problem? Like with trying rewards, threats, and consequences?

Darryl: Duh-uh!

Dad: Well, we were wrong. We forgot the golden rule of our family: we work on stuff together, because we're a team and each one of us is needed to make things better. Mom and I weren't working on this problem with you. . . . We were putting it all on you to fix, son, and we're so sorry and so sad we did this.

[Darryl crosses his arms with an angry "hrrummph."]

Dad: Come here and let me put my arm around you so I can tell you what we've figured out . . .

[Darryl stays put with arms crossed and an angry brow.]

[Dad waits.]

Darryl: Okay, have it your way. [Scoots over a bit nearer to Dad on the sofa.]

Dad: [Pulling Darryl closer.] There, see, we are together in this. . . . You're not alone with it anymore. [Side-hugs Darryl.]

[Darryl is still stiff, but begins to soften as his mom comes to sit next to him on his other side and Dad proceeds to talk to Darryl about the revelation.]

Mom joined Darryl and his dad on the sofa, and as they talked, Darryl's parents wondered aloud whether anything scary ever happened in a bathroom, maybe even a long time ago. Darryl flashed on a "bad man in the bathroom," whom Darryl's parents guessed must have been one of his birth mom's many unsavory boyfriends they had heard about. Darryl went on to say the bad man had scared him in the bathroom of "the house with the blue curtains that me and Mommy lived in a long time ago." Such an incident apparently had never been reported, and as a result Darryl's avoidance of the bathroom hadn't been linked to the abuse but rather to the neglect. Additionally, Darryl's foster mom had found a toileting solution that had worked for Darryl (placing the portable potty chair near the kitchen where foster mom was most of the time); thus, no one had pursued his avoidance of the bathroom as being a problem.

Darryl's mom made a mental note to contact Darryl's therapist regarding his disclosure so she could explore and process it with them at the next appointment. In the meantime, Darryl and his dad and mom came up with a plan that would prove to gradually lessen Darryl's association between the bathroom and fear. Initially, with his dad's help and support, Darryl began to be able to stay in the bathroom long enough to aim accurately. Dad (or Mom if Dad was gone) would stand just outside and next to the open door as Darryl went in to use the toilet. While Darryl was doing his business, Dad would read aloud the next paragraph or two of a book on wizards that Darryl loved and had chosen for this intervention. This plan worked because it took Darryl's mind instantly away from its automatic leap to fear, and with a parent nearby, Darryl felt he was not alone.

~

Darryl's mom and dad had used the power of LSC by joining with their son to work through his troubles, rather than continuing to administer punitive parenting solutions that were failing to address the behavior. In carrying forth their new approach, Darryl's mom and dad discovered that forming an alliance with Darryl was also the foundation they had needed to help him begin to remember trauma he had experienced early in his life. Joining together had created the safety Darryl needed to talk a bit about what had happened in the past and permitted Darryl's parents truly to support him in the present in dealing with the trauma's lingering effect.

As you begin to use Language of Supportive Control, start by joining with your child. He needs the safety of your consistent presence to navigate through his world. Your child will need you to hang in there with him for the long run. The question parents must continually ask themselves as they are working to heal their child is, "Are we joining with our

Ask yourself: are you joining with your child and working on a true alliance, or are you trying to get him to do something?

child in this moment and working in a true alliance?" If the answer is "no," then parents need to regroup before moving on and start over using LSC fundamentals.

Reviewing an "x-ray" of the philosophic underpinnings of Language of Supportive Control will help you acquire a deeper feeling for the building blocks that provide the foundation for the supportive relationship you are building with your child. The component parts of Language of Supportive Control philosophy include its mind-set, values, attitude, viewpoint, and emotional tenor.

Language of Supportive Control Foundational Philosophy

MUTUAL RESPECT VERSUS POWER AND CONTROL—being the parent that educates, not dictates; you have the life experience, knowledge, and wisdom your child needs you to convey in your role as his best resource

UNCONDITIONAL POSITIVE REGARD—being continually accepting of your child, even if you do not always accept his choices or behavior

CONSIDERATION OF YOUR UNIQUE CHILD—considering your child's particular temperament, his current capacity for self-regulation, and his individual likes and dislikes to maximize his chances for success

SOVEREIGNTY—respecting the dignity and separateness of your child, his mind, and his emotions by helping him make sense out of his experiences in the world

RESOLUTION—not keeping a scorecard of your child's unhealthy choices, focusing instead on your resolve to support the growth you do see

JOINING—teaming with your child to overcome problems together

ATTUNEMENT—allowing your own state of mind and being to align with those of your child, using his rhythms and his expressional vocabulary to connect with him

EMPATHY—experiencing and communicating your understanding of your child's world view and accurately perceiving his emotions, not imposing yours upon him

MINDFULNESS—being in the present with an acute awareness of all that is in this moment; your child lives in the present but needs your active, global awareness to understand it

COMPARTMENTALIZATION—helping your child learn when, where, and to whom to talk about his therapeutic issues; home life cannot center on resolving your child's specific trauma

HONEST EXPRESSION—making what is internal for you extant for your child in order to reify his internal knowing of you, because he can tell if you are being honest or not

PLAYFULNESS—teaching your child how to have fun and play, to reduce his flow of stress hormones and shift his focus, which for so long has been on survival

CLARIFICATION—noticing and ameliorating that which is unclear or unseen by your child so he can be in sync with you in the present

Language of Supportive Control is an entity of its own and a paradigm that needs to be experienced as it is learned. After each layer of relational progress you make with your child, your understanding of LSC philosophy will deepen. Upon review, the words you read here initially may even seem to shape shift and their meanings may seem to morph in ways that may surprise and enlighten you. So make it a point to revisit this as well as the other sections of this handbook frequently throughout your journey with your child. Something that seemed meaningless to you the first time around may pop out at you later and be just the idea you have been searching for. Use this resource and mine it for all of its knowledge, which will continue to emerge as you spiral up its staircase of wisdom.

Structure and Attunement:
The Two Pillars of Language of Supportive Control

Parents can make great headway in their relationship with their child by ensuring their use of Language of Supportive Control consistently includes both structure and attunement. Structure includes family expectations, norms, rhythms, rules, values, permissions, routines, and modeling. Attunement, as discussed in the last chapter, is the state in which parents stay emotionally close to and connected with their child and his experience as they accurately read and respond to his feelings and needs. A child feels safer with his parents when they hold to and follow through with a set structure, and closer to them when they attune to him by matching his emotional intensity while accurately putting words to his experience.

Structure refers to the daily routine and expectations for your child. Children coming into your care may need more structure than you would typically use since they need to know what to expect next.

Through the use of LSC, parents can meld the necessary security the child's parent-controlled environment provides (structure), with their responsiveness to the uniqueness of the child's world view (attunement).

The ultimate and most important form of structure is line-of-sight supervision, which is an essential tool parents must use daily, hourly, and minute by minute, especially at the beginning of their relationship with their child. All children at some point may need line-of-sight supervision to be tightened to match the "three-foot rule," in which the parent keeps the child within three feet of her at all times. As you are getting to know your child at a depth necessary to create a trusting relationship, your child needs to be with you continually, as if he were an infant. The process of healing an emotionally distressed child requires proximity, which serves as the powerful nonverbal binding agent between parent and child. Note that the use of *line-of-sight supervision within LSC is never presented or used as a punishment.*

In being close to your child, you are immediately available to provide regulation for him when he cannot regulate himself. Closeness is indispensable as a condition that allows for the mirroring and narration of experience the child needs to get to know himself. This closeness and responsiveness are what the child missed when he was an infant, and he cannot fully develop in any realm without having these experiences. *An emotionally distressed child needs his parent to teach him who he is, show him what he needs, and guide him through reregulation because he cannot yet do these things for himself.*

Proximity also creates the healing space that your child needs to experience being dependent on you, a state that is vital to the development of an intimate one-on-one relationship with you. Your child's trust in your care and trust that your control is for his safety will naturally grow as he experiences your consistent presence. Furthermore, when you use proximity with your child, you greatly simplify your life as a parent. All of the expectations, norms, rhythms, rules, values, permissions, routines, and modeling within the family structure are carried out naturally, simultaneously, and without ado as you work closely with your child.

Keeping your child close, while monitoring his tolerance for closeness, allows you to teach your child the structure of your family naturally

What happens when a child is so emotionally distressed that close proximity seems to exacerbate his problems? When a child shows his parents his level of distrust, distress, and active avoidance through either externalization or internalization, the scope of the parents' work becomes evident. To see and work with these defenses in their child, parents need a certain proximity to their child. Additionally, a child's level of distress with closeness reveals the depth of relational neglect he has experienced, so to heal, the *child* also needs proximity. However, when proximity causes distress and yet is necessary for healing, parents need to find a distance that works for their child in the present situation.

Every child has a shifting comfort zone when it comes to intimacy, and you will need to discover and honor where this zone is for your child in the moment. Being the parent of a highly distressed, distrustful child requires a large dose of patience along with very realistic expectations. If your child only feels safe sitting in a chair across the room from you right now, you honor his need. In order to unlock the door to your child's world, you need always to acknowledge and begin where your child is, and then remain with him wherever he needs to go. Well paced equals child paced, and when you are really *with* your child, he knows it and can begin to let down his guard.

Closeness Plus Choices

Keeping your child close enough to be safe but not so close as to be intrusive is crucial to enhancing any interaction with your child. The use of choices helps the child maintain a much-needed sense of control. The key to giving choices is to limit the options to *two* things that ensure that you remain in charge while at the same time keep the child safe. It is much like the strategy that you might use with a two-year-old, e.g., "Would you rather have your bath before or after we read a story?" This gives two choices and some control, but you remain in control of the central requirement—taking a bath. In giving your child choices, you neverthe-less are containing him, creating a simple and defined emotional holding

Giving a child choices
allows him to feel some control while you remain in charge

environment that allows him to experience trust in your care, even if he is not aware of it. Limiting choices also prevents the child from feeling overwhelmed by the possibilities, which is a sure trigger for dysregulation for most children. All children, especially those who are emotionally distressed, need to have some control in their daily lives, and need that sense of control to be embraced within their parents' limits and care in order to build trust and reliance upon caregivers.

To illustrate the use of proximity plus choices with a highly distressed child, we will look at a morning in the life of Juli, a six-year-old girl who was adopted out of foster care when she was almost five.

Juli's Story

Juli came into foster care with welts on her legs from being beaten with sticks, so closeness was most likely experienced by Juli as hurtful and dangerous. Adoptive mom and dad determined that the closeness was best with the "three-foot rule"—wherein the parent keeps the child within three feet at all times—in order to help regulate Juli in the moment but give her enough distance to feel safe. Juli's parents gave her a choice of *where and how* she sat within her three-foot radius, and most of the time she had her choice of two appropriate activities she could do while there.

One week before Juli's seventh birthday, Mom was putting dishes in the dishwasher and Juli sat cross-legged on the countertop right above the dishwasher, a spot that Juli had chosen, and worked on her bead stringing. As Juli was threading on the last bead, the bead stopper on the end of the shoelace came off and all of the beads immediately slipped off. A few beads ended up in the basket in her lap, but most fell onto the floor, where they bounced and scattered. Instantly, Juli let out a harsh scream, threw the basket with the remaining beads at her mom, jumped off the counter, and ran to the kitchen table, sweeping all the items—the salt and pepper shakers, the plastic vase with fabric flowers in it, the cloth napkins, the placemats—off the table onto the floor and across the room. Juli was in a full-blown rage, and as she continued screaming, Juli started to kick the wall and topple over the chairs.

Instead of escalating in response to Juli's tantrum, Mom calmly sat down on the kitchen floor right where she was by the dishwasher, folded her legs, placed her hands in her lap, and started her slow, even breathing. As Juli's mom continued to sit and breathe calmly, Juli's wall-kicking started to slow and became more of a weak gesture, her screaming had less intensity, and she began to lower her head as if feeling shame. These behavioral cues signaled to Juli's mom that Juli might now be ready for some soft words.

Juli's mom said soothingly, "It's okay, Jules . . . it's okay." Juli's mom's soft posture, her stationary position on the floor, her calm voice, and her reassuring words began to shift Juli's reactivity. Juli then slumped to the floor, hugged her knees to her chest, leaned against the wall opposite her mom, put her forehead on her knees, and got still and quiet.

"Jules," Mom said, "are you okay with me sitting a little closer to you right now?" Mom could see Juli shrug her shoulders ever so slightly, and she knew that it was probably going to be all right to scoot in a bit closer, which she then did. Still seated on the floor, Juli's mom was now about five feet away from her daughter, where she paused and took a few deliberately audible deep breaths, knowing that this would help shift Juli into a more regulated breathing state.

Finally, Juli's mom softly asked Juli if she was ready to scoot forward to be closer, or if she would rather have Mom move closer to her. There was a pause, and then Juli slowly began to scoot in inch by inch, still maintaining her leg hugging and forehead-on-knees posture, until she was about a foot away from her mom, still not touching her.

Juli's mom knew from her past interactions with her daughter that when Juli was through raging, became calmer, and could move closer to Mom on her own that Juli was probably somewhat receptive to her mom beginning to explore what happened. *Mom was careful to use an empathic approach, absent of blame and criticism, when she began to talk to her daughter.* Mom reflected to Juli that it seemed like she was having a hard time right now and that her frustration with the bead project was understandable. After all, Juli had worked so carefully in stringing the beads, to have them all slip off without warning had to be very, very frustrating and maddening. Juli had been feeling good about herself for the accomplishment of stringing all of the beads on her own, and when the beads let loose without her permission, it was as if they were telling her, "See, you can't do anything."

This accurate reflection of Juli's feelings had the effect of easing Juli, and although she hung her head, her posture shifted to a more open stance of legs crossed, hands in lap. At this point, Mom continued and expressed compassion for how difficult everything has been in Juli's life and how none of it seemed to be fair: "It wasn't fair at all, Jules. Not one bit!" Mom then conveyed her thankfulness that Juli now had someone to help her so that her life might be less difficult, and that *she* was glad to be the one who was there to help. Mom's additional words had the effect of softening Juli a little bit more, and Juli began to sneak quick peeks at her mom. Mom assured Juli that no matter what, she would be here for her and that there was nothing Juli could do, "nothing at all," that would make Mom go away.

Juli's mom sensed that she had said enough about the incident and began to shift the emphasis to the present. Mom was imagining herself and Juli getting silly, crawling around on the kitchen floor, dodging the knocked-down chairs and other stuff, as if they were in a video game, to collect the beads together. In a playful, squeaky voice Mom said, "Hey! I know: let's play 'catch 'em' with the beads like that new video game where we race to get as many pieces of candy as possible." Juli looked up briefly and saw that Mom was seriously suggesting that they do this. Mom caught Juli's gaze, put on a mischievous face and a sly smile, and turned and crawled quickly away to begin gathering up the beads. Juli initially was reluctant, not sure if she really wanted to become playful, but then she began lethargically crawling after her mom. Then Juli perked up a bit, grabbed the bead basket, and joined in the game.

When all of the beads were in the basket, Mom got that mischievous look on her face again and began crawling around, playfully picking up the placemats and other items Juli had pushed onto the floor. Juli joined in for the last few items and then helped Mom as she put the chairs upright and tucked them into the table. Then Juli and her mom looked at each other and broke into smiles. "Want some juice, Jules? I know I do. I'm really thirsty now." Mom and Juli each had a cup of juice, and then together decided they would sit on the couch and Mom would read Juli the next chapter in her new fairy book.

The next day, Mom found that Juli was more receptive to talking about the incident. Aware that Juli's birthday was imminent, Mom sat with Juli and told her a story about a little bunny who was just about to have her next birthday, but was so mixed up about her birthday coming that she was having a hard time being happy. This little bunny had lost her mama and papa bunnies and had been all alone until she was taken in by the squirrel family, who came to love her as one of their own. As time went on, the little bunny began to feel safer and even was able to let in a little bit of her squirrel parents' love and care. Yet every year near her birthday, Little Bunny started to have mixed-up feelings—like lots of mad and sad.

"I wonder why Little Bunny had all of those mixed-up big feelings before her birthday." Juli shrugged her shoulders, paused and thought about it, still not looking at Mom, and hanging down her head. Then Juli spoke almost inaudibly and said that Little Bunny probably missed her bunny parents. Mom said that she agreed with Juli.

Next, Juli's mom wondered what Little Bunny's squirrel parents could do about her big feelings, which came out as she loudly thumped her little rabbit feet all around the house for days before her birthday. Juli's mom continued, "Before Little Bunny's squirrel parents thought of something they could do, Little Bunny told them that she didn't even want to *have* a birthday this year. Then, mommy and daddy squirrel thought about this and decided that's just what they'd do—they wouldn't celebrate Little Bunny's birthday this year." Juli's mom said that Little Bunny seemed very relieved upon hearing her parents say this, and the three of them talked about what they could do instead. They all agreed that they would go to the frog pond to swim and have a picnic of Little Bunny's favorite foods— cabbage and carrots—which is exactly what they did.

Mom talked with Juli about what she thought Little Bunny and her squirrel parents had done to help Little Bunny feel better about her birthday. Then, Juli told her mom that *she* actually *did* want a birthday, but she did not want her parents or anyone else to make a big deal about it. Juli and her mom decided that they would have her favorite spaghetti dinner with just cupcakes for dessert and no candles or singing the happy birthday song or presents. For the next few days before her birthday, Juli was calmer and actually wanted to spend extra time reading with her mom, a request that Juli's mom happily accommodated.

⟋

This incident took about a day to resolve, and some might say that is too long to deal with a "tantrum." However, this wasn't just a tantrum; losing control of the beads unleashed big feelings of deep loss and powerlessness in Juli's life that had been building up inside her. If Mom had used authoritarian discipline instead of structure and closeness, Juli would have learned that she and what she wanted really did not matter, and she would not have learned that it is safe to talk about feelings. Juli's mom had had to learn how to approach Juli's episodes of dysregulation in the successful way she did, and it had taken much practice.

Being able to stay calm and grounded in the face of a child's aggressive and potentially destructive behavior is definitely a learned skill for almost all parents. While composure is an essential stance for parents to take in order to be able to help their child regulate, it is not easy to come by. As we discussed in Chapter 1, parents must be conversant with their own history, their issues regarding authority, and their triggers, as well as have a much-practiced plan in place so they can address their child's dysregulation in a productive and relationally enhancing manner. Remembering the power of being present, employing the simplicity of sitting, and using intentional breath are tools that parents can rely upon in the most distressing situations to reestablish a healing milieu.

Helping Your Child Find His Story: Creating a Narrative

Language of Supportive Control is also the medium through which parents work to provide their child with his *narrative*. A child's narrative is the story of his life—past, present, and future—that helps him make sense of his life. Imagine any single event in your life without the larger picture of your life story—it would be like seeing a portrait of yourself as a dot on a huge, empty canvas. You, alone, without a world to be in or people to be in it with: this singular event would render you storyless and with no way to understand the past, enjoy the present, or have hope for the future. Trauma, incomplete brain development, and lack of a constant, nurturing primary caregiver early in life disable the distressed child from being able to formulate his narrative. The hurt child's world exists only in this moment, and without the organizing influence of your supportive control, he is left in "nowheresville" like the dot on the canvas because he does not have a coherent story as a context in which to see himself.

Each of us needs a story—our own personalized, unique story—to make

Your child needs a story that includes both the good and the bad that has happened to him so that he can understand the past, be fully present, and have hope for the future

sense of life; otherwise, living is just experiencing a bunch of random events. We do not think about this because we all have our story already and are able to integrate successive experiences into it without thinking about what we are doing. How are we able to do this? Most of us had a childhood with an adequate primary caregiver, who narrated our life to us from the very beginning. Mom may even have talked to you about her experience of you while you were still in utero. After you were born, mom continued narrating your experience and integrated each new event into your story as you grew: "I see you are so happy right now because you can grasp that toy ring!" When you were old enough to begin narrating your own experiences, mom and close others helped you integrate them into your developing story. This process continued and seamlessly became something you could do on your own by the time you reached adulthood.

However, some of us did not have adequate care by a primary caregiver when we were children; thus, we are not able to construct a cohesive, coherent, accurate narrative even as adults. In fact, the ability to construct a coherent narrative is the bellwether that determines our adult attachment status. For example, an adult might *think* she is securely attached because her childhood was "great" and her parents were "great." However, if this adult is not able to go deeper and recount the events of her childhood—good and bad—or describe her parents with accurate examples, her generalizations indicate that she has not yet attained a secure attachment status. The good news is that, even as adults, we can work with a therapist who functions as our singular, nurturing caregiver to acquire the ability to construct a coherent narrative. A commitment to working with an attachment-focused therapist in a consistent manner can give us the relational experience we missed in childhood that will allow us to "fill in the blanks" of our story. The ability to construct our own coherent narrative is an essential capacity that all who work with distressed children need to have, as it is an indicator that we have achieved a secure attachment status. We simply cannot take a child further in his growth than we have come ourselves.

Distressed children carrying unresolved trauma cannot construct a story that sticks together and makes sense of the good and the bad that has happened to them. If you ask such a child to tell you the story of his life, he will not understand the concept because he does not view his life as a *story*. Instead, his life is something that is happening right now. Like Darryl in the example earlier in this chapter, the distressed child does not consciously think about his past, but with support, he probably can talk a bit about a past experience and be helped to connect the present with the past through a current emotion or event. An emotionally distressed child might be triggered into a rage when his mom leaves in the evening to attend a meeting. Later, when mom is talking with her child about the situation and translates the rage into her child's fear that she was never coming back, she can wonder if he had ever felt this way when he lived with his birth mom, then help him create a story about whatever comes up for him. In this way, over time, a parent assists her child in piecing together a complete narrative of his life, which he can own and repeat because he understands his life history through emotions as well as through words.

As your child heals, you will be helping him reconstruct his past so that he can have his own story into which you will help him integrate new experiences. Having a complete story—one that needs to include traumatic and abusive times as well as joyful and loving times—finally will give your child a context in which to see himself and feel like he truly exists. It is through your use of Language of Supportive Control that the collaborative construction of your child's narrative will occur naturally in the course of your growing relationship with your child. As your child's primary caregiver, you will be narrating his present moments: "You seem to be really struggling with trying to be kind to me right now." Then, you will meld his present with his past: "I wonder if the 'mad' about your birth mom is wanting to come out and push away the 'kind' in you." Finally, you will be connecting the present with the future in a way that includes the element of "hoping forward": "You're really getting good at letting us look at the mad inside you, and I can see that someday you'll even be able to *say* you're mad when you are feeling it."

In making sense of Darryl's present by integrating newly surfaced knowledge about his past, Darryl's parents helped him develop as well as revise his narrative. Prior to working through the current problem, Darryl's standing belief about himself was, "Mom and Dad really think I am a bad kid who can't do anything right, especially something so easy like peeing into the toilet.... I'll never be able to do *anything* right, and they'll make me go live somewhere else, just like what happened before I came here." After being enveloped in an alliance with his parents to resolve a shameful situation, Darryl could own and recite a narrative that reflected his growth: "I used to feel like I was no good because I couldn't even pee right. Now I can do it right because Mom and Dad helped me figure it all out so I don't have to be so scared. Maybe I really *will* be able to do some stuff right."

Although Darryl's parents initially put it all together and gave Darryl the words for both his old belief and his new narrative, he was able to own and repeat them because the *meaning of the words had hit the mark for him, factually and emotionally.* Using supportive language, Darryl's parents had tied his past to his present, as well as connected his present to a future in a way that encouraged hope. Alone, without an alliance, Darryl had felt completely hopeless about his life. With his parents joining him to traverse a difficult situation together, Darryl was able to reach toward a future where *something* might be okay. Darryl's parents will have to continue helping him make sense of his life, and in each go-round help him constructively add to his narrative by giving him language and meaning for what he is experiencing in the present, by tying his present experience with his past, and by instilling hope in him for the future.

Not only does your child need his own story, he needs a *"hoping forward" story*—one that acknowledges his sufferings in the past, yet includes a genuine hopefulness for the future based on the positive changes he is making in the present. As we have witnessed in Darryl's family scenario, "hoping forward" is an essential part of the successful use of LSC. Your child can begin to experience himself and others in a new way in the now, within his relationship with you, his present caregiver, and break out of his cemented past into a more fluid world of possibilities. No longer will your child be alone with the hopeless beliefs about himself and his life he has dragged around with him like a dank, dirty blanket. With your help, he will be creating a cohesive, coherent narrative that will continue to reflect his hard work and growth in the present, with which you can help him to see the possibilities in his future.

Eventually your child's developing narrative will eclipse his old beliefs, but until then, he will fall back upon his old beliefs to bring him comfort because they are all he has ever known. Therefore, it is important to understand that *you cannot take away your child's negative perspective of himself*, nor should you try. He needs you to *acknowledge and respect* what he thinks of himself in the present and integrate that into his narrative for now. Otherwise, his trust in you will diminish because he senses you do not "get" him. It is also important and necessary, however, for you not to *accept* the negatives he believes about himself because you need to hold a picture in your mind *for him* of the child he is growing to be. "Right now, you still feel like you're a bad kid when you can't do what you *think* you should be able to do. That's why I'm here . . . to help you find those things you *can* do and have goals you *can* reach." Sustaining a tangible construct representing the objective you want to achieve in the healing journey with your child helps you both "stay on message" and refocus when you and he have temporarily lost your way.

Key Points for Chapter 9

1. Traditional approaches like punishment or an authoritarian stance evoke fear, frustration, and shame in the distressed child.
2. It is helpful to see your child's problem as an opportunity for your child to grow within the relationship.
3. *Supportive control* means providing structure, kind words, and non-threatening body language that help the child name and understand his feelings.
4. Language of Supportive Control is a way of speaking that identifies and names the need, keeps the relationship as the medium of repair, weaves the past, present, and future together into the child's story, and plants hope into even the most dire of situations.
5. Important aspects of Language of Supportive Control are addressing and reframing the need, joining with the child in the solution, attuning, putting hope forward, conveying your competence as an adult and the child's competence as a growing individual, using a teaching approach, and decreasing failure.
6. Keeping your child close while monitoring his tolerance for closeness allows you to teach your child the structure of your family naturally.
7. Giving a child choices allows him to feel some control while you remain in charge.
8. Your child needs a story that includes both the good and the bad that has happened to him so that he can understand the past, be fully present, and be able to have hope for the future.

10.
What Do I Do When?
Structure, Discipline,
and Relationship Interventions

**Raising children uses every bit of your being—
your heart, your time, your patience, your foresight,
your intuition to protect them, and you have to use all of this
while trying to figure out how to discipline them.**

NICOLE ARI PARKER

〜 IT IS MONDAY MORNING before school, the day after spring vacation. Rusty, now six, had been adopted at eighteen months. When it was time to put on his coat to leave the house for school, Rusty fell apart. One sleeve on and one sleeve off, Rusty collapsed on the floor in the front hall. Because Rusty's sobs were inconsolable, his mom had to quickly call on the neighbor (a prearranged "plan b" for just such occasions) to take her other children to school so she could stay and address Rusty's needs. Mom quickly assessed the situation and concluded that because the past week was spring break, Rusty had gotten used to being home where he has always felt the safest and most comfortable, and now he had to leave his safety zone to return to school.

Mom took off Rusty's coat (a signal to him he was not going anywhere) and pulled him into her lap in the overstuffed rocker so she could soothe his fear by hugging and rocking him. As they rocked together, Rusty's mom softly narrated what had just happened, laying out the series of events, naming his emotions and needs, and talking about how, in the present, she and Rusty together were meeting those needs.

Within the hour, Rusty was back to feeling safe and reassured as his mom could see by his lack of tears, his regular breathing, and the relief on his face. They then decided together that Rusty would stay home that day and go to school the next day when he would be more ready. They could spend the day together and also make a plan to allow his transition back to school to feel safe. Rusty's mom had recognized her son's distress as well as his inability to self-soothe. Mom had identified that Rusty's displayed developmental age when he broke down was that of a very young toddler who was about to be separated from his safe person. Thus, the goal in Rusty's mom's intervention was to regulate his distress because, just as if he were still a toddler, Rusty was not yet able to regulate himself.

What Do You Want Your Child to Learn?

While the intervention in this example may appear to be clear and straightforward, it probably would not be most parents' first response. Traditionally, responding to a child's unregulated behavior may have had a less empathic, more authoritarian bent to it. Using a more traditional approach, Rusty's mother may have picked him up, finished putting on his coat, and shuffled him toward the car to take him to school. Rusty might have been told that he could not have dessert that night if he didn't go to school. Yet what capacity would these more matter-of-fact approaches have fostered in the child? In the end, after many such repetitions, Rusty would have learned to "manage" his emotions on his own by squelching them in order to do what was expected of him. Furthermore, in dismissing Rusty's emotions and needs, his parent would have lost an opportunity to continue to build a trusting relationship with him while helping him learn who he is and how to manage his needs. Knowing the goal you are trying to attain through your relationship allows you to choose the intervention that will help you meet both your objective and your child's needs.

Let's change the story above just a little. Let's say that Rusty is ten, and leaves his coat at school on a regular basis. Now we don't have just an episode of being emotionally overwhelmed but a habitual behavior that Rusty needs to take some responsibility for. This chapter will outline some helpful ways of teaching emotionally distressed children how to handle responsibility and how to talk about what they need instead of acting on their frustrations and anxiety. As a parent, you first need to understand what need the child is expressing and what approach is developmentally appropriate.

Discipline or Consequences?

The word "discipline" comes from the Latin word "disciple," which means one who is a follower of a master's teaching. A disciple is a voluntary student who is seeking knowledge and inspiration from a teacher he respects and admires. In the same sense, a well-nurtured child can be seen as a seeker of the knowledge, acceptance, and approval offered by his parents. This child not only admires his parents but also strives to be admired by them. This reciprocal relationship demonstrates the bonding and trust that have developed over time as the child has come to rely upon his parents and as they have come to embrace him. In the case of the emotionally distressed child, however, such a reciprocal relationship has not been part of his experience, nor is it something he will be able to understand or live until he and his primary caregiver co-create it starting from scratch. Developing a reciprocal relationship takes much time and patience as well as a conscious focus on *connecting before correcting* (Neufeld, 2005) on the part of the parent.

Traditional disciplining techniques such as authoritarianism, using punishment and time out, employing chronologically age-appropriate expectations, and relying on parental relationship as leverage are inevitably ineffective when used with emotionally distressed children. A child who is distressed will interpret adult authoritarianism as a threat to his safety, and his difficult behaviors will likely escalate as a result of the stimulation of his core fear. Parents who assign punishment as a consequence for unregulated behavior do so believing that this deterrent will inspire their child to learn from and thus mind his behavior. In "teaching the child a lesson" by assigning punishment, parents falsely assume that a child does not know he did something wrong. The fact is, a child is almost always fully aware of his wrong actions; thus there is no "lesson to teach." What the child needs is not parent *reprimand*; he needs a parental *response* that targets understanding the "why" of his misbehavior. Moreover, the punishment approach will be perceived once again by a distressed child as a threat, which will trigger shame and reactivity, which often increases the undesired behavior.

A troubled child experiences *time out* as rejection, and feeling rejected will plummet him into shame—a sure trigger for behavioral dysregulation. Therefore, if a child needs to take a moment to regroup, *time in* is used instead, and so the child sits with his parent to become regulated. If a parent believes that having chronologically age-appropriate expectations for her developmentally younger child will somehow inspire this child to "rise to the occasion," she places the bar higher than her child can possibly reach, which again will ignite a shame reaction in the child who already feels "less than." Accurate assessment of the child's present developmental age,

---

Focus on *connecting* with your child
before you move on to taking any action to correct

as we discussed in Chapter 5, is necessary to intervene effectively. Relying on the parental relationship for leverage assumes the child is invested in the relationship to the degree necessary for him to value and strive for his parent's approval. While a birth child who has received adequate care and nurturing from the time of conception will surely want to please his primary caregiver in order to maintain her acceptance and love, a child with an attachment disruption will have no such motivation. The distressed child, in fact, is leery of relying on an adult for anything and associates caregivers with uncertainty, fear, and pain rather than with safety, love, and acceptance. Thus, the distressed child's behavior will not pivot upon the weight of his parent's approval. Instead, challenging behavior functions more as a remote-control device the child uses to try to *manage his parents* in a way that will keep him feeling in charge and safe.

What, then, is the parent of a distressed child to do when it comes to shaping her child's behavior? The most effective approach to intervening in a child's challenging behavior involves using your relationship with your child to further bonding while enhancing your child's developmental growth as well as his knowledge about himself and the world. Practically, what this means is responding to your child's actions as learning events that the two of you share and explore together. With this mind-set, you support your child in experiencing the *consequences* of his behaviors, whether they flow naturally or logically from his actions. Allowing consequences teaches your child that from every one of his actions flows a reaction—one that is both inevitable and educative. In contrast, using *punishment* elicits shame, teaches the child that parents are scary, and encourages the child to be sneaky so as not to get caught next time. Punishment, therefore, "teaches" the child to be better at relying upon himself, which is the antithesis of the goal of building a trusting relationship with him. In allowing consequences, parents are building their child's cause-and-effect thinking capacity, a must-have skill that is either weak or nonexistent at the time a distressed child enters his forever home.

An example of a *natural consequence* is if a child refuses to wear his winter coat out into the snow, he will get cold. Another is if a child is truly capable of doing a homework assignment but chooses not to do it, he would receive zero points for that task from his teacher. In both cases, the child's parent would work with him to understand what is going on for him internally that led him to make unfortunate choices. An example of a *logical consequence* is if a child throws her marbles across

> A *natural* consequence is what naturally happens in the real world
> as a result of a behavior. A *logical* consequence is created
> as a response that follows logically from a behavior. A *punishment*
> is an assignment of something painful to the child
> that is intended to teach the child a lesson but shames him instead.

the room, she must gather them up. Another logical consequence would be if a child hurls a rock through a picture window, he must help pay for, clean up, and replace the window. Logical consequences are carried out to the child's level of ability, with parental assistance as necessary for completion. Both natural and logical consequences are relationally educational for the child as he is learning that everything he does affects someone or something in his world. Using consequences enhances the child's relationship with his parent, who does not just levy the consequence per se, but rather talks over the action-reaction dynamic of his behavior with him and supports or assists him as necessary in taking responsibility for his actions.

In addition to using natural and logical consequences in response to an event wherein parents want to connect *and* correct, they can use "do-overs." A do-over allows both parent and child to go back and modify their interaction in a way that works better in achieving the momentary goal. A simple example of a do-over is for the parent to gently stop the action with, "Wait, let's redo that before we go on," and then have the child go back and ask, "Please, may I?" instead of screaming, "Gimme that!" A do-over provides a learning experience and a practice tool the child needs in order to learn to act in a way that is more beneficial to him. The mutual reenactment that takes place in a do-over fosters a closer relationship between parent and child in the moment as well as in the long run. Do-overs allow the child to take away a successful behavioral experience, which will naturally increase his sense of "can do" and, thus, his self-esteem.

The distressed child cannot stand on his own as he is building neural pathways for cause-and-effect thinking and self-reflective ability. This means

> A *do-over* is a chance to repeat a behavior more appropriately.
> A *rescue* is taking responsibility for an action away from the child.

**The first and last thing parents must do when giving a consequence
is to establish and maintain a trusting connection with their child**

that the child's parent must walk through each event with her child much as she would do if he were a younger child. Placing chronological age-appropriate expectations on a developmentally younger child poises the child to become enveloped in shame because he cannot achieve what he is expected to achieve. In working to close the developmental gaps of an emotionally distressed child, parents must actively be engaged in a relationship with him *at the level of his functionally ability.* Consequences, when used as lessons that are worked through *between parent and child* at his level of understanding, are the most educative and relationship-enhancing responses to challenging behavior.

Indeed, parents are looking to help their child communicate and express himself through verbal rather than behavioral means. However, parents must learn to look at their child's misbehavior in a way that differs from an action that merely needs to be corrected. As we discussed in earlier chapters, a child's behavior is the language he uses to express his emotions, thoughts, and feelings about his experiences. If parents can enter a new paradigm of understanding, wherein misbehavior is seen as an opportunity to get to know their child on a deeper level, they can respond in a way that fosters that knowing as well as nurtures growth in their relationship with their child. Authoritarianism, assigning time out, punishment, or holding unrealistic expectations for your child to "rise to the challenge" hinders the *development of trust in care and control—the ultimate goal when working with an emotionally distressed child.*

One additional, but ineffective type of response to challenging behavior is called a "rescue"—the act of *the parent taking responsibility for the child's actions.* An example of a rescue is the parent picking up the scraps of a drawing the child tore up and left when he was mad and stomped out. Parents might try to rescue their child as a way of managing their own anxiety or relieving a felt pressure to solve the problem. A parent may employ a rescue to avoid a confrontation with the child. Whatever the reason a parent attempts a rescue, it is counterproductive because rescuing does not teach a child how his behavior affects himself, others, or the world. Instead, it induces shame in the child if he interprets a parent's rescue as "Mom thinks I'm stupid and can't do it" or substantiates a feeling of control the child has over the parent, who just did the child's job. Rescuing can rob the child of the opportunity to prove himself, instill a hopeless, "he'll never do anything right" feeling in the parent, and cause relational divisiveness.

Each of the following examples falls into one of these five categories: natural consequence (N), logical consequence (L), do-over (D), punishment (P), or rescue (R). Identify the type of parental response described in each vignette below, and then check your answers at the bottom of page 193.

Name the Response

1. **SITUATION:** Sarah wants to play video games. Dad had said she could do this after dinner, so Sarah rushes through dinner, chews with her mouth open, and leaves the table abruptly without permission.
   Parental response: Dad sends Sarah to her room instead of letting her play video games because she failed to use proper table manners.

2. **SITUATION:** Sarah wants to play video games. Dad said she could do this after dinner, so Sarah starts rushing through dinner, chewing with her mouth open, and talking with food in her mouth.
   Parental response: Dad says, "Sarah, you need to slow down and use your manners during dinner. I'll know you can handle the privilege of playing video games if you are able to pay attention to your manners now while you're eating."

3. **SITUATION:** Scott forgot to take his lunch to school for the second time this week.
   Parental response: After the bus has come, Mom once again finds Scott's lunch box sitting on the kitchen shelf where she always puts it after making it for him. For the second time this week, she drives over to the school to take Scott his lunch. As Mom hands the lunch to Scott, she sighs, "I wish you would be more responsible because I'm tired of having to interrupt my morning to bring you your lunch all of the time." Scott hangs his head, turns, and slowly shuffles back into the classroom with his lunch box.

4. **SITUATION:** Scott forgot to take his lunch to school for the second time this week.
   Parental response: Mom empties the lunch box into the fridge and will repack it the next day. When Scott calls her at lunchtime, Mom says,

"It sounds like we'll need to sit down soon and figure out how to help you remember your lunch. But for now, you ask your teacher for some milk and one of the snack bars she keeps in the classroom for when her students forget their lunches. Neither she nor I want you to go hungry."

5. **SITUATION:** When his mom steps into the family room and asks him to take a break from his Lego project and come into the kitchen for lunch, Jack, who along with his mom has been working on his behavior during transitions, has a mini-tantrum—throwing Legos, pounding his fists on the floor, and yelling, "Ahhhhrrggg."

Parental response: "Whoa, Jackie! Looks like you must have been right in the middle of making a really cool building when I came in to call you to lunch. I saw it just briefly before you threw it against the wall, and it was quite something! [Mom sits down near Jack, and he settles fairly quickly.] I'm sorry your building project got ruined. I'd like us to have a do-over on this because I think both of us could have done a better job on this transition." [Jack lets out a big tension-relieving sigh and Mom takes this as a signal to proceed. She gets up, goes back to the door from the kitchen into the family room.]

"Okay, Jack, this is our do-over—'come to lunch, take two.'" [Mom claps her hands shut like the jaws of a crocodile, imitating the clap-board that starts the film rolling.] "Hi, Jack! Can I see what you're making?" [Mom walks over to Jack and leans down, pretending to ad-mire his Lego building.] "That's a cool building! Looks like you've been working hard on it for a while now. Can I see it? [Jack holds up his Lego building for his mom to see.] "Cool!" Mom exclaims. "I like the way the window and door open." [Jack shrugs his shoulders as his way of taking his mom's compliment.]

"Hey, Jackie. We're going to need to take a lunch break pretty soon. Do you think you could take a break from your project in about five minutes?" Jack responds, "Yeah, okay, Mom. But I'm bringing my house with me so no one wrecks it." Mom says, "Sounds good." [Mom and Jack look at each other and start to smirk at the silliness of the "play" they have just performed. Mom reaches her hand down to Jack and she pulls him up, exaggerating the movement as if he has sud-denly gotten very heavy. They laugh and move on into the kitchen.]

Answers: 1) P; 2) L; 3) R; 4) N; 5) D

Considerations in Giving a Consequence

When it comes to giving a consequence to a distressed child, parents have the potential to ignite the powder keg that is their child's core shame. However, consequences give a child a real-world experience of the cause-and-effect reality we all face. So, rather than avoiding a move into giving a consequence, parents can proceed successfully if they have some guidance to help them navigate this potential for dysregulation. The first and last thing parents must do when giving a consequence is to establish and maintain a trusting connection with their child.

Guidelines for Giving a Consequence

➤ Establish and maintain a trusting connection with your child.

➤ Remember the goal is to make the consequence a learning event for the child.

➤ Is the consequence directly related to the behavior? (What does eating without manners have to do with going to your room?)

➤ Is the consequence reasonable? (Is having the child pick rocks in the back field for a week a reasonable consequence for taking some quarters out of the change jar without permission?)

➤ Does the consequence allow choices so that the child can feel his power? (The child has the choice between doing his homework and getting credit or not doing his homework and receiving a zero.) Accept any (safe) choice the child makes, and later use the result, whether positive or negative, as a teaching lesson.

➤ Is the consequence enforceable? (It is ineffective to say "no TV" if you are not around to check.) Following through in a neutral, non-shaming manner is essential for the child's trust in you to develop.

➤ Is it the right time to give a consequence? (Neither child nor parent can think logically when flooded with emotions.)

➤ Is your spouse/partner in agreement with the consequence? (If not, the child has a wide-open invitation to split the two of you and gain control, which leads to him feeling insecure in the end because parents are not united and in control.)

➤ Have you assured your child that he will have the chance for another try? ("I think that when this happens again, you might be able to choose differently.")

WHAT DO I DO WHEN?

With these guidelines in mind, review the following vignette to see how it feels to be in the parent's shoes as you use the guidelines to teach while growing the parent-child relationship.

Cody's Story

Cody, a fourteen-year-old boy, is a young teen who does not like being away from home even though his neighboring town, which is three miles away, is quiet and safe. Cody is angry about a decision you have made to have him work off money that he had taken from you by doing extra chores around the house. He decides to run away. As Cody is headed for the door, you respond, "Cody, right now you have a choice. If you run away, it will be difficult for you. It is three miles to anywhere, it is hot, and you have no one to stay with. *And* your work will still be waiting when you return. If you decide to stay, you might need some time to settle down and run around the property a few times before you get back to the work you need to do. When you're done with the work, you can get on with life and do what you want to do."

Cody decides to leave. Two hours later, Cody calls home and says that he is sorry he ran away. He wants a ride home. You respond, "I'm also sorry that you made the choice to run away. It is not the one I would have made for you, but it's the one you made. You know how to get home from where you are. I'm glad you've decided to come home, and I will be here waiting for you." Cody slams down the phone and starts grudgingly walking back to the house.

After walking the three miles back, Cody finishes his work. He is very tired at the end of the day. You say, "When this situation arises again, I hope you will make a choice that works out better for you." He responds, "I hate it when you do this." However, the sense of safety Cody has grown to feel within your kind and consistent care and control eventually settles into him again, and he goes right to sleep.

A few weeks later, after you have given Cody another consequence he does not like, he stomps off toward the door. You weigh whether to reiterate the choices Cody has in the moment. You decide doing so would reinforce the sense of security he feels within your relationship due to your consistency. So you say, "Cody, right now you have a choice—" Cody turns, cuts you off midsentence, and quips, "Do you think I'm *crazy*? If you think I'm walking to town you're *nuts*. I'm *never* doing *that* again." You respond lightly as you walk back to the kitchen, "I'm *so glad* you're not crazy and I'm not nuts."

Pitfalls in Giving Consequences

There are some potential pitfalls parents need to avoid when they are giving a consequence. As you review this list of pitfalls, make note of the ones that are likely to trip you up, and then consider what you could do to avoid each one.

Pitfalls in Giving Consequences
- ➤ *Not establishing a connection first.* Without having a connection with your child, a consequence is a surefire way to set off an explosion of shame in your child.
- ➤ *Being unaware of your own level of anxiety* or anger before giving a consequence.
- ➤ *Feeling sorry for the child or giving in.* The child gains the upper hand in the moment, which leads to him feeling insecure in the end. You have also lost an opportunity to teach your child something.
- ➤ *Fearing the consequence is too easy.* It is not necessary for a consequence to be gigantic or difficult; learning will occur by giving the *right* consequence.
- ➤ *Not being firm* with consequences because it is hard for you to see your child's disappointment. Your child may withhold hugs or refuse to comply in an attempt to get you to give in. However, you can be consistent and firm with consequences while soothing your child's feelings of disappointment: "I know that you feel really disappointed with yourself for making this mistake, and I also know that if you clean it up, you'll feel better."
- ➤ *Immediately giving your child a second chance.* A child needs some time to digest the action-reaction dynamic of his choices.
- ➤ *Taking a punitive attitude,* showing impatience, ridiculing, invoking shame or humiliation, or acting out of retaliation. All lead to shame and disruption in your relationship with your child, which is fragile to begin with.
- ➤ *Creating a consequence that is too difficult* or too unpleasant for learning to occur. If you stay attuned to your child, you will be able to gauge what is "just enough" for your child in the moment.

➤ *Showing inconsistency or not following through.* Your word establishes an expectation that if left unfulfilled will damage the trust you are building with your child. You cannot afford this kind of avoidable setback in your relationship with your child, who needs to be able to count on you at all times.

➤ *Working on too many behaviors at one time.* If your child is following through with the given consequence but has a glare on his face, do not give an additional consequence for glaring. However, if your child's behavior escalates and he becomes dysregulated, reflect that you can see that he is not ready to do what was asked of him and tell him he will get another chance later. Help your child reregulate, then let him know that as soon as he finishes his assigned task, you and he can move on and do something else.

➤ *Feeling guilty about giving consequences.* Remember that consequences are the learning experiences your child needs to complete his development. If your guilt endures after this reminder, your consequence may be too harsh or inappropriate.

➤ *Arguing or talking too much.* Use a few simple words, get straight to the point, and say it in a calming voice. Your child's stress level is elevated when he is faced with taking responsibility for his actions, and he is operating out of his primitive brain, which cannot take in or understand a flood of words. Ask your child to repeat what you are saying so that you can be sure he understands.

➤ *Thinking that using a consequence will take too much time.* Remember what your goal with your child is and reprioritize if need be.

➤ *Allowing yourself to feel pressured.* Responding to your child's actions in a way that teaches him and improves your bond with him takes some thought. Letting your child know that you need to think about it and that you will follow up later is an effective response when you need time.

➤ *Expecting behavior from your child that you do not expect of yourself.* Children learn what they live, and they look to parents as role models.

➤ *Conveying an "I told you so" message to your child* verbally or nonverbally. Using snide remarks only puts a wedge between you and your child. Remember your goal.

➤ *Using an angry, demanding, demeaning, or sarcastic tone of voice.* You will immediately set your child's defenses into motion if you are not monitoring your emotions.

➤ *Using time-limited consequences.* This invites your child to stall and challenge you, taking the focus off of building trust in your relationship with him.

➤ *Not taking the "high road."* Tempting as it may be at times to want to punish your child, taking that "low road" will be a setback in building your relationship with your child.

➤ *Not being vigilant about minding your own triggers.* First and foremost, when parenting your child, you must strive to remain in an objective state of mind for your interactions to result in healing for your child.

If two parents are involved in responding to an event with their child, both must be in agreement about the consequence. If you are not on the same page, a shift will occur and the marital/partner relationship will become the focus instead of the child's behavior and choices. The child will sense this and try to further divide the parents in their decision-making process. It is easier than it might seem for splitting to happen "under the radar" of the parents, while the child quickly recognizes a chance to take control. If this is happening, address it. It is never too late to right the foundering ship. Join with your spouse to figure out why you are not working together and change what needs to be changed to reunite the two of you. Your child will sense the strength returning to your partnership, and while this will reduce his own power in the triad, he will be able to relax again into the safety of his parents' care.

The objective of intervening in your child's challenging behavior is to teach him self-control—not to take control away from him. Practically, you cannot be by your child's side every single minute, twenty-four hours a day, so your child inevitably needs to learn to make decisions for himself. If you are attempting to control all aspects of your child's life for fear he will fail or, worse, that you will look like a bad parent in the eyes of others, you are being counterproductive, and your child's development will suffer. Even though it may feel burdensome or time-consuming, you must weigh the risks and the opportunities in each event you negotiate with your child in making a decision about what is best for your child's growth and your relationship. Keeping in mind that you are only the teacher and that progress truly happens only when your child solves the problem can be your guiding star as you continue your work with your child.

"Taking a Seat" and "Time In"

One of Intermountain's signature interventions within Language of Supportive Control is "taking a seat." The purpose of a child sitting, or "taking a seat," is to promote the development of self-regulation, to afford a learning opportunity which takes place *within* the relationship (the parent remains present with the child), and to provide practice in taking responsibility for one's behavior. The action of deliberate sitting is not a punishment; rather, it makes it clear to your child that the problem belongs to him and establishes the conditions necessary for pushing through an issue, if appropriate at the time. The child is taught "how to take a seat" at a time prior to its first usage, when he is calm and thus available for learning. When taking a seat, your child sits erect, remains quiet, and does not initiate interaction. The child can practice sitting and the parent can talk him through what he is to be thinking about as he sits, as a preparation for the time when taking a seat will be used therapeutically.

The choices of where to sit and what to sit upon in the room can be ceded to your child, as this modicum of control may allow him to feel a bit safer, and therefore less oppositional. Parents decide whether the moment calls for just the child to take a seat or if it is more appropriate for parent and child to sit together for the seat. This decision is made based on the child's current capacity for supporting himself in becoming regulated. Sometimes the child might be able to become regulated on his own, while at other times the same child might need the parent to sit with him in order for him to become regulated. If the child is highly dysregulated and will not take a seat, then the parent quietly takes a seat first, an action that will eventually lead to the child calming and following suit. In this situation, the parent sits and focuses on her breathing and posture—not on what the child is doing. When the conditions for sitting have been met by the child, the parent can begin to talk with him about the situation.

Asking the child to take a seat means that the child sits quietly and thinks about what is going on beneath his dysregulated behavior

Steps for Taking a Seat
The parent's steps for facilitating sitting are as follows:
➤ **STOP:** Ask your child to take a seat. Regulate yourself with conscious breath until you are calm.
➤ **THINK:** Identify the trigger for your child's behavior and the feeling underlying the behavior.
➤ **PLAN:** Establish a plan: Is there enough time and is this a good location to address the behavior and the issue? If so, how are you going to approach the discussion? If not, how are you going to transition from here and when can you have the discussion?
➤ **DO:** If taking a seat does not regulate your child enough to allow the two of you to discuss and resolve the issue, then implement a different intervention as a first step, for example, taking *yourself* for a time out.

The child's steps for taking a seat are as follows:
➤ **STOP:** Stop and take a seat, because what you are doing is not working out well for you.
➤ **THINK:** Name the problem behavior, accept responsibility for it, and think about why it is not working.
➤ **PLAN:** Plan what you can do differently next time so that it will work out better for you.
➤ **DO:** Try it again using what you have learned.

Taking a seat is an intentional intervention on the part of the parent, used to pull the child into the present and help him reregulate, moving him from his reptile brain into his cortex so that he can begin to reason and think about how he can make his life work better for him. In order for parents to achieve these goals, it helps for them to follow guidelines until they become more familiar with the process.

Guidelines for Taking a Seat
1. When you ask your child to "take a seat," you are looking for a demonstration of your child's trust of your control as evidenced by him following the instruction. Once in the seat, if your child is playing with items or calling out, then he can't be thinking about what he is doing that is not working well for him; he is actively avoiding taking responsibility for his behavior. Handing your child a "taking a seat" card that spells out what he is to be doing in the seat can be

a useful nonverbal response to your child when he is evading the process.

2. Stay present, but do not interact with your child while he is settling into his seat. Your child knows what he needs to do while in a seat, and you are waiting for him to make a statement describing the problem behavior and accepting responsibility for it. As your child is thinking, you have time to become clear about exactly what the issue is and who is responsible for what. This is also an opportunity to establish a goal for the sitting, although you will need to remain flexible because your child may take you in another, more meaningful direction.

3. When you ask your child to tell you about why he is taking a seat, he needs to communicate ownership in the here and now. If he blames others, he is not ready to talk with you. Being able to make and sustain eye contact is indicative of there being trust in your relationship. If your child cannot make eye contact when you ask him to look at you, then he is not ready to talk. Let your child know what you are looking for as a signal he is ready.

4. Be aware that your child may tell you what he thinks you want to hear. If you think he is doing this, then he is not ready to talk, so have him think in his seat awhile longer. If you find yourself going back and forth with your child, let him know that he is still not ready to talk. "I am feeling like you may need a bit longer to think because you keep saying that you are ready to resolve this, but you're showing me that you're not, so I'm going to put it on my timetable now. I will get back to you when I think you are ready."

5. When your child is ready to talk, he needs to be involved in the process. If you find yourself doing all of the talking, then your child is not participating. Likewise, if you find yourself doing all of the problem solving, then your child may need more time to think in his seat before you proceed.

6. When your child is ready to talk, your conversation needs to include the following: (1) "What is it that is not working out well for you?" (2) "Did that choice get you what you wanted?" (3) "What can you do differently next time so that it will work out better for you?" (4) "Are you ready to try it again using what you've learned?"

7. If a child is new to the seat taking process, you may have to help him think through the situation and formulate the answers to the

questions. As time goes by, you can expect your child to know how to negotiate the sitting process as well as come up with alternative behaviors.

8. Taking a seat does not negate your child's responsibility for the results of his behavior: a natural or logical consequence is often an appropriate adjunct to sitting, especially if your child's behavior caused harm to something or someone. Work with your child to help him come up with a suitable consequence.

Another intervention that on the surface may look similar to taking a seat is "time in," which is the opposite of "time out," wherein the child is sent to his room alone to calm himself or reset his attitude before he returns to the family. In using time out—separating child from parent, ostensibly for the purpose of giving the child time to cool off and think—the relationship is not being addressed, and, in fact, the relationship suffers because the child feels shame and fear when sent away. Contrastingly, "time in" involves the parent and child sitting together, first to help him become regulated, and second to help him grow his narrative by understanding how his present behavior is conveying a need, and how it relates to his past trauma.

Initially, this "time in" approach is similar to the parent and child "taking a seat" together, in that the parent first sits with the child to help him regulate. However, after the child is regulated, "time in" differs from "taking a seat" in its objective. "Taking a seat" focuses upon the immediate behavior, provides the child with an opportunity to learn what is and what is not working for him, and gives him the opportunity to practice a more functional behavior. "Time in," on the other hand, focuses upon helping the child make a connection between his immediate behavior and his history.

As with the use of "taking a seat," consequences can be used with "time in." The child still needs to be accountable for the results of his behavior because his past does not excuse him from taking responsibility in the present. The difference between the use of consequences in "taking

---

"Time-in" involves sitting with your child to help him reregulate and make a connection between his current behavior and his history

a seat" and "time in" comes with the level of parent participation. In general, a child who is able to take a seat on his own will be more capable of taking responsibility for the completion of a task related to the consequence. In this situation, a parent may need to be present or nearby to lend a supportive presence to what the child is doing, but the parent does not help the child in finishing his task.

On the other hand, a child who is receptive enough to address his past in the connective context of "time in" may need and/or benefit from his parent's active support in completing a task related to the consequence. When a child is emotionally accessible, parents have the opportunity to "move in" and capitalize on their child's openness to relationship by having a bonding experience based on the parent's direct assistance to the child. In this scenario, to cement trust and respect, the parent needs to elicit from her child a sincere request and then appreciation for the parent's help. "Time in" can be used by itself as an intervention or in addition to "taking a seat." The decision to use one or the other is made according to the parent's judgment as to whether the child is receptive enough to talking about his past so that narrative building will be productive.

Helping Your Child Solve Problems

When you solve your child's problems for him, it allows you temporarily to feel competent and needed. But it also denies your child the opportunity to learn to think for himself and to attain the feeling of "I can do," which is the core element of self-esteem. Allow and encourage your child to solve his own problems as much as he is capable of doing so. Otherwise, power struggles will arise out of your child's feelings of being powerless and unworthy. Evaluate each situation carefully in terms of what your child is truly capable of handling in the moment, and give him as much latitude to make decisions as will lead to success. As you let your child make decisions within limits that will yield a positive outcome, he can learn to use personal power in a constructive way and he can feel what it is like to be responsible for his own choices.

Be aware of attempts on your child's part to use behaviors to distance himself from you or to save him from taking responsibility for a problem. Do not allow your child to put the problem between the two of you; instead, join your child in solving the problem. As you approach a problem with your child, it is important to frame the situation in terms of helping

**The problem of getting what he wants belongs to your child,
and you are there to help him succeed**

your child get what he desires. As you conceptualize the problem with your child, do not view his behaviors as either good or bad, but rather as helpful or not in having things go well. As you help your child, remain conscious of who is doing the most work. Your child does not gain anything in terms of self-responsibility if you bear the burden of solving his dilemma. The following are some examples of successfully using this "I'm only an assistant in my child's problem-solving process" approach.

Assist Your Child in Solving His Problems

"Thomas, I want you to be able to play with Ralphie too, but in order for it to be fun for both of you, it has to be safe, and hitting is not safe. Let's figure out what's happening that makes you want to hit Ralphie when you are playing. When we solve this, you'll be able to play safely and have fun with Ralphie."

"I know you want to have friends, LaShandra. It seems there's something happening that makes that hard for you. I wonder if you have any ideas about this. I want to help you have friends."

"Jeremy, it sounds like playing on the playground can get too rough for you and you end up getting hurt a lot. Let's see if together we can figure out how you can stay safe on the school playground while still having fun."

"I wonder what you could do to make things better between you and Mom, Terry, now that she knows you were the one who stole money out of her purse."

"Yes, Randa, I can see how frustrated you are when you try to do your math homework and don't understand it. Maybe there's something we can think of that will help you so you can understand it and feel like you know what you're doing."

"It's so scary for you, Shawn, to think what Mr. Coles might say or do when he finds out you dented the school's tuba. I'm thinking that together we can come up with a plan to get it fixed so that when you tell him about the accident and show him the instrument, you also can show him how responsible you are by having a solid plan in place to get it fixed."

"Chelsea, I bet it will be hard for you to get past the shame you feel for shoplifting that CD. I'm here to help you figure out what to do now to make things right. What ideas do you have?"

"Danielle, it must be difficult for you right now to think about when you kicked me when you were angry. But I feel certain that we can work through this and be okay with each other again. I wonder what might begin to make things better."

If the problem is one that the child has no motivation to solve, but it is one you need him to assume responsibility for, you have to create an incentive for him. Let us say that it is your seventeen-year-old son's responsibility to take out the garbage. He has a job and girlfriend that he values as being far more important than doing chores, so he does not prioritize his family responsibilities. If you are tired of waiting and decide to take out the garbage yourself to get rid of the smell, your son will have no motivation for changing his behavior. Instead, he will conclude, "If I wait long enough, Mom will do it for me." You have to assist your son in changing his priorities if you want him to take responsibility for his chore. If *your* discomfort in seeing that his chore is incomplete is greater than *your son's* discomfort, then *you own the problem.*

To make it your son's problem, you will need to make it more uncomfortable for him to ignore the chore than to assume responsibility for it. For example, you might tell him he has a choice: he can take the garbage out or do another chore that requires more time and energy in return. You could allow him to go out and play *after* he completes chore a or chore b. You are again employing the use of choices here, giving the child a choice between two options, both of which satisfy your conditions and goal.

Each child has specific motivators that are sufficient to get him to assume responsibility for things he may not want to do, and as a parent, you *can* find the one that works to motivate your child in any given moment. What motivates a child is surely changeable and shifts with circumstance and developmental age, but there is always something that will "inspire" your child to do something that is not of his choosing. It seems like just when you think you can count on a particular motivator to work—one that has worked well in the past—your child's interests will shift, making

Try to make solving the problem
more motivating than avoiding the problem

it necessary for you to search for a new form of motivation. Keeping up with this quest for the right "carrot" can make parents feel like *they* are always on the donkey's end of the stick—forever reaching out for that carrot, which remains just out of reach.

Focusing on problem solving within the relationship with your child can feel like playing an involuntarily game of catch-me-if-you-can. When *you* are ready to approach your child to work out an issue or solve a current problem, he seems to slip away either physically or psychologically. Out of fear, children distance from adults by interrupting physical closeness, by preventing or dissuading confrontation, thereby interrupting gratification and fun, and by preventing, interrupting, or evading opportunities for receiving nurturance or fostering trust. These behaviors protect the child from what he fears most about relationship: that intimacy will lead to abandonment. Therefore, parents have to keep one eye on pursuing their relational goal with their child and the other eye on their child's self-protective attempts to secure emotional distance and safety for himself with controlling behaviors. Finding a balance between these opposing objectives can be a daily, sometimes minute-to-minute dance.

Tracking your child's distancing behavior can be easier for you if you know what your child is seeking with the behavior. In most cases, the child is looking for security and safety—commodities he is fearful of gaining from his caregivers and is used to providing for himself. Parents only add to the problem when they mistakenly only see the child's *drive for control* instead of what lies underneath: his need for security and safety. Control battles often arise out of this oversight and eclipse the need, which remains unmet and even gets more deeply buried by the child's fear that increases due to the turmoil. Being alert and recognizing the child's controllingness for what it truly means is essential for parents as they negotiate their relationship with their child. There are myriad ways a child may try to use control to meet his need for safety.

Controlling Behaviors a Child Uses to Feel Safe

➤ Taking over the adult role through pseudo-adult competencies

➤ Distancing adults through stimulating their fear, anger, revulsion, fatigue, frustration, and indifference

➤ Attempting to influence adults by being endearing and charming (promiscuous false self), resulting in adults minimizing their child's pathology and idealizing him

➤ Attempting to sway adults by engaging in "seductive" (meaning overly cooperative and exaggeratingly helpful) behaviors that reduce the adults' normal and appropriate demands and expectations

➤ Behaving in ways that control the adults' opportunities and desire to gratify and nurture the child

By becoming familiar with the ways your child attempts to keep a barrier between you and him, you have made the first move in building the bridge of trust he will need to cross in order to move from isolation into relationship. When you join your child in solving the problem at hand, you are working within your relationship with him to meet a mutual goal. *Keeping the focus on solving a problem together instead of focusing on the result of working together—being in relationship—actually gives your child the psychological distance he needs to feel safe enough to stay close and in relationship.*

Deciding to Intervene: When, How, by Whom, and Why

Jim FitzGerald, Intermountain's CEO, developed a protocol for making a decision about intervening in a child's behavior in the inpatient setting called "Seven Lenses for the Cottage Floor" (FitzGerald, 1996). For this parent handbook, the protocol has been adapted for use by the child's parents in the home to help them to perceive, think, and take action in a dynamic way—that is, to apply it as needed in any given situation. Because the lenses are designed to be used dynamically, they may be used differentially, depending on the adult-child combination. For example, use of the lenses by the primary caregiver with the child may differ at times from use by those who provide the primary caregiver with support.

Two factors to be considered when the lenses are used are 1) the functional *developmental* age of the child and 2) the *nature* of the relationship between the child and the adult in charge at the time. The set of lenses can be used by the child's parents in concert with the therapeutic team in the process of establishing a treatment plan, as well as by the caregivers themselves in the family's daily home life to assist them in thinking on their feet. If you cannot answer the questions based upon *your relationship with your child*, you are not empathically attuned to the needs of the child and will be relegated to mindless irrelevant rules and structure that will never be dynamic or powerful. *Only attuned relationships will be powerful in providing corrective emotional experiences.*

The Seven Lenses

1. **EXPECTATIONS.** What is going to be expected of the child (behaviorally, emotionally, etc.) where and why? Some expectations need to be universal for caregivers, such as we do not hurt others, while most need to be defined within each child/adult relationship.
2. **CONFRONTATIONS.** "Confrontation" is helping the child see what is not working for him. What are you going to confront now that you did not in the past and why? What should be held off on until later and why?
3. **STRUCTURE.** Structure is adult oversight, supervision, proximity, emotional engagement, restrictions, activities that you engage your child in or prevent the child from being engaged in. What does structure look like for an emotionally "messy" child who is working through his difficulties and anxieties as opposed to a child who has attached to his caregivers and feels safe?
4. **SUPPORT.** Support is human interaction: soothing, nurturance, engagement, empathy, affirmation, etc., determining how much support, by whom support needs to be provided, and in what settings for your child's optimal functioning.
5. **TOLERANCES.** What will be tolerated by whom, in what settings, and why?
6. **HERE AND NOW.** To what extent do your child and you need to be emotionally present right here and right now? This means no talk about history or the future, just how are you together right here and right now? How emotionally present can you be?
7. **STRENGTHS.** What strengths, talent, interests does your child possess that will be built upon?

All seven of these lenses are interrelated. For example, your decisions about how much support your child needs today must inform and align with the expectations you will place on your child today. There are not any correct answers for all situations. The correct answer for your child in each situation is a product of your relationship with the child, thorough and reflective thinking, allowing yourself to be open to your full experiences of the child, the child's level of developmental functioning, and consideration of the treatment plan.

In reviewing Rusty's story from the beginning of this chapter, we can see how Rusty's mom used the Seven Lenses to meet Rusty's needs.

The Seven Lenses: Rusty's Story

1. **EXPECTATIONS.** Rusty's mom used his *developmental age at the time of the incident* as the gauge to set her expectations for her son and make the decision to let Rusty stay home. Emotionally a toddler at the time, Rusty needed to be close to Mom so she could regulate, comfort him, and prepare him for the transition back to school, which she had not foreseen the need for the night before.

2. **CONFRONTATIONS.** In this incident, the "confrontation" was Mom narrating for Rusty what was going on for him when he melted down. She would be considering whether it was also an opportunity to tie this transition problem with his past experience of being taken away from his birth parents.

3. **STRUCTURE.** Providing structure for Rusty in meeting his expressed toddler needs for safety and security meant keeping him close, organizing his day, and giving him appropriate limits.

4. **SUPPORT.** Rusty's mom used the lens of support throughout her intervention with her son, as this is exactly what he needed during his day to reregulate him and bring him back into his six-year-old self in order to transition him back to school.

5. **TOLERANCES.** Mom would tolerate behaviors that were more typical of a toddler to meet Rusty where he was in order to attune to his needs because Rusty's *behaviors* were his way of telling his mom what he needed.

6. **HERE AND NOW.** Mom and Rusty needed to be in the here and now during the day because Mom recognized that in his toddler state, Rusty could not perceive past and future; he could only experience the present.

7. **STRENGTHS.** Rusty's mom saw that Rusty's strengths included his ability to "tell" her what he needed by melting down before school as well

as Rusty's increasing resilience that was the result of his ability to take in her support and nurturing like she gave him during the transition day. Each one of these strengths showed his mom how reliant on the relationship he had become over time since the adoption.

Choose Your Battles Wisely

For many parents, it can seem like the battles they need to fight are endless when waging war on the effects of their child's trauma and the developmental delays it has caused. Without having criteria for judging which battles are worth fighting, "choosing your battles" can feel overwhelming and arbitrary. Once parents decide which battles to choose, they need to know when and how to intervene in a way that moves the relationship forward and prompts growth in their child. Prioritizing battles can be done at a general level or at a situational level, which is defined by the parent's present emotional state, energy level, and available time; by the receptivity of the child in the moment; and by the current aspect of treatment being done. Realistically, the criteria for choosing which battles to fight and which to let go have to include both general and situation-specific elements in order for parents to discern what to address and when to address it.

Ultimately, there are battles that are just not useful or helpful to wage, because either they are relatively inconsequential and/or they are battles parents can never win. Examples of battles that are not useful to wage because, in the end, they are relatively unimportant, include the following.

Non-Beneficial Battles
- ➤ clothing choice—e.g., wearing unmatched socks, clashing colors, wrinkled clothes
- ➤ hair condition—e.g., insisting that hair is always brushed, neat, and clean, or of a parent-acceptable style
- ➤ participation in an activity—e.g., playing team sports or taking music lessons
- ➤ homework, especially multilayered assigned projects

Whether a child wears mismatched socks, yesterday's shirt, or his favorite pajama bottoms to school does not matter in the larger scheme of things. School dress code violations can be removed as potential arguments between parent and child because the school will enforce its own standards. The natural consequence of the child having to change clothes after a reprimand by the principal helps the child see that there are rules and expectations he needs to heed, even in the world outside his home. Parents may argue that the child's consequence becomes the parent's consequence when the child needs a change of clothes. However, parents can anticipate this eventuality and prepare for it by leaving a change of clothes at school for the young child or by suggesting to the teen that he carry a change of clothes in his backpack, reminding him that unless there's an emergency, there will be no parent trips to the school that day, so he might spend the day in in-school suspension. This approach leaves the consequences with the child, who hopefully will make better decisions for himself the next time he wants to see if he can get away with wearing his cutoff T-shirt to school.

If parents are concerned, for example, that their younger child's choice of clothing or hair condition might trigger a call from the principal or a visit by social services, they can preempt such a response by having a meeting prior to the start of the school year with the child's teachers, the school counselor, the principal, and any other school personnel who might have reason to question their child's welfare. The meeting should include any community professionals who are working with the child as well to lend credibility to the parents' position and to solidify the team that surrounds and supports the child on all fronts. An emotionally distressed child needs for all adults who are involved with his care and healing to be unified in purpose and approach. Creating this team and maintaining a meeting schedule that is sufficient to support and advance the course of the child's healing is an essential part of the child's care and treatment.

There are battles that parents should never engage in because they are battles parents *cannot possibly* win. Unfortunately, parents get stuck in such conflicts because they are concerned (unnecessarily) that their child's negative choice will lead to physical or developmental harm. The following are potential battles that can trigger a parent's hyper-concern, but are unwinnable.

Battles Parents Cannot Win
➤ potty training and keeping dry during the night and/or day
➤ learning
➤ eating
➤ sleeping

Just as no one can push a river or make the sun rise, no one can *make* a child potty, learn, eat, or sleep on demand. Attempting to require a child to do any of these acts sets up a no-win conflict within the parent-child relationship that can arrest progress he is making toward trusting in his parent's care and control. Requiring a child to perform one of these actions is not only fruitless but can be shame inducing, because without a natural urge or an interest on the part of the child to attempt these actions, he truly cannot *make* himself perform. Anytime a child cannot do what is expected of him, shame stirs within, which can unleash negative behaviors. Especially where the four actions mentioned above are concerned, parents must respect the child where he is in terms of his developmental age, his level of trust in care and control, and his progress in treatment.

Accommodations can be made to allow the child to go at his own pace where these four basic functions—elimination, learning, eating, and sleeping—are concerned. The "child's way" can be integrated into his daily life in a manner that is both respectful and functional for the time being. For example, a child who is chronologically five may be expected to be out of diapers and self-sufficient in toileting, but he may also be a two-year-old emotionally. Parents need to coach themselves where their expectations and emotions are concerned, assuring themselves that yes, their child someday will be potty trained, but that no, now is not that time and it is okay that he wears pull-ups. Supporting a child where he is emotionally is more effective and essential than is pushing him physically. In prioritizing their *child's needs* as more important than their *own needs*, parents actually reach their own goals for their child more quickly than if they push him.

On a general level, a parent can ask herself, "Do I need to win this battle?" If the answer is "yes," then the parent must ask herself, "*Why* does this battle need to be won?" If the answer to that question is anything other than a safety-related issue (e.g., my child must stay out of the street because it is not safe), winning the battle, in the grand scheme of things, is not necessary. However, when there is imminent danger, the decision tree is aborted and the parent uses whatever means she has to win the battle. Safety is always the first consideration, and sometimes the *only* consideration parents need to reflect upon when they are deciding whether to intervene. Since a child can only fully develop within relationship with his parents, the quality of that relationship becomes the paramount consideration in any intervention decision parents make. Development is biologically driven, and parents can be in harmony with and support that naturally unfolding process or they can thwart it. In focusing on *their unique child's true needs*, parents move in concert with biology to give the child the experiences he needs *at the time he needs them* to grow.

After safety is ensured, parents consider present situational factors in determining whether there is time in the present and if they have the capacity for dealing with a challenging event in a constructive way. If you can catch yourself thinking, "I've *got* to win this one *to feel better*" versus "My child needs _____," you presently are out of sorts, are not objective, and have needs of your own that have to be addressed first. For example, parents may feel they need to win a battle because they are feeling insecure in their position of being in charge of their child. Parents also might be feeling inadequate, publicly humiliated, tricked, or challenged by their child to "fight." When parents slip into a reactive position, it is impossible for them to respond in an appropriate and educative manner because they are not operating out of the logical part of the brain. If they are reactive, parents must assess what it is that has replaced their objectivity and deal with it so that they can approach their child from a more neutral stance.

When parents are not in a place of balance in their own emotions, they risk being controlling, punitive, and petty, which can damage the relational progress they have made with their child. Achieving emotional balance may require eliciting the support of a third party such as a spouse or friend who can help talk through the issue before addressing it with the child. It may mean taking a time out for yourself, whether that is a few minutes, an hour, or a whole day. It is definitely okay for parents to delay responding to a charged situation as long as they communicate to their child what they are doing and make sure they follow up at a later time to revisit the event with their child when they are of a calmer mind. Raising children requires a certain degree of unselfishness, as the needs of the child are paramount most of the time. Putting a child first when necessary can take its toll on parents' reserves, however, requiring that they *make and take time for themselves* to reenergize, hopefully before their needs cloud their judgment or take them over the edge.

In choosing your battle, ask yourself, "Do I need to win this?" and "Why?"
If the answer is other than a concern for safety,
taking action may negatively affect relational development.

Considering the receptivity of the child in the moment is the next step in responding on a situational level. This appraisal determines if the parent moves forward with an intervention that targets a child's issue based on whether it will "take" in the moment. If the child is not in a state wherein he can receive his parent's intercession, the parent holds off on intervening, again unless there is a safety issue. If the child is receptive, that is, not in a high state of distress, the parent can move into the situation with an intervention that will edify the child while supporting the relationship. Finally, when evaluating whether the time is right to intervene, consideration of the place in which the child is in treatment helps determine whether the battle is worthwhile. Keeping pace with the child's growth and developmental readiness to benefit from an intervention will aid parents in deciding to intervene in the present or wait until later on when the child is in a better position to benefit from the experience.

Making Repairs

What does it mean to make a repair? In all relationships, there is an ebb and flow of interaction as well as various levels of attunement within those interactions. Most of the time, relationships flow smoothly as the parties engage in relating. At times, however, mistakes in understanding, communication, and responding occur that temporarily disrupt the relationship and the trust in the connection with the other. These disruptions can last for seconds, minutes, or days, and sometimes even for years. The goal in any relationship is to stay committed to another person and to the shared process; perfect interaction or attunement is not only impossible, but aiming for faultlessness can become a distraction because attention shifts from the relational partner onto performance. Ebb and flow in the level of understanding within relationship is actually the rhythm necessary for interaction to evolve. If perfect understanding and attunement were possible, the relational participants would be of one mind, and thus would not need to communicate anything, as they would have the same thoughts and feelings about their experience. The richness in and draw toward relationship—like positive and negative magnets—lie in difference, not sameness. Occasions of misunderstandings and misattunement result from the clash of unique experiences of the world, those that when noticed and acknowledged enrich the life of each person in the relationship.

Resolving conflicts with those with whom we have daily contact is essential to maintaining a solid connection. When clashes result in hurt feelings, distancing, and a break in the relational flow, making a repair can reconvene the relationship and actually provide an opportunity for increased closeness. However, effective repair involves more than just saying, "I'm sorry." This mere utterance is often not a sufficient response to mistakes we make that distance the person to whom we are relating. A sufficient apology is, in the end, defined by the recipient, but in most relationships most of the time an apology must have some depth to it. Acknowledgment of the *exact* transgression is usually necessary for the recipient to feel the sincerity of the errant one making the apology. For example, saying, "I'm sorry I yelled at you," would be more effective if it included a descriptor such as, "I'm sorry I yelled at you *when I asked you to get ready for bed.*" In addition, acknowledgment of the *impact of the transgression* upon the other often makes a difference in the felt completeness of the apology and in reestablishing trust. For that reason, a person desiring to make a *full repair* might say, "I'm sorry I yelled at you when I asked you to get ready for bed. *It looks like I made you mad and maybe even scared you*, which definitely was not my intention. I'm sorry for this and hope we can get back on track when you're ready."

Repair is, in effect, a reattunement following a shame-inducing or hurtful experience. The repair cycle, then, is this: *attunement gets interrupted by misattunement, and misattunement gets healed with reattunement.* Parents, especially, need to use repair in their relationship with their child because it teaches him that he is valuable to the parent and also that making a mistake is not the end of the world. Repairing also models how to make a meaningful apology and reinforces that repair is an essential part of relationship. *In fact, an accurate, empathic repair actually serves as a relationship strengthener* in that trust blossoms when the child feels valued because parents are making the effort to apologize. The child also feels understood when parents acknowledge the feelings their error has aroused in their child. Therefore, although not often thought of as important or sometimes not thought about at all, making repairs is an essential part of growing any relationship, especially the one you are fostering with your child.

Repair is the essential act of "reattuning" following a hurtful interaction

Repair also works when you realize that you have misapplied a consequence because of your anger or lack of objectivity. When you apologize to your child, again, be specific: "I'm sorry I took my anger out on you when you threw your Legos at the wall by assigning you that awful task of picking up the toys in the backyard while it was raining. Having you work out in the rain must have made you feel like I really don't care about you. I want you to know that I really do care about you and that I was wrong to have you carry out any consequence in conditions like that." You can repair the sense of unimportance your child felt during his unreasonable penance by revisiting with him the situation that prompted the consequence. As you work together with your child to come up with a more reasonable consequence, he regains the sense that you do value him and his ideas. This collective approach underscores your valuing the alliance between you and your child and reinforces the idea that a consequence is *not* a punishment.

When the tables are turned, however, saying, "I'm sorry," usually marks the extent to which a child can apologize for a misstep until he feels safer in the relationship and more valuable to himself. For a distressed child, apologizing for a wrong action can send him into deep shame—not for what he has done, but for *who he is*. The hurt child cannot make the distinction between *doing something wrong* and *being wrong* in his mere existence. When he makes a mistake, the distressed child feels like he *is* the mistake, so for him, making an apology is like saying, "I'm worthless." Nevertheless, it is still essential to help the child own his hurtful action with an apology, even if at first the parent has to speak for the child or give him the words. In helping the child be specific, such as, "I'm sorry I kicked you when I was mad, Mom," he gets the practice of using language that describes his *action*. Anytime the child needs to make an apology, the parent can coach him through it beginning with, "I know when you've done something wrong and you have to apologize, it's hard for you because you feel so much shame, it's like admitting you're a bad kid. The fact is, you're *not* a bad kid; you're a kid who made a mistake."

No one gets it right all of the time, and realistically, most days do not go by without at least one blunder, not only on the part of the child but also

**If you're in your non-thinking, primitive brain,
give yourself some time to get back to your cortex**

on the part of the parent. Therefore, it would be unwise and misleading to hold yourself out to your child as being invincible. Rather, when you model being attuned and taking responsibility for your actions, the child feels less like an outcast because he can see that parents make mistakes just as he does. An apology from an adult, especially a parent, is a powerful act and often the precursor to the trust in your relationship with your child taking not just a step, but a leap forward.

When Nothing Seems to Be Working

Sometimes parents feel backed into a corner or are so frazzled they cannot think of a single thing they can do to ease the challenging situation at hand. Having a list of actions that can move you out of that stuck place can feel like a lifesaver in a stressful moment. The following actions have helped other parents when things got tough. You might have additional actions that you know work well for you. Create your list, write it down, and put it on the refrigerator.

When Nothing Is Working

➤ Make it the child's choice: Give your child two options that you can live with for now. "You may play quietly with your Legos in here on the carpet, or you may sit quietly over in that chair and read a book for ten minutes while *I* take a time out."

➤ Engage the child in finding the solution: Curiously explore the problem with your child, asking, "How were you hoping things would go?"

➤ Redefine it: Break the static of seeing a problem in the same way by telling a different story about it. "I wonder if you were just in a bad mood when you kicked the chair, or if you were telling me you were mad at me."

➤ Momentarily remove expectations you are holding for your child (and for yourself): Let the homework go for now/give yourself permission to leave the dishes in the sink.

➤ Change it up: Move outside, use a chipmunk voice, or give your child the reins in the moment.

➤ Let go of needing your child's approval: You are the adult; you gently steer the situation where it needs to go.

➤ Catch your child doing something right: Turn a negatively heading situation around by shifting the focus to what's going well, even if it's the most minute positive you can think of. "I love it when you catch my eyes for a second!"

➤ Make it fun: Make a game out of an unpleasant chore, or allow your child to set up such a game.

➤ Provide care and nurture and let go of the rest: Some days, all you can do is cover the basics—eating, snuggling, napping—and that's perfectly okay.

➤ Set it aside and come back to it later: When you are not getting anywhere fast, move on and save it for another time.

➤ Give yourself a time in (with your child) or time out (away from your child): Shift the moment by taking a timed break from it.

➤ Do nothing: Sometimes just sitting down right where you are and regulating your breathing can unstick the situation.

At times, even with all of the tools available, parents find they just can't "get it"—that is, understand what their child needs in the moment. This is frustrating for both parents and child. Yet one of the most obvious avenues for discovery can lay hidden in plain sight. For example, when one adult does not understand another adult, the one simply asks the other, "I don't understand what you're saying. Could you clarify what you need?" However, within the therapeutic parenting mind-set, directly requesting, "Explain why you did that" or "What do you need?" of the child is rarely helpful because, in most cases, the child does not know why he did something or what he needs. Nonetheless, a parent can always let her child know, "I'm sorry, I just don't understand what you need right now, but I can see you're upset and *I would like to help.*" In the moment, this message is often sufficient to calm the child because what he ultimately needs is to know that he is not alone and that you are committed to helping him feel better.

Parents can use active "listening" in the event neither the child nor the parent is able to articulate the child's need. Active listening in this case involves the parents narrating their observations to their child (e.g.,

---

When you've run out of ideas, stop, acknowledge you don't know what is going on, and listen to your child

"I can see you're upset right now, and maybe a bit angry"), even if they are not sure what their child's feelings mean. That the parent "gets" even *part* of what the child is communicating can help the child to calm down because he senses his parent cares enough to try to understand his emotional expression in the moment. It is also okay to sit with the child and let him have his feelings without talking much. Sometimes your child just needs to experience his feelings in your presence because you provide a felt, nonverbal, safe container for his emotionality. With you by his side, your child may feel freer to express himself because he senses your support, which allows him to feel safe.

Children, especially those who tend to internalize their feelings instead of acting them out, worry that expressing big feelings might make others reject them, an experience they may have had in the past. A child, therefore, may hold on to his feelings or be hypervigilant, interpreting the slightest shift in your demeanor as a sign rejection is on the way. For this reason, *resist the temptation to move in right away to try to "fix it," lest you quell your child's expression of feelings.* When you remain with your child throughout the arc of his expression, it lets him know, perhaps unconsciously, that he and his feelings are *not* too much for you and that you will not leave him. If you are feeling uncomfortable being with your child in his pain and hurt, remain with him nonetheless, and focus on deepening and evening out your breath. Regulating yourself this way has the added benefit of ultimately regulating your child as his mirror neurons bring his breathing into alignment with yours. By supporting your child's emotional expression along with providing your reflective interpretation, you can help his process flow more easily to free up a stuck situation.

Keep in mind that the way you frame things with your words can create for your child either a positive or a negative catch phrase—one that he embraces and understands or one that puts him off and ends the conversation. Saying, "Don't make this a bigger problem" or "You're digging yourself in deeper," can feel alienating to your child because it frames the situation such that he is alone and has to turn things around by himself. Chances are this "you're on your own, buddy" approach will feel like rejection to your child, and behaviors will escalate. Conversely, you can create an alliance with your child using the same basic words by saying, "Right now, it's a small problem—I can help you prevent it from getting bigger" and "You're in a pretty deep hole right now, and I can help you climb out before it gets deeper." Each of these positively framed phrases promotes a connective relationship with your child as being the way out of a negative spiral that your child probably cannot arrest on his own. Once you have found particular catch phrases that work positively for your child, you can use them to bypass the long and drawn-out escalation/resolution process by nipping the behavior in the bud.

A child not only can sense when his parents are ambivalent toward disciplining him, he also can sense their ambivalence in their emotional attachment to him that may lie underneath. This feeling can amplify the child's acting-out behavior, triggered by the perceived threat that ambivalence ultimately leads to abandonment. Equally, parents who fear demanding too much of their distressed child may inadvertently begin a pattern of lowering their expectations, which eventually places their child in the position of "running the show." Child-in-control results in the child becoming more anxious, insecure, and unable to focus, which in turn gives rise to challenging behaviors that aim to test the strength of his bond with his parents. With his behavior, the child is asking, "You've given me the power here. . . . Is that because you're not strong enough to handle me (which maybe means you're planning to give me up)?" Being aware of your true underlying feelings about your relationship with your child can help you avoid putting up relational road signs that say "dead end" to your child, and can eliminate one source of reactivity to the threat of abandonment.

When nothing seems to be working, it might indicate that in the moment the problem that needs to be addressed is on *your* side of the equation. Using a self-check at times when you sense your frustration is creeping up or your reaction does not match the situation can avert potential problems. Sometimes, if recognized and caught before it grows, a momentary resentment toward your child can be eliminated by just sitting and talking with him. "I'm trying to figure out what just happened, and I'll need your help in remembering how we got here." Taking action this way gives you a means of focusing low-grade frustration and using it in a positive manner. The key to poising this approach for success is making an accurate self-assessment. Obviously, when you are past the point where

---

If the child feels he is in control, his behavior will get worse. Remember, you only have to be "bigger, stronger, wiser, and kind."

you can arrest your accelerating negative feelings, taking a time out would be a better choice. Stemming personal reactivity before it takes over is a skill parents can and must learn to master, further benefitting themselves and their child by modeling self-regulation.

When you are struggling, consider how your child may be interpreting what you are saying. Each of us filters what we hear through the sieve of our own experience. If perceived threat causes your child's filter to stop content from passing through his non-thinking, flight or fight brain to his "thinking brain," he will get stuck in a reactive mode. Interpreting danger from the tone, intensity, cadence, or meaning of the words you use can trigger your child's negative memories and flashes of traumatic experiences, which will then trigger reactivity. If your child has become negatively activated, he can no longer hear what you are saying because his filter has trapped him in his past. *When your child senses your emotional intensity or confrontational energy, he truly cannot think,* he can only act.

For example, even if you were to say, in a kindly tone, "You seem to be having trouble following instructions today. How can I help?" your child might hear, "You are such a screw up! Can't you do anything right?" If you know or have discovered the hard way that your child tends to interpret what you say in the most damning way possible, becoming a word crafter is your only option. In reworking our example, you might have to word the sentence like this: "I know: let's take a break right now—I know I could use one . . . How 'bout you?" In avoiding reference to what your child is having difficulty doing in the moment, you bypass the likelihood of a shame reaction. Creating a non-shame-evoking way of communicating with your child is an art, but it is worth mastering so you can eliminate a known source of triggers.

Relationships are never perfect. When the going gets really tough, your consistent care and constant presence provides an underlying foundational sense for your child that you will not give up on him. An adoptive dad said to assure his twelve-year-old daughter, who was acting out once again, "You can't push me away, no matter what you do. I'm your dad, I love you, and you are stuck with me." The preteen really took in what her dad meant when he said she was "stuck with" him. That conveyance of commitment was just what she needed to hear, and in fact was *what she was pushing for with her behavior.* Regardless of what may be offered in return, your assurance of dedication to your child is crucial for him to have and to hear, not just once, but often. As you speak your allegiance loudly

**For the most part, your child's behavior is not about *you*, the *person*;
it is about your child's history, perception, and expectations**

in your behavior, and then use your words for reinforcement, both you
and your child can be reminded of that solid bottom line.

In the end, remind yourself that it is not about you. Although you may
make mistakes at times, this journey is about healing your distressed
child. As you continue building a relationship with your child, there are a
few helpful things to remember when things get rough.

When Things Get Rough, Remember
- ➤ Your child will carry his original primary attachment pattern into
  his relationship with you, and this is not about you.
- ➤ The closer your child gets to you, the worse his behavior may initially get due to his fear of becoming intimate with caregivers, and
  this isn't about you.
- ➤ A child typically gives his worst to his mother because she represents the child's birth mother in the relationship of his original
  abandonment, so this is not about you.
- ➤ Just like an adult, a child can have different attachments with different people (e.g., attachment to father may be different from attachment to mother), and this is not about you.
- ➤ Keep in mind that even if you have given your child everything he
  needs in all realms, he still may feel he does not fit in or may not feel
  safe enough, and this is not about you.
- ➤ And, no matter what, you are okay.

What is it that pulls you through all of the struggles of life and gets
you from one day to the next? It is the people that you love, that you are
attached to, and that love you back. It is the sense of security that you
find with those loved ones. They are your refuge in a storm, your safety
zone. Your child may not yet (or may never) be one of these safe people
for you. Having gone through his early life as a child without someone to
enjoy him, protect him, or nurture him, *your child does not have it in him
to be a giver during his healing journey.* It will take many years of having
a dependable relationship with you for your child to learn he can trust in

your care and control, and thus become capable of giving back. Remember this when you become overwhelmed, so you can turn to those whom you *can* lean on for the support, comfort, and understanding you will need.

Tips for Preventing Problems

"Prevention is the best medicine." We hear this adage frequently but rarely act on it. When you are working with an emotionally distressed child, you cannot afford to ignore this wisdom. Both putting preventative measures in place and revisiting them periodically to make supportive adjustments need to be priorities for parents who are parenting a challenging child. Acknowledging those measures you are presently using and scrutinizing them in terms of efficacy, in addition to implementing any additional helpful supports, will go a long way toward minimizing the potential for problems to arise. The following are some ideas that can help you assess your current situation to ensure you are maximizing the use of preventative measures in your work with your child.

Tips for Preventing Problems

RELATIONSHIP FIRST. Your expectations of your child cannot come before your relationship with him because, ultimately, it is your bond with him that will motivate and heal your child.

CREATE AND MAINTAIN A SENSE OF SECURITY FOR YOUR CHILD. By using structure, safety, a set schedule, supervision, simplicity, sensitivity, soothing, and support, along with managing your own triggers, you create a milieu that promotes the development of trust.

START WITH MORE STRUCTURE THAN YOU THINK YOU MIGHT NEED. You can always decrease structure as trust builds, and it is difficult to increase structure and limits after your child has had more freedom.

CREATE A NURTURING ATMOSPHERE FOR YOUR UNIQUE CHILD. Soft lighting, comfy furniture, subtly healing scents, softly flowing music, cuddly blankets, an overstuffed rocking chair, gentleness, and few, if any, electronics establishes a relaxed baseline that affords you the best chance for maintaining calm environs throughout the day, especially for a sensory-reactive child (one who gets stressed by too much sensory stimulation). A nurturing atmosphere for a sensory-seeking child (one who requires heavy sensory stimulation) may need to be brighter, louder, and rougher and contain equipment that meets the child's need for high activity.

CRAFT A SPACE OR A ROOM INTO A SENSORY-STIMULATING ENVIRONMENT for the sensory-seeking child. A child whose lower brain was under-stimulated in his infancy will seek out high stimulation via hyperactive behavior unless adequate stimulatory measures are put in place for him.

USE *PACE*. Using playfulness, acceptance, curiosity, and empathy allows you to get the most bang for your buck as you grow your relationship with your child and as you intervene in his challenging behaviors (Hughes, 2004).

CREATE A SAFE PLACE FOR EACH CHILD. Everyone needs a place to call his own, and helping each child establish one for himself reduces conflicts and jealousies.

TAKE CHARGE GENTLY. A calm voice, gentle delivery of sentences, and limited gesticulation slow down your child's chaotic sense of the world and allow you to remain relaxed as well.

BE HONEST. Your child can be incredibly perceptive and will pick up on inaccuracies, white lies, and any discomfort you are feeling.

SET AN UNHURRIED PACE. Your child's insides are going a million miles per hour, and the only way to help him down-shift is to set and maintain a slow tempo for yourself. An unhurried pace for a sensory-seeking child may be jogging instead of running.

AVOID NEGATIVITY. Even though it might seem obvious, being conscious of setting a positive tone with your thoughts and words wards off a downward spiral.

GREATLY LIMIT OR WHOLLY ELIMINATE ELECTRONIC STIMULATION. TVs, electronic games, cell phones, computers, radios, raucous music, glaring lights, and atmospheric hyperactivity (clutter, too much stuff, overly deco-rated rooms) all contribute to overload for your child (and maybe you!).

BE CONSISTENT BUT NOT RIGID IN SETTING LIMITS. Your child needs to build his trust in you, and consistency will enable him to be more relaxed and listen with greater ease, which will allow you to feel far more comfort-able and effective.

STAND YOUR GROUND. Following through instills an atmosphere of predict-ability for your child that allows him to feel safe.

LET YOUR CHILD KNOW WHAT TO EXPECT. Within your child's relative concept of time, let him know what's next (e.g., delay discussing a dental appointment with a developmentally young child until you are on your way) and reassure him that you'll be returning home when you're done. *You* know you are coming back, but your child associates change with abandonment.

STAY IN THE ZONE OF MUTUAL RESPECT. When you approach your child from a place of power and control, his resistance goes up and his trust goes down.

PROVIDE YOUR CHILD WITH ENJOYABLE EXPERIENCES. Measure your child's in-the-moment ability to navigate in the positive and fun realms, and meet him there often.

HONOR YOUR CHILD'S PRESENT SELF-CONCEPT. Your child is who he thinks he is, even if he thinks he is bad, and you cannot empower him to change unless you respect and meet him where he is in the present. If you contradict your child's self-concept—"No, honey, you're not a bad kid"—he will feel you do not "get" him, and his trust will go down and his defenses will go up.

KEEP IT SIMPLE. Your child needs a simple schedule, not an overstuffed day, which will increase stress, thus benefiting no one.

DEMONSTRATE PATIENCE AND FLEXIBILITY *in your expectations about outcomes*. Your child is watching you and learning how to pace himself realistically from what he sees. "You know, I'm now thinking we've done enough for one day. Let's come back to it tomorrow."

SET CLEAR LIMITS. Adjust your limits so they are few, simple, to the point, and aimed at protecting your child physically, emotionally, and psychologically. Trying to enforce (and remember!) a plethora of rules sets you and your child up for failure and creates a negative atmosphere.

TALK TO THE "GOOD KID" INSIDE. If you address the positive part inside your child, he will be more able to do his best and will be more likely to rise to the occasion.

BE PLAYFUL WITH YOUR CHILD. Playfulness reduces the flow of stress hormones, so both you and your child will have more of yourselves to give.

REINFORCE DESIRED BEHAVIOR. What you pay attention to will continue, so pay attention and reinforce what your child is doing right to avoid the trap of him seeking your attention negatively.

BE CAREFUL WITH PRAISE. If your child's self-concept is negative, global statements such as, "You're a great kid!" will bounce back at you in the form of challenging behavior. Instead, be very specific: "I like how you hung up your coat when we got home." Your child can own his action and take in your appreciation for it.

STOP AND ASK YOUR CHILD PERIODICALLY WHAT HE HEARD YOU SAY. Find out if your child is listening, and ensure he perceives your meaning correctly. "Just so we're both on the same page, I was wondering what you thought I just said."

BREAK IT INTO SMALL STEPS. You and your child are more likely to reach the top of the mountain if you take small, measured steps to get there. Leaps are difficult and in the end can be unsuccessful. Plan to "camp out" when making progress is not possible in the moment.

REFRAME YOUR DEFINITION OF SUCCESS. Reexamine and adjust any unrealistic expectations; highlight even the smallest successes, as these become the building blocks of larger achievements.

ALLOW YOUR CHILD TO START OVER. Minute by minute, hour by hour, or day by day, make it clear to your child that this is a fresh start and the past is the past. Carrying around the burden of shame from past mistakes and transgressions instills hopelessness in your child and leaves him stuck in an overwhelming sense of himself as worthless. "Let's start over!" is a reset button for you both, and using it increases the possibility of success.

SET ASIDE DAILY PARENT-CHILD QUIET TIME. Set a time during the day, every day, for you and *each* child to be together to talk quietly, read a story, or relax to soothing music. *Honor this time no matter what*: do *not* make it dependent upon his behavior, good or bad.

BE CAREFUL HOW YOU SAY "NO." Your child hears "no" as a *criticism of himself*, which induces shame and spawns negative reactivity. Be creative in how you manage each situation so that you steer it in the right direction without igniting your child. Instead of "No, you can't have a cookie," try "Yes, you can have a cookie, right after dinner. In fact, let's pick it out and put it in a safe place right now."

LIMIT CELEBRATIONS. Especially at first, your child will have a limited capacity to handle high, unpaced stimulation. As well, he will be harboring a feeling of unworthiness, so gifts and celebrations will feel antithetical to his sense of self, creating a dissonance he will be driven to resolve with disruptive behavior.

ADDRESS IDENTITY ISSUES. If your child is with you via foster, adoptive, or guardianship placement, he will have identity issues that far exceed those of a birth child who is naturally searching for himself in his teens. If of a different color, race, or culture, your child will have additional identity issues that must be addressed, not just one time, but frequently. Actively and continually addressing your child's identity issues reifies and legitimizes his struggle in coming to terms with his past and in accepting who he is.

HOLD REALISTIC, FLEXIBLE EXPECTATIONS FOR YOURSELF AND YOUR CHILD. You can maximize your and your child's sense of success by strategically placing the bar within reach. Instead of picking up the whole room, just pick up the clothes for now.

USE PARENTAL DETACHMENT AS APPROPRIATE. Keep some of your emotional investment in your child in reserve, being careful to match his ability to receive so he will not feel the need to push you away for coming too close, too fast.

"PUT ON YOUR MASK FIRST." As in an airplane emergency, when you put on your own mask before helping others with theirs, make it a priority to take good care of yourself so you will have the desire and energy to meet your child's needs.

ACCEPT YOUR LEARNING CURVE. Your job as a therapeutic parent is akin to a graduate-level occupation; thus it takes education, time, and experience to "get your degree." Honor the gravity, commitment, and scope of your undertaking by noticing how hard you are working to learn and to apply your knowledge strategically.

SEEK AND ACCEPT SUPPORT. If raising a child takes a village, then raising an emotionally distressed child takes an even larger community. Realize you cannot do it alone; set up personal, familial, professional, educational, online, and peer components as parts of your community, and make use of whichever of these supports you need each day.

SET UP RESPITE. It is impossible for you to be on duty 24/7 for fifty-two weeks per year. Arrange for a regular two- to four-hour weekly respite period for yourself and your spouse, and an overnight once a month. Regularity will benefit both you and your child, who will come to see your time away as part of the family routine.

KEEP UP THE HOPE. Hope is the fuel of change and is the guiding light that will see you through the inevitable dark moments.

Key Points for Chapter 10

1. A *natural* consequence is what naturally happens in the real world as a result of a behavior. A *logical* consequence is created as a response that follows logically from a behavior. A punishment is an assignment of something painful to the child that is intended to teach the child a lesson but shames him instead.
2. A *do-over* is a chance to repeat a behavior more appropriately. A *rescue* is taking responsibility for an action away from the child.
3. Asking the child to take a seat means that the child sits quietly and thinks about what is going on beneath his dysregulated behavior.
4. "Time in" involves sitting with your child and helping him make a connection between his current behavior and his history.
5. *The problem of getting what he wants belongs to your child*, and you are there to help him succeed.
6. Try to make solving the problem more motivating than avoiding the problem.
7. In choosing which battles are important, ask yourself, "Do I need to win this?" and "Why?" If the answer is other than a concern for safety, taking action may negatively affect relational development.
8. Each of the Seven Lenses is an important way to think about intervening with your child, before and after the intervention.
9. For the most part, your child's behavior is not about *you*; it is about your child's history, perception, and expectations.
10. Preventing problems may mean thinking ahead, keeping yourself regulated, and remembering that this is a process that will change both you and the child.

11.
The Process of Healing
The Dance of Relationship and Healing

**Coming together is a beginning; keeping together is progress;
working together is success.**
HENRY FORD

∿ IN OUR FIRST YEAR TOGETHER, I honestly didn't know what had happened. The darling little girl that we had adopted who was all smiles and thank-yous for six months turned into a monster. She destroyed my favorite quilt and hurt the dog. Sometimes I got so angry with her I felt like hitting her and I actually thought about duct-taping her to a chair. Who was I becoming?

Eight months later, although we still have our battles, we are connected. She is becoming more of the "real her," and when she cuddles into me at night and asks for a story, I treasure each moment of peace. The storms still come, but I can calm her down now with a look of reassurance or reproach, depending on what is going on. I can trust her to go outside, play, and call me if she needs me.

Coming Together

The process of healing an emotionally distressed child and integrating him into a permanent family is daunting for many parents. Without a clear sense of direction, parents can get mired in feelings of helplessness and hopelessness. Fortunately, healing and integration is a relatively predictable and orderly process, one that can be clarified and quantified. The healing task can feel arduous at times, but if parents plot their progress, they can see their efforts in the context of the bigger picture. Parents need and benefit from a road map as they work their way through treatment with their child.

Decades of experience in healing distressed children and unifying them successfully with permanent families has allowed us to identify the stages and treatment factors associated with the permanency process. The details of the permanency process are represented in the chart below and are fleshed out in multidimensional segments, each of which we will be looking at closely throughout the rest of this chapter. At the end of the

Stages of Treatment / Significant Treatment Factors Matrix

STAGES OF TREATMENT ⟶

	ENTITLEMENT AND CLAIMING			WORKING THROUGH			RELATIONSHIP RESOLUTION	
	Honeymoon	Unmatched Expectations	Engagement	Deepening Attachment	Grief and Loss	Family Integration and Reformation	Identity Development and Increased Autonomy	Rite of Passage—Mastery and Control

SIGNIFICANT TREATMENT FACTORS

Trust in Care: Progress toward the child allowing adults to care for him and increasing the child's dependence on adults to meet his needs

Trust in Control: Progress toward the child allowing adults to direct him, make decisions for him, and provide structure

Trust in Self: Progress toward internalization of attachment such that the child and family can operate autonomously

Integration of Past Trauma: Process of differentiation between old and current family

Adaptive Functioning/Social Skills/Benefit of Fun: Progress toward appropriate community and family functioning and the bonding fostered through enjoyment

Quality of Relationships: Depth of attachment, level of empathy, conscience development, emotional intimacy, reciprocity within relationships, object permanency, adjusting the focus to interpersonal relationships

Emotional Awareness and Regulation: Ability to identify feelings, to be congruent in expressing feelings adaptively, and to risk seeking to meet needs

Progress toward Permanency: Resolution of feelings about adoption/permanency by child and family, making mutual choice to be a new family

chapter, we will look at the dance of permanency in an overall representation of the trajectory of your developing relationship with your child.

In the chart above, the segments of the permanency process are plotted within the confines of horizontal and vertical axes that represent the breadth and depth of the treatment process, respectively. Along the horizontal axis lie the stages of treatment: Entitlement and Claiming (Honeymoon, Unmatched Expectations, Engagement); Working Through (Deepening Attachment, Grief and Loss, Family Integration and Reformation); and Relationship Resolution (Identity Development and Increased

Autonomy, Rite of Passage—Mastery and Control). Down the vertical axis run the significant treatment factors the child and the family encounter in each stage (horizontal axis) of the process toward permanency: Trust in Care, Trust in Control, Trust in Self, Integration of Past Trauma, Adaptive Functioning/Social Skills/Benefit of Fun, Quality of Relationships, Emotional Awareness and Regulation, and Progress toward Permanency. Each of these treatment factors manifests uniquely within each stage of treatment from placement to resolution.

Bringing a new child into the family requires both the child *and* the family to transform in significant and foundational ways. As the child and the family move toward permanency, each entity develops and changes to the point where neither can nor will be the same as they were prior to the child entering the home. Like the addition of an object to a mobile, the integration of a child into a new family necessarily shifts all members into a new configuration, which will take time to rebalance and stabilize. Becoming familiar with this evolution helps the child and the family track progress, which serves to sustain hope for all. In this chapter, we will look more in depth at each of the stages and each of the significant treatment factors in healing and integrating a distressed child so parents will be able to identify and follow their child's and family's growth, as well as their own personal growth.

Stages of Treatment: The Dance

When parents think about raising a child, they may think about what they are going to do to care for, parent, and mold that child as he grows. Parents of an emotionally distressed child, however, will find this one-sided perspective of the process to be an inaccurate expectation. The truth about parenting a hurting child is that the process is actually a dance, which *both* partners—parent and child—learn to "perform," eventually in unison. Never static in their development, both parent and child constantly adjust to one another within this dance as treatment progresses. Rhythms change from simple to complex, tempos shift and slow down or speed up, and the melody and chords have their consonances and dissonances. The inherent changeability of the dance requires availability, flexibility, open-mindedness, and acceptance on the part of the parent, while it requires the child simply to be willing to engage to the extent that he can in any given moment.

> **It is the child who leads the dance steps of relationship**
> **while it is you, the parent, who determines the path across the floor.**
> **You are the dance partner as well as the coach.**

Perhaps surprisingly for parents, it is *the child who leads the dance* as the parent navigates his needs, moods, and developmental changes. The dance begins long before the curtain rises and the parent sees the child for the first time. Consequently, the parent must work diligently to catch up with the child in order to step into the flow. The transition to becoming a new "dance team" will undoubtedly be difficult for both child and parent: there will be confusion, conflict, and missteps. Fortunately, the parent has dual roles—dance partner and coach—so there is an objective presence as well, one that oversees the dance to guide it toward success. Not without its discouraging moments, learning the healing dance can be, in the end, a joyful endeavor that becomes its own reward. Neither parent nor child will be the same when it is time to rest.

First Steps: Entitlement and Claiming

Honeymoon (placement months 1–3)

When a child is first placed in a permanent home, there is usually a period of quiet before the storm. Both parents and child are displaying their best selves while working hard to hold back the full expression of their feelings and thoughts about the new situation. This "honeymoon" period can feel both hopeful and fragile, and the home atmosphere may be infused with the quality of blind optimism as well as the sense of walking on eggshells. Humpty Dumpty is waiting to fall, but everyone is invested in staving off the inevitable for as long as possible. Then again, while the family (and community) may be honeymooning at the beginning of treatment, infused with visions of success, the child might enter the home with guns blazing.

HONEYMOON: TRUST IN CARE

Upon placement, the child is awash with feelings of fear: fear of parents, fear of their rules and reactions, fear of abandonment, and fear of having to make his way on his own and take care of himself in an unknown environment. The child lacks a sense of self and place, while feeling loss and grief for the familiarity of the place from which he came, even if he was neglected or abused there. Especially at first, the emotionally distressed child cannot separate the past and present; thus, he will try to re-create the environment of his previous home to regain the familiar atmosphere he is used to. The child will very often be indirect with his feelings, for example kicking the wall, dog, or couch when he is lonely and scared. He will actively attempt to push his new parents away because he does not trust in their care. The child's security rests in his ability to control every situation and to control all others.

Parents must stay in an observant mode and begin to identify the behaviors the child is using to push them away, such as soiling the bed, leaving tasks unfinished, being sneaky, and refusing their attempts to comfort him. In reminding themselves that the emotionally distressed child is fighting as hard as he can to survive in a new world, which from his point of view was forced upon him, parents can maintain their crucial stance of empathy and understanding. When they notice themselves straying from that stance, especially when thoughts and feelings that the child is personally rejecting them creep in, parents must pull themselves back into a place of objectivity and remember what the child is actually experiencing.

To prepare themselves to recognize the child's self-protective rebuffs of their attempts to care for him, parents can refer to the following list of distancing behaviors they may encounter.

Child's Initial Self-Protective Behaviors
➤ Maintenance of interpersonal distance from everyone by defending against emotional and physical proximity, or at the other extreme by taking on an excessively adult-pleasing persona
➤ Actively living out a fantasy of having the most wonderful new parents who will care for him, shower him with gifts, and dote on him in every way
➤ Active denial via pretending to have no problems, seducing parents into believing he does not need help
➤ Sustained hypervigilance, paying close and constant attention to everything the parent does, perhaps even asking every five minutes, "What's next?"
➤ Emotional promiscuity, calling new parents "Mom and Dad" right away and/or going to any adult for care or giving hugs upon meeting someone new
➤ Self-parenting on the part of the child, which can be highly misleading to parents, lulling them into complacency until the underlying

issues arise, at which point parents may become hurt and disappointed and feel personally attacked or tricked by their child

➤ Pretending to have fun when feeling no true gratification

➤ Being impulsive and controlling, exposing his low frustration tolerance

➤ Trying to maintain control through manipulation, sneaking, or lying

➤ Becoming emotionally unglued when activity slows down, such as at bedtime

After recognizing the child's initial defensive behaviors for what they are—self-protection—parents can have some strategies in place that both respect the child's need to take care of himself for the time being and help him begin to adjust to his new home. For example, to start to lay the foundation for the parent-led rhythm that needs to pace the day, parents can schedule "slow down" times throughout the day to make space for feelings to surface that the child may be avoiding through activities, so the feelings won't get backed up only to spill out at bedtime.

At first, to avoid putting pressure on the child and themselves, parents can view themselves as "professional parents" who are committed to caring for the distressed child and meeting his basic needs for food, shelter, love, and security, instead of as "Mom and Dad." In seeing themselves in this more objective role, parents avoid the conscious and unconscious expectations they and their child would place upon them if they were to function in the more intimate and gendered mom/dad roles.

Parents can quickly become overwhelmed with the addition of a distressed child to their family because there are now additional outside responsibilities such as meetings, school transition, and therapy to assume. In exposing themselves to these new venues, parents may begin to worry about others passing judgment on them regarding their parenting decisions and abilities. Raising an emotionally distressed child is a task that few outside the child's parents and therapeutic team understand. External judgments and criticisms often abound, and parents feel that much more pressure to justify why they do what they need to do.

Concentrating on the challenges of parenting a distressed child is more difficult when parents feel they also need to be looking over their shoulder to appease others, especially family members. Meanwhile, parents also need support in the form of approval and affirmation from those same

The honeymoon period is the tender time full of hopes, worries, and newness. Your child may be on his best behavior or at his worst, as his anxiety about being acceptable is high.

family members, friends, and community members. Professionals on the child's team can be extremely helpful when, with the parents' permission, they sit down with those the parents need as allies and educate them in what is going on and in how they can support the parents and the process.

Swimming in the newness of the situation, parents are often caught off guard when their unique child's issues activate their own past trauma and affect the way they relate to the child. Especially in the beginning, parents need to mind their personal triggers to recognize and avoid getting "hooked" by the child. By paying attention to behaviors that make them anxious or angry, parents can arrest their reactivity in the present and later come back to assess why they reacted so strongly. Keeping a personal reactivity log from the very start helps parents track their own patterns so they can more readily address them at the appropriate time.

Complicating the scenario, emotionally distressed children are often hypervigilant. Almost immediately it seems, these children can zoom in on their parents' reactivity and readily identify their parents' triggers, which they will exploit as often as parents let them. However, the child's need to trigger parents is not grounded in "gotcha" pleasure, but rather in a quest to find ultimate safety and security, which exists for him only in a *nonreactive* parent. If the child has the ability to create a reaction in his parents that throws them off-balance, this proves to him that he is stronger than they are. Trust in care dissolves, returning the child to a state of self-reliance.

In the beginning, it also behooves parents to keep in mind that taking in a child is an endeavor that is not about the parents getting their needs met through their child, but rather about meeting the child's needs and accepting the growth curve inherent in learning to fully accept another human being for who he is. Because discovering what a child needs can be so difficult, parents often slip into the mantra, "Why doesn't this child *just ask* for what he needs or wants?" Remembering that their child will express his feelings and needs *with his behavior* helps to keep parents oriented in the right direction. Parents need to afford themselves the breathing room necessary to begin to understand their child, for this is a process that will unfold over time. Not immediately "getting" their child in every situation actually helps parents hone in on his needs more closely as they eliminate possibilities along the way.

In tandem with their child, parents also have defenses and behaviors that arise in the honeymoon stage of permanency. These occur naturally for all parents undertaking the responsibilities that come with bringing a new child into their home.

Thoughts and Behaviors of Parents during the Honeymoon

➤ Wanting to see everything as normal
➤ Misperceiving their power to "love this child into mental health"
➤ Fantasizing about how the process will unfold
➤ Being anxious about being able to be a parent for this child
➤ Wanting the child to like them, therefore establishing inadequate structure while walking on eggshells
➤ Being overbearing with care that becomes engulfing
➤ Feeling sorry for the child, trying to make up for his past
➤ Trying to feed the child's fantasies about being in the "perfect" family
➤ Resisting outside support, or being too dependent upon it
➤ Trying to be a "super parent" under illusion that they have omnipotent control
➤ Striving to always appear "perky" and to have high energy
➤ Being overly protective of their fantasy about the child, thus not seeing behavior problems
➤ Assuming that the child has more competencies than he has
➤ Having an initial false sense of knowing the depth of the child's grief
➤ Believing in and trying to assert a traditional parenting paradigm

The emotional dance the family is going through during this honeymoon stage tends to be one of loose structure in which each family member is trying to please and be liked by everyone. There is a false perception that the new family/adoption will magically fix all. However, the illusion of being the "forever family" can lay extreme pressure upon both the child and the family to "bond" and to work together to avoid all conflict. Behavior problems are for the most part kept hidden or remain low-keyed compared to what they will become.

Parents are excited and want their new child to "know" them, so they prematurely may share deep values, morals, and personal feelings. Taking caution in not revealing too much too soon will greatly benefit the early family dynamics. Too much intimate information given too early becomes leverage for the child to push parents away in the present and in the working through stage. Moreover, *the child does not care about his new parents or about what they think and feel.* Imposing such information upon the child convinces him that just like all other adults, his new parents care only about themselves.

During the honeymoon, parents generally keep the child close, even when the child is distancing. This can be done by keeping the child in close physical proximity doing activities that will be gratifying to him such as baking cookies, playing a game, or feeding the family pet. Parents can have fun with their child by dancing, giving high fives, and being silly and playful in their approach to the "have tos." Most of all, having no expectations of the child to be one way or another, giving lots of unconditional nurture within the child's comfort zone, and making sure the child has everything that he needs, not what he wants, sets the stage for the child's new home to be a warm and welcoming place.

HONEYMOON: TRUST IN CONTROL

In the first three months, during the honeymoon phase, the child most likely is going to balk on some level at parents' efforts to control him and his environment. In trying to maintain *his* control, the child may actively or passively try to assert his power in most situations. These attempts may be obvious, or they may elude parents, passing beneath their radar. Awareness is the first step in helpful intervention, so parents may want to begin actively to notice the way their child tries to hold on to his power. Here are some of the ways a child might reveal this either conscious or unconscious intent:

Child's Assertion of Power against Trust and Control in Parents
➤ low frustration tolerance
➤ impulsiveness
➤ active controllingness
➤ resistance to basic interventions or being overly compliant and placating
➤ being indirect with feelings
➤ passive aggression

➤ being condescending
➤ acting fearful of parent and/or parent's reactions
➤ superficially trusting parental control

As in many of the stages of treatment, parts of the parents' trust-in-control process during the honeymoon phase can parallel that of the child. The phenomenon that parent and child do parallel work at times during the course of the permanency journey may come as a surprise to parents who are of the mind-set that they are there solely to help the child though *his* growth and development. Where trust in control is concerned, some of the dynamics in the parent-professional relationship appear similar to those in the child-parent relationship. The parents desire to control the honeymoon process just as their child does.

Parents' Assertion of Power against Trust and Control in Professionals

➤ Parents want to rely on their own past experience with parenting instead of trusting the treatment model, professional guidance, and prescribed interventions.
➤ Parents are overwhelmed with and sometimes balk at new structures they need to institute as well as by outside responsibilities such as meetings and therapy appointments that have been added as part of the permanency process to their already full daily lives.
➤ Dad wants to hold on to his role "as is," while mom struggles with negotiating her child's negative projections ("You are a 'mom,' and moms cannot be trusted"), which are part of the inevitable and necessary transference process that comes with permanency.
➤ Parents worry about their ability to contain their child's behavior as well as their own physical and emotional reactions to it, and tend to get controlling in the effort to handle both.
➤ Parents want everything to be normal; thus they try to control the experience by attempting to sculpt daily life into the "normal" configuration they envision.
➤ Although placement is a time when support is needed the most, parents want to "do it themselves" and are most resistant to intrusiveness.

The phenomenon that parent and child do parallel work at times during the course of the permanency journey may come as a surprise to parents who are of the mind-set that they are there solely to help the child though *his* growth and development

HONEYMOON: TRUST IN SELF

During the honeymoon phase, the child fights hard against his fear and insecurity, trying to hold on to the sense of trust in himself he has used all along to survive. The "trust in self" the child arrives with was born out of necessary defensiveness, and contains elements of desperation, fear, and entitlement that are absent in the true trust in self the child is on the road to learning. The components of the type of trust in self the child will be learning include mastery of self-regulation, the capacity for accurate assessment of self and others, and a foundational sense of "I can" that will carry the child through whatever life brings his way.

Parents also struggle with trust in self, especially at the beginning of placement. Not knowing how the process will unfold or who their child really is, as well as not having confidence in what they are doing, parents either take on a persona that exudes false bravado or they give up their power and become excessively treatment program–dependent, hoping that the program has all the answers. Both overly and under confident parents hold on to their respective positions, understandably needing something to cling to, but at the expense of having the willingness to make the changes that would truly help them succeed. Other ways parents slip away from really trusting that they can, indeed, handle what may come is assuming their child has more competencies than he really has or that he needs more extensive protection than he really does.

HONEYMOON: INTEGRATION OF PAST TRAUMA

During the honeymoon phase of this entitlement and claiming stage, evidence of the child's trauma experiences begin to appear but are not addressed directly with the child. Rather, as time passes, behaviors with their origins in trauma "leak out" despite the child's efforts to remain in control to attempt to create safety for himself. In the honeymoon phase, not at all trusting his new parents, the child tries to hold on to his dysregulated parts and keep them undercover lest they get exposed and trigger another abandonment. The child is working very hard to be the child he thinks he needs to be so his parents will keep him. Although this scenario depicts the self-protective, defensive stance taken by most children entering permanency, sometimes a child will enter his new home in a wide-open way emotionally and behaviorally, essentially skipping the expected honeymoon phase.

Some behaviors of a child who is defending himself, trying to keep a cap on his trauma, that parents can look for during the honeymoon phase, follow.

Keeping Trauma "Under Wraps"—The Child
➤ General denial of any prior negative experiences
➤ Resistance to parental relationship and attempts to excavate feelings and memories
➤ Inability to separate his past from present—i.e., "that was then, this is now"
➤ Lack of congruency between behaviors and feelings
➤ Bedtime behavioral problems based on fear, such as creating delays, attempting to make everything "just so"
➤ Toileting issues as evidence of anxiety and/or underdevelopment

Parents can expect themselves to experience some predictable feelings, thoughts, and behaviors during the honeymoon as well. Keeping one eye open to observe themselves and their reactions will help parents focus on the child's needs during this phase. Some of the things parents can watch for in themselves include the following.

Keeping Trauma "Under Wraps"—The Parents
➤ Denial that the child had, and has, problems: "It was the other caregiver that had the problem, not the child, and now that we have the child, things will be better"
➤ Resistance to acknowledging the real child within, thus resistance to meeting his true needs
➤ Feeling sorry for the child, thus being too lenient
➤ Remaining unaware that from the very beginning, the child's issues can trigger parents' own unresolved past trauma and affect the way they relate to the child

HONEYMOON: ADAPTIVE FUNCTIONING/SOCIAL SKILLS/BENEFIT OF FUN

Not surprisingly, day-to-day behavioral tendencies of the newly placed child are defensive in nature, as the child once again tries to maintain as much control as he can to ward off anxiety. During the honeymoon, the child can be placating, and he may work hard at trying to convince his new parents that he is okay, independent, and not in need of their support. He may appear to be very capable and "adult," even to the point of trying to assume parental responsibilities. The child may try to display a "fun" and agreeable persona by pretending to have fun, when inside he actually feels no gratification.

At the same time, a child just entering his permanent placement may be using such an agreeable persona to conceal his covert acting-out behaviors, which when discovered by parents he may steadfastly deny, saying, "It wasn't *me*." Or he might be unable to entertain himself, effectively shifting the locus of control for the responsibility of having fun outside of himself, expecting his parents to orchestrate his day with plans and activities.

Like puzzle pieces that fit perfectly together, parent and child may unconsciously collude with each other during the honeymoon such that the parent actively supports some of the child's defensive behaviors. Parents can be misled by apparent competency and believe that the child is more mature and adaptive than he is. Likewise, parents may think that they, too, are more competent than they are, feeling that they can do it all without needing outside resources and support. In wanting to give the child the benefit of the doubt, parents may allow themselves to be swayed by the child's convincing lies.

Parents also may feel they are responsible for entertaining the child, as if he were a guest during the initial phase of giving him a new home. It is difficult for honeymooning parents to retain an objective view of their new child, yet it is crucial that they strive to do so. Even inadvertently allowing the child to take charge on any level during the honeymoon period can cause the child undue anxiety triggered by the lack of safety he feels when a parent is not in control.

HONEYMOON: QUALITY OF RELATIONSHIPS

Relationships during the honeymoon period tend to lean toward superficiality on the part of both the child and the parent, each trying to be on their best behavior to make a good first impression. Either by being interpersonally distant or by seeking affection and care indiscriminately, the child likely will attempt to keep his true self from emerging. At the same time parents strive to be super parents, the child may reject parent overtures of protection and concern by increasing his self-parenting behaviors.

Meanwhile, parents may worry that the professionals supporting the placement are judging them. Or parents may turn over their power to the professionals, feeling they cannot function without continual hand-holding, or they may desire to be rescued outright. The initial parent-child relationship is usually fraught with an anxiety and tentativeness, which when acknowledged as expected can actually somewhat reduce the stress.

HONEYMOON: EMOTIONAL AWARENESS AND REGULATION

Consumed with adjustment on all levels, certainly the child and likely also the parents remain unaware of their underlying emotions during the initial phase of treatment. Often, parents also do not see behavior problems that are there because these behaviors tend to happen under their radar due to the "new kid" bias. Parents also can have a false sense of the depth of the child's emotional disturbance and grief as they are honeymooning with a child who is trying very hard to look okay.

Similarly, if the child enters the home in a storm of acting out, parents have difficulty accurately gauging the extent of the child's trauma because they may feel the child is making a bigger deal out of everything than is necessary. Misunderstanding about the process and timeline of family integration can come about during the honeymoon, especially if everything is going well. Due to everyone being on their best behavior, parents may be lulled into believing that their situation is unique and that the transition is going to go easily for them.

Parents may also find themselves caught up in a crazy whirlwind of their own making during the honeymoon phase if they treat this period as an endless celebration, parading their new child around to outside family, friends, and community for approval and affirmation. Although it is expected that the child entering a new placement will show at least some dysregulation, upset of the entire family system can be a "given" if parents are not consciously and objectively stepping forth. Deliberate structuring, reasonable expectations, and intentional moderation on the part of the parents can yield a transition that is less disruptive than one entered into with abandon.

HONEYMOON: PROGRESS TOWARD PERMANENCY

Riding high on false hopes that adoption will magically fix everything for the child is common for parents during the honeymoon phase, again, especially if everything is going well. The notion that the child has landed in his "forever family," thus the integration process will unfold smoothly and naturally, romanticizes the unpredictable demands that healing an emotionally distressed child can place on parents. For permanency to become a reality, parents need to set aside preconceived ideas and expectations of how they *think* things should be and focus on the needs of the child in the *here and now.*

If they focus on the present, parents will be able to see daily progress and can be assured they will make a positive difference in the child's life by taking it one day at a time. Also, reassuring the child regularly that *he does not need to be perfect or anywhere near perfect* helps take the pressure off of everyone as the process unfolds according to the child's developmental timetable.

Unmatched Expectations (placement months 3–6)

During the stage of unmatched expectations, the differences between preconceptions and reality begin to emerge, initiating rumblings of conflict between parents and child. While parents bask in the joy of finally having the child join the family, the child is struggling with a deep sense of loss, sadness, and despair, feelings he cannot identify or articulate for himself. The child may hold a vision of what a "family" should be that is unrealistic in either a positive or negative sense, or he may have no preconceived idea about family at all. Notions of loving fantasy families may have come from TV or videos, while the child's very real experiences might be the source of his belief that families are scary and bad.

As the child moves through this period, he can become frustrated and angry when the reality of what his new parents are like does not match up with the parents in his fantasy. Some of the questions the child may have on his mind are: "Who is this family?" "Will I fit in with them?" "Will living with this family be like living with my last foster/adoptive family, who ended up not wanting me?" The child also may long to be living back

---

Through his negative behaviors, the child is now working to script his new parents' roles to match those of birth parents or other previous caregivers

with his birth family, thus unconsciously beginning to re-create his birth family dynamics in his new family.

To avoid underlying feelings of intense sadness and fear, or to fuel denial that his past problems may be reemerging, the child may seek distraction by pushing to play video games or to watch TV or movies. He may hound his parents to buy him things he does not need but thinks he wants or to take him places as a diversion. The child may try to behave the way he thinks parents want him to, but his overwhelming feelings may prompt him to act out despite his efforts to contain himself. Parents may begin to notice the child's angst but may not want to acknowledge it because of their desire to maintain their run on happiness.

Nevertheless, there now begins to be movement between emotional tectonic plates that will result in a chasm opening up between the child's and parents' realities—a chasm that will have to be dealt with readily if permanency is to progress. Yet parents may not be ready for this reality and may suppress their awareness of the widening gulf between them and their child by becoming controlling in an attempt to defend their fantasy of how they want the child to be. Accordingly, parents may begin to set rigid boundaries by proclaiming, "*This* is how we do it in *our house*." Or parents may push for the child to "act his age" and be more self-sufficient.

During this time, parents may start to ask themselves, "Will I be able to parent this child?" If they are raising or have raised other children, parents might become concerned if their previous parenting approach is not working very well with their new child. Parents may try to defend against their sense of crumbling confidence by denying or minimizing the child's behaviors and problems, or they may disavow the intensity of emerging feelings—the child's and their own. Parents also may be harboring fear that taking in the new child is having negative effects on their birth children. Concerns may emerge for the parents regarding their abilities to live up to community or extended family expectations. As the phase of unmatched expectations advances, parents' feelings of inadequacy may creep in as their child's distress deepens.

Professionals supporting the parents might notice a split forming between mom and dad initiated by the child's negative projections about "the mom," whom he sees as the "bad" one, while dad is the "good" one. Parents may also start to question their decision to parent the child but suppress their doubts by revisiting the reasons they decided to care for and become a family for this child. At this point, it is helpful for those who are professionally supporting the parents to encourage them to identify more realistic expectations and to help them understand that the child's behaviors were less intense in the honeymoon stage because relationship fear was not involved.

Parents also benefit from a reminder that the child, through his negative behaviors, is now working to script their roles to match those of birth parents or other previous caregivers. In the face of this phenomenon, validation that parents' strong reactive feelings are linked to their defensive stance of "But *that* is not who *I* am" is also helpful. Embracing the whole child is often difficult when parents feel misrepresented by their child's projections; thus they may tend to see the child only in two ways—as either "good" or "bad." To manage their growing sense that parenting the child may be more challenging than they could have imagined, parents can find themselves intellectually "parceling off" and claiming only the "good" child—the one they feel competent parenting.

Engagement (placement months 6–9)

During the engagement phase, the relational dance becomes more realistic. Both the child and parents are starting to give up their fantasies of how their lives were going to unfold. The child's behaviors begin to bring out and magnify the *problematic family dynamics existing before the placement*. More than ever, parents need strong outside support and guidance to help them stay objective and to help them interpret the dynamics that are beginning to deepen. The magnetism between the child's needs emerging through challenging behaviors and the parents' reactivity to these behaviors strengthens. The perspective outside professionals can lend to parents can function like a dam that holds back the flood of parents' negative feelings from engulfing the child. In other words, *parents need reliable and accessible support during the engagement phase to feel they can handle the challenges this period delivers*.

ENGAGEMENT: TRUST IN CARE

As engagement unfolds, the child is more invested in testing adults with the goal of determining if they will keep him, and if so, if they can keep

---

Parents need reliable and accessible support during the engagement phase to feel they can handle the challenges this period delivers

him safe. Each time the child pulls the parent into reactivity, he takes one step back on the road toward trust. If parents can stay on top of this dynamic of the child testing for security, they can see that a large portion of the child's behaviors aims to serve this goal. The child's testing also reveals his lack of self-definition and his poor boundaries, pointing to just some of the developmental tasks parents need to help the child master.

The child can be emotionally and physically intrusive, and parents learn to respond to this invasion of personal space in a kind, teaching manner. For example, if the child is needing one-on-one attention and is caught up in literally reaching for it when a parent has her hands full, she can take a minute to narrate and meet his need, or she can just meet his need and later process the scenario with him. With the child tugging on her jacket, mom may put down her multiple bags of groceries near the car and get down at the child's level to say, "You really do need me right now, don't you? And it's so hard for you to wait sometimes, even if I'm just about in a place that I can respond to you. Let's first have a hug, then I'll put these groceries in the car, and then we'll try this over using words."

During engagement, dad continues to be the "fun guy," while mom is riding an emotional roller coaster due to the child's "come here, go away" pattern, which is based in his fear of trusting her. Dad wonders what is going on and worries mom may be on her way toward a nervous breakdown. Concurrently, mom is questioning her own ability to parent or even to hold it together as an adult and also fears that she may be going crazy. Both parents are trying to figure out why the professionals supporting the family keep insisting on structure, when it is obvious that relational dynamics are heating up. Although parents sense correctly that they are moving into closer proximity with their child emotionally, they need to adhere to structure so that through the ups and downs of this phase parents have a stable place to dock. More than ever, the child needs for the parents to be steadfast and unwavering in their stability because he is pushing harder behaviorally than he has in the past.

At the same time the child is seeking connection in his defensive, roundabout way, parents are starting to get frustrated because the child

---

**Engagement is a more realistic time in which your child's issues
may begin to come to the surface. Keep structure high.**

will not take in all of the nurturing they are giving. It is easy for parents in this phase to want to give more than the child can handle, so reminding themselves to be more restrained and match the child's pace helps them relax. Resentment about the child not appreciating their care can creep into the parents' emotional mix because in some ways, the child seems more capable than ever of acknowledging their efforts. Unfortunately, holding on to the expectation that the child will *someday* express appreciation for what they have done is not helpful either and eventually brings parental heartache because this outcome is the exception rather than the rule when taking in an emotionally distressed child. Due to the lack of positive feedback from the child and his increased demands, feelings of inadequacy can arise for parents who allow themselves to take the child's resistance to trusting in their care personally.

ENGAGEMENT: TRUST IN CONTROL

In addition to the child's struggle with trust in care, during engagement the child begins to wrestle harder with trust in his parents' control as well. Parents can expect to encounter the following needs, challenges, and dynamics as the child tries to come to terms with the control aspect of their caregiving.

During the Trust in Control Phase of Engagement . . .

➤ the child may need to take more seats and have more time in with his parents as he increases his testing behaviors.

➤ there is a dichotomy between the child's unquestioning acceptance of dad's control due to the phenomenon of "identification with the aggressor" and his escalation of behaviors with mom, especially in dad's absence, due to his negative projections onto "Mom."

➤ the intensification of the parental split is fueled by dad's emerging inaccurate notions that his wife must be doing something wrong to make the child test her so harshly.

➤ the child is pressing even harder to try to change his new parents by provoking them to react like his birth and foster parents did so he can feel safe in the familiar.

➤ parents are feeling the urge to become more punitive and have the tendency to revert to parenting methods learned in their own childhoods even as they are more open to professionals' suggestions because they cannot yet be consistent with the new strategies.

➤ parents may be allowing themselves to feel disrespected by the child, who, again, is pushing to see if they are strong enough to make him feel safe.

➤ parents may find themselves getting locked into control battles with their child, a dynamic they need to recognize and resist.

➤ parents strive to maintain the bridge that is forming between structure and relationship.

ENGAGEMENT: TRUST IN SELF

As engagement proceeds, forays into the zone of true trust in self are occurring more often for the child as he experiments with newfound power in relationships. The child engages in bargaining: "Why can't I do this myself?" and "If you would just do _____, I'd be who you want me to be." The strength parents feel emerging from the child, however, lulls them into believing that the child has a higher level of healthy trust in self than he actually does, and they find themselves having to correct their decisions more often, even as they continue to want the child to become more self-sufficient than is possible.

In this phase, parents are beginning to trust in themselves more as they develop the strength and the will to separate fantasy from reality. Parents are becoming more capable of catching themselves before they react, though because of the child's increased testing, it may seem not to be the case. Finding support in peers is becoming more amenable to parents as they begin to realize that the dynamics in their home are the norm rather than the exception for families taking in emotionally distressed children. This shift to seeing and accepting themselves more clearly as they meet other parents is timely and necessary as parents move toward the working through stage with their child.

ENGAGEMENT: INTEGRATION OF PAST TRAUMA

The child's past trauma experience almost becomes an entity of itself in the family as engagement progresses. The child strives to re-create his past in the home environment and ramps up his transference as he more frequently interprets family members' behavior as trauma-inducing. However, neither child nor parent is sufficiently aware of this re-creation; therefore, it is not yet possible for the implementation of the corrective emotional experience. The child vacillates between pulling back and prematurely disclosing traumatic episodes from his past, unable to regulate

When the child inevitably projects "bad parent" on his new parent, the parent can begin to feel and behave just like the original parent

the emerging associated emotions. Yet in seeking one-on-one attention, the child persists in trying to connect with parents either by withholding or by making up things to maintain the therapeutic intensity level.

When the child is stressed during this period, he exhibits more occasions of poor ego functioning and more episodes of regressed behavior. This is also a time when the child may engage in subtle or even not-so-subtle testing of sexual boundaries, depending on the nature of his trauma history.

The parents' process again parallels that of the child in terms of re-enactment and boundaries. Still unaware of their "buttons" and the issues those buttons represent, parents find themselves responding to the child's projecting past relational dynamics onto them by turning into the "bad parent." That is, the child takes the image of "parent," which has been wired into his brain during his first few months and years, and places it onto his new parent. When the child inevitably projects "bad parent" on his new parent, *the parent can begin to feel and behave just like the original parent*, which can effectively re-create the traumatic relationship of the child's past. In some ways parents find the worst parts of themselves, much as did the parent at the beginning of this chapter who got so angry she felt like hitting her child and duct-taping her child to a chair. In the moment, this circular pattern can be hard to identify as a reenactment of trauma from the child's past, but if parents can get the support they need to step back, they not only can observe this, they also can put a stop to it by not "taking the bait."

Similarly as for their child, parents' boundaries are diffuse during this time of engagement because they lack the clarity to discern whose issue it is or who owns the problem at hand. The tangle created by this back-and-forth dynamic is largely responsible for creating the unclear division between parents and child. Also, parents are not yet highly skilled in the minute-to-minute process of stepping back from the present situation to gain the objective perspective they need to determine what, exactly, is going on and whose "stuff" is causing the issue. Though they will, in time, be able to readily and automatically perform this feat, parents still need consistent, present support to engage in the art of being objective.

ENGAGEMENT: ADAPTIVE FUNCTIONING/SOCIAL SKILLS/BENEFIT OF FUN

During the adaptive functioning/social skills/benefit of fun phase of engagement, the child becomes more dysregulated and less able to contain himself to preserve a more "together" version of himself. This increased dysregulation can show up in the child's behaviors and feelings in the following ways.

The Child's Increased Dysregulation Leads to . . .

➤ increase in acting out
➤ showing fear of and/or avoiding consequences
➤ emergence of sexual acting out
➤ unveiling of the inability to adapt to changing circumstances
➤ more episodes of regression
➤ less inhibition in letting his inner self show (being bad feels good)
➤ triggering of parents' public humiliation during transference, so that they "have his feelings for him"
➤ display of a broader range of emotions
➤ vehement declaration that he is not "different"
➤ using the power driving his anxiety to sabotage whatever is important to the family
➤ appearing socially awkward compared to same-aged children

Parents begin to get somewhat dysregulated and their frustration level elevates with their child's increasing behaviors. The difference between the parents' fantasy child and the actual child is now plain to see, and disappointment wells up. The parents' growing awareness of their child's developmental delays and behavioral problems emerges at this point, but they do not yet perceive these deficits as involuntary. Instead, parents may be stuck in the perspective that a child's challenging behaviors are purposeful, and therefore they continue to be drawn to the use of authoritarian parenting strategies. Parents may start to be concerned that all of their energy and focus are being rerouted toward the new child as they and/or their other children begin to voice their frustrations regarding this shift.

ENGAGEMENT: QUALITY OF RELATIONSHIPS

As the child pushes to re-create past attachment patterns, he also begins verbalizing how hard it is to be in a family. The child may want to go back to the former foster home or treatment center where such intimate relational demands were not being made of him. He may want the professionals supporting his parents to disappear because he feels vulnerable and senses their presence is making things more difficult for him in his relationship with his parents. Internal and external pressures begin to move the child toward his primary attachment figure, his adoptive mother. This shift stirs deep emotional reactivity and pain as he struggles with making sense of where "mother" fits into his life. Meanwhile, because he sees mom getting mad at dad more often, the child starts noticing the split that exists between his parents and is drawn to it like a magnet as an opportunity to once again test if parents are more powerful than he is so he can feel safe. If parents do not get on top of their differences at this point, the child has the power to divide them further by playing one off of the other.

Adult relationships bend under the weight of the child's needs during engagement, yet couples cannot readily recognize they do not have time for themselves. Problems that existed in the family system prior to the arrival of the child become magnified, and what were just irritants become outright difficulties. Parents tend to call on their support professionals more often, especially now because they are getting triggered by their child's behaviors more intensely and often cannot step back without outside help. The child's relational push-pull becomes more apparent and frustrating for parents, and the strain leads them to question their abilities to parent even more. They still try to hold on to the image of having an ideal relationship with their child, but this vision may start crumbling and disillusionment may set in.

ENGAGEMENT: EMOTIONAL AWARENESS AND REGULATION

The child is showing more congruency between his inner and outer self, which allows parents to have glimpses of the real child. However, with these glimmers of reality being exposed, the child becomes scared and retreats in fear that this placement will fall apart if his whole self were to come out. Unconsciously, the child has sentiments creating inner conflict running through his mind now: "If I become vulnerable, how will they hurt me?" and "I can go back to my birth family if I fail here." These under-the-radar thoughts stimulate a regression in the child's feelings and needs. The child's ability to mask his feelings and needs with passive-aggressive behavior obscures them, making it difficult for parents to sort them out. The child does not have the capacity to compartmentalize all of the inner and outer experiences he is having; thus, he exists in a whirlwind of emotion that is not easy to arrest.

During the engagement phase of emotional awareness and regulation, parents see the child's dysregulation and become frustrated that the child will not talk about his feelings and his needs, forgetting that he is incapable of doing so. As an extension of this expectation, parents can take the child's inability to make sense of his experience as a personal affront, falsely concluding that the child does not want to be in relationship with them. Emotions are running high for the parents as well as for the child during engagement. Parents can get upset and embarrassed about their own emotional reactions to their child's strife, and fear that they, too, are becoming dysregulated. Dad may try to avoid this discomfort by staying occupied or absent doing other things, while mom feels she has no such option to escape the craziness.

ENGAGEMENT: PROGRESS TOWARD PERMANENCY

The concept of a "forever family" creates internal conflict for the child, making him feel trapped. The child sees everything as all/none or win/lose and fears that making one mistake will cause his parents to reject him. At the same time, he senses that in making an allegiance to his permanent family, he is rejecting his birth family, which results in an intolerable conundrum for the child. The churning internal conflict causes a downward emotional spiral, which results in the child developing a flight/fight response.

To counteract this emotionally charged predicament, the child may stay and "fight" by zinging his new parents and family with assertions that his foster and birth families provided much better and, in fact, superior care and environs than his permanent family ever could. Despite their efforts to suppress reactions to these inaccurate declarations, parents may tend to fall into the trap and begin defending themselves or trying to "talk sense" into their child. In not recognizing the child's inner conflict, parents can spend hours of unfruitful time engaging with his defenses.

**The child does not have the capacity to compartmentalize
all of the inner and outer experiences he is having;
thus, he exists in a whirlwind of emotion that is not easy to arrest**

In making an allegiance to his permanent family, the child is rejecting his birth family, which results in an intolerable conundrum

In keeping their perspective clear and objective, parents can traverse the stage of engagement with relatively few forays into the dead-end emotional side streets that await them.

During the engagement stage, the child's parents are the most critical pieces of the healing puzzle. This means that in order to be available and energized enough to meet their child where he is, parents must be in a good space. Staying healthy physically through eating nutritious food, getting adequate sleep, and exercising daily, and tending to their emotional needs by making time for themselves and their spousal relationship each day, by consulting supportive friends and professionals often, and by using regular respite where they can leave child responsibilities in the hands of trusted, capable others is essential for parents in order to completely recharge. Neither parent nor child can drink from an empty well. Staying open to the reflections of others who often see things more clearly because they are not involved in the daily push and pull of the relationship is critical. If parents find themselves giving up "me time" or letting go of all activities with others that they enjoyed prior to the child joining the family, then they are likely to get off kilter. Parents must stay tuned in to themselves and give themselves what they need before they give to their child.

Second Steps: Working Through (placement months 9–18)

Deepening Attachment
Just as when we fall in love, deepening attachment brings forth our greatest joys and hopes as well as our deepest fears and wounds. As attachment deepens, the child's early formative experiences with others move right into the center of the current, real relationship.

Working through is the time in which the child begins to feel safe enough to show you and himself who he really is

DEEPENING ATTACHMENT: TRUST IN CARE

As attachment deepens, so does trust in care; however, the deepening continues to occur in fits and spurts. The overall trajectory of treatment reaches toward secure attachment, while the day-to-day progression resembles more of a two-step dance—two steps up and one step back. Nevertheless, the child's attachment behaviors—those of approaching and retreating—are more visible and less obscured by passive aggression and other smoke screens. As the child becomes more connected, the issues that brought him into your home—the loss of his birth parents, the trauma and fear of relationships—come into his relationship with you and have to be "worked through," that is, integrated into his new relationship with you. Parents can begin to see certain trust in care dynamics during this time of deepening attachment.

Working Through: Trust in Care Dynamics—The Child
➤ The child is being more tolerant of parental care and nurture
➤ Either an increase or decrease in the child demanding attention, depending on the child and his temperament
➤ The child showing a preference for mom
➤ The child's emerging loyalty binds to permanent family are developing, but he still expresses wanting to be out of the family on and off
➤ The child not understanding how this family can possibly love and care about him
➤ Noticeable shift in the child's demeanor to vulnerability being an easier choice

Meanwhile, as the child is generally moving closer to parents and the family, the parents are still wrestling with some of the issues that have dragged on from the first nine months of placement, while new issues begin to arise as well.

Working Through: Trust in Care Dynamics—The Parents
➤ Mom is still getting the brunt of the child's negative behaviors and continues to feel overwhelmed.
➤ Mom gets mad because she does not feel that dad is supportive and still does not "get" the child's transference of birth mom issues onto her.
➤ At the same time, dad tries to support mom, but may confuse

support with being protective of mom where the child is concerned, so he senses he is missing the connection and feels left out.

➤ Parents may continue feeling guilty about the impact on birth children and others of bringing a new child into the family.

➤ Parents may question their original choice to take the child in.

➤ Support professionals step up to intervene when the parents say they want the child out of their house "right now," which can happen two to three times as attachment deepens via the child's amplified push-pull behaviors.

DEEPENING ATTACHMENT: TRUST IN CONTROL

During the deepening of attachment, parent and child may face less frequent, but deeper challenges to the parents' control. On a positive note, however, the child is now responding well to structure, and when the child's demands increase, parents are wise to increase structure as well. The child may need to take fewer seats, but his need to process his feelings and flesh out his narrative is stronger than ever, so parents may want to have more time-in sessions to accommodate this need. The child still carries significant abandonment fear and may seek to quell this anxiety through pushing for limits. He also continues not to believe in himself and will try to prove his worthlessness through increased acting out.

DEEPENING ATTACHMENT: TRUST IN SELF

The child's trust in self is still not developed, and although he wants to work hard, he fears he cannot do it, so he returns to using his tried-and-true defenses. The child's lack of self-acceptance spawns his resistance to allowing anyone else to accept him. Standing on the precipice of allowing himself to be vulnerable and move more deeply into attachment evokes fear and self-doubt in the child. This inner conflict is palpable to parents when they are able to tune in to the child's process, and they can help the child understand what is going on inside of him by giving him words for his feelings and further fleshing out his narrative. Ideally, this process gets carried out by the parents, but they may need specific coaching both to see and to verbalize their child's reality. Professionals stepping in to help parents navigate their child's inner world can give a much-needed boost to the parents' confidence, for during this time, parents are prone to feeling guilty that they are not able to affect the child more: "Is *anything* I'm doing making a difference?"

Understandably, parents do not want to face their own feelings of incompetency that rise up when they feel powerless to help their child

Just as the child is more raw as he flirts with his vulnerability, as attachment deepens parents may start to show more primitive aspects of their own emotionality as well, displaying more angry and unregulated reactions. Again, the child and parents' processes tend to parallel one another during this phase of moving closer together as they all get the jitters about their capacity to succeed. Parents see more of the child's primitive affect as it emerges through his risk-retreat pattern. At the same time, in their relatively raw and needy state, parents wonder again why the child cannot *just talk about what is going on* for him. This is their wish, but parents know it is not possible for their child to be self-reflective at this point: it is just that parents do not want to face their own feelings of incompetency that rise up when they feel powerless to help their child through his present difficulties.

DEEPENING ATTACHMENT: INTEGRATION OF PAST TRAUMA

During the time of deepening attachment, the child struggles with integration of his past trauma. The child relives his past traumas in the present, unable to distinguish past from present. The parents' anxiety rises as the child increasingly treats them as if they were his original family, trying to re-create his past. Not only do the parents struggle with their own integrity, but they can succumb to the child's drive to re-create the dynamics of his former environments. Unconsciously, parents may feel the urge to reenact trauma. Parents may find themselves wanting to hurt their child as they begin to identify with his birth parents. If they can use this urge as a warning signal and resist falling into this role, parents can avert reenactment. Similarly, if parents heed this warning sign, they can also sidestep reengaging themselves in their own personal past trauma.

The child's fear of intimacy can give rise to bizarre behaviors as the child desperately attempts to defend against closeness. The parents may find themselves falling into the victim-rescuer dynamic as dad tries to defend and rescue mom from the child's defensive aggression. In renewing their awareness of this tendency, parents can avoid getting hooked into this unhelpful pattern in which mom gets angry when dad tries to step in.

DEEPENING ATTACHMENT: ADAPTIVE FUNCTIONING/SOCIAL SKILLS/BENEFIT OF FUN

As attachment deepens for the younger child, he may become very clingy with his primary parent to avoid feeling overwhelmed by the world outside the home, whereas an adolescent may feel drawn to over-identify with his peers to avoid attaching to his parent. The younger child at this time will begin to experiment with pleasing his parents. At the same time, he may sabotage community activities because he does not feel safe or want to rise to the increased expectations and demands of being successful outside the home. The younger child has not yet internalized being a "good citizen" for its own sake and instead avoids the stress of external demands. Parents also struggle with taking risks in allowing the child to attend outside events and are loathe to "raise the bar" for the child to go out for fear of his negative behaviors in public.

For the adolescent especially, peer relationships can become compromised because shame is so easily triggered during this time, making acting out more likely to increase. For younger children, problems with competition may arise, especially for boys. Unstructured play does not work well, and parents begin to understand the difference between their child's developmental and chronological age. Understandably, parents can become afraid during this time if they fall into "future think," worrying about the possibility their child will not catch up developmentally. Outside support is essential in order to prevent this fear from throwing the family into crisis.

Parents must now strive to prioritize their relational work with the child over putting their efforts into helping him progress toward social adaptability. Although "helicopter" parenting is normally discouraged, parents need to revolve their lives around their child at this stage to maximize the opportunity they have to deepen the attachment. The child expects and needs the locus of control to be external, which becomes the natural bridge to trust in the care of his parents. He will exhibit behaviors that will need to be tolerated, such as the tendency to be competitive and bossy, and cannot accept fun on the adults' terms, negating or sabotaging his parents' efforts to direct activities. The child is still learning to have

---

Parents may find themselves getting so overwhelmed and involved with the child that they forget to have fun

fun and does not yet value fun as a means to create or maintain successful peer relationships.

DEEPENING ATTACHMENT: QUALITY OF RELATIONSHIPS

During this time of deepening attachment, parents will feel more on top of the process if they can remember and anticipate what their child will be struggling with. Referring to a list such as the following can be a sanity saver for parents in this phase.

> **As Attachment Deepens, the Child May . . .**
> ➤ operate out of anxiety about placement permanency
> ➤ intensify his behaviors due to his struggle to assimilate the reality that his present parents are his "Mom" and "Dad"
> ➤ be heavily entrenched in a narcissistic, it's-all-about-me stance
> ➤ exhibit challenging behaviors due to his fear of intimacy
> ➤ protest the loss of his biological family, which will result in him struggling with loyalty binds
> ➤ attempt to divide his parents in a "competition for affection" as his Oedipal issues reemerge
> ➤ engage in behaviors indicative of sibling rivalry, protesting his siblings' positions and roles in the family

Especially in families with more than one emotionally distressed child, the "identified patient" role may be passed around. The emotionally distressed child's pathology will tend to define all relationships within the family. Parents may find themselves getting sidetracked by negative behaviors stimulated by increased intimacy, and become so overwhelmed and involved with the child that they forget to have fun. Any real or perceived division between parents is magnified at this time, and other family members may want to quit or protect mom due to her pain. The pressures may result in the parents' tendency toward fight or flight, which may potentially come in the form of collapse. Therefore, at this time especially, parents must dig in with the attitude that they will "win," lest the child's placement gives way to disruption.

DEEPENING ATTACHMENT: EMOTIONAL AWARENESS AND REGULATION

This phase of deepening attachment marks the child's last-ditch effort before surrender, as well as coincides with the exposure of the weak links in the family dynamics. *This is the most vulnerable time for placement permanence and where families drop out if they are going to.* While the child's defensiveness was initially all-pervasive, as his defenses get more brittle and fall apart, acting out increases, but it is no longer gratifying to him. Vulnerability actually becomes an easier choice for the child, but his demeanor remains incongruent with this inner feeling. The child continues to be overwhelmed by his feelings and has difficulty sorting through them as wide mood swings keep him off-balance. Although he is beginning to be able to articulate the feelings of anxiety and depression ("mad" and "sad"), the child still tends to act out his emotions.

Survival guilt about birth siblings and other family members becomes more tangible for the child as he begins to be aware of differences between his permanent and birth families. The child engages more than ever in projective identification—meaning when feelings are intolerable, he "projects" or puts his feelings inside of others—and in doing so, he sets up siblings and parents to act out his rage and shame. At this time, the child attacks family values at their core, blames, is passive-aggressive, and creates chaos.

Meanwhile, parents become divided as they "swallow" the classic family dynamics models for the "perfect" dad and mom personas: the emotionally disconnected, analytical, and avoidant dad and the emotionally connected, feelings-oriented, and protective mom. This splintering puts the family on shaky ground as the protectiveness in mom calls forth a choice between the child and the marriage, creating at the very least a psychological divorce. If parents remain united, however, they may begin blaming the system for letting them down and others for not meeting their needs. Parents also may seek medication solutions to handle overwhelming family emotions.

DEEPENING ATTACHMENT: PROGRESS TOWARD PERMANENCY

As the placement progresses toward permanency, parents who have failed in the past may begin to make connections between the dynamics of the current and prior placements, identifying conflict and the causes of the previous disruptions. For parents, this awareness brings out particular feelings.

As Permanency Nears, Parents May Feel . . .

➤ terrified of "forever" due to lack of trust that their child's behaviors will change

➤ like they are losing hope

➤ desperation about completing the permanency plan

➤ high anxiety

➤ overwhelmed, thus forgetting to use resources and interventions already identified

➤ controllingness, resulting in the tendency for parents to become punitive

➤ ambivalence about "family"

➤ fear of being severely judged by outside agencies because of their doubts and ambivalence

➤ frustrated with their child's difficulty in talking about feelings and needs

Meanwhile, as the adults struggle in their parental realm, the child swirls in the confusion brought on by the felt pressure to "make it or break it" in this family.

As Permanency Nears, the Child May Feel . . .

➤ high ambivalence about permanency, which results in his verbalizations of "what adults want to hear" intermingled with behavioral communication of rejection

➤ an inability to manage the conflicting desires of wanting his birth family and his permanent family, not able to hold on to "both" as an option

➤ like experimenting with family name, identity

➤ more primitive emotions such as shame, rage, and fear—a sense that something is looming

➤ overwhelmed by feelings and have difficulty sorting through them

➤ an inability to care about others or give them empathy because he does not yet care about himself or have empathy for himself

➤ longing for and worrying about birth family

➤ a sense of grief and loss close to the surface

The child's fear of connecting with his parents, of accepting them as "Mom" and "Dad," along with his anxiety about permanency cause regression and acting out to increase because he cannot meet presumed expectations or talk about feelings in the way he was becoming more capable of doing. This situation calls for parents not to get stuck in a behavioral spiral with their child as they must be the ones to keep all family members' heads above water. Parents cannot fall victim to their feelings of anger and inadequacy; they must lead the way toward the light of achieved permanency.

"Working from the head, not the heart" becomes a critical skill for parents to practice in this phase. This may sound counterintuitive as we are talking about attachment, but displaying heightened "mom and dad" personas at this time puts increased pressure on the child to become a part of the family. Now more than ever, parents must not push, instead letting the child come to them, lest he turn in the opposite direction out of fear of closeness. This does not mean parents need to stop interacting; it means they must love their child as if from afar, respecting his present ability to tolerate intimacy.

In this penultimate phase of permanency, families often forget to have fun because of the swarm of negative behaviors. Yet parents must not lose sight of having fun with their child, even though it is very hard to do as they struggle. Tactics for successfully having fun include mentally separating the child from how the child is behaving, choosing an appropriate location, and not taking the child's rejection of the attempts at fun personally. If the child does not want to join in, parents can have him be close and watch the activity, giving the child the message that they hope someday he will allow himself to have some fun because he deserves it. This approach prevents the child from wielding his power to control the parents' decisions and emotions.

Parental communication is crucial: parents must work as a team, support and believe in one another, and share feelings as they arise. Remembering the intervention tools such as taking a seat, time in, and giving choices, and the nurturing strategies such as rocking and carrying the child, attunement, and meeting the child where he is developmentally helps parents focus on the now. Balancing unconditional nurture with relational boundaries, conveying total acceptance of the child but not his behaviors, and carefully increasing expectations that the child express what he wants and needs verbally instead of through behaviors helps build a

---

Parents must not fall victim to their feelings of anger and inadequacy; they must lead the way toward the light of achieved permanency

bridge between the present uncertainties of the working through phase and the confidence of permanency success so that hope can be sustained.

In using natural and logical consequences instead of grounding or other punishment, parents can continue to build the platform of trust while keeping their child safe as well as accountable. In avoiding close-ended time frames, parents can ensure the "when" of things is all about the relationship. In letting their child know clearly what they expect, that they are not "keeping score," and that every day is a new day, trust has fertile ground for growth. Parents must allow for change and tell their child "I don't know" rather than make promises they cannot keep. They must let the child come to them when he is ready. The push-and-pull dance of working through represents the child's final attempts to keep from surrendering to his parents' attachment pattern. If the family can withstand this time of relationship-in-high-motion, the placement is likely to sustain over time.

Grief and Loss

For the emotionally distressed child, issues of grief and loss are nearly always present, but without specific help from his parents, he cannot cognitively connect these feelings with their behavioral manifestations. Therefore, if parents would like to help both the child and themselves navigate the tangle of feelings and behaviors, they need to remain cognizant of the fact that loss has been and will continue to be an enduring issue for the child. This is not an easy task, for during this time in the process of working through, the pressure of the dynamics—family integration, separation, loss and grief, and attachment—that are going on at the same time has parents maxed out emotionally and leaves them without the energy it would take to focus sufficiently on the child's pain. Yet if parents could remind themselves regularly of the grief and loss their child may be experiencing, they will be able to remain in a place of compassion more often and succumb to their feelings of frustration less often.

The Child's Defenses and Behaviors. The child is comparing his new parents with his birth parents and will react to them as if they were his birth parents. It may feel counterintuitive for parents to ride this out rather than fight it, and difficult for them to quell the temptation to justify that they are, indeed, different from their child's birth parents. What is happening is that the child is beginning to "fall in love" with his new mom, and feelings

The child at once wants this placement to work
and yet is terrified that it might work

of disloyalty emerge for him in the process. The child's behavior belies the fact that his new parents are becoming "Mom" and "Dad" to him.

At an emotional level, the child begins to recognize the conflictual dynamics that led to disruption in previous placements emerging in his current placement, which greatly increases his anxiety because he at once wants this placement to work and yet is terrified that it might work. Dysregulated behaviors occur as the child swims in the emotional confusion of the then and the now. If the child has struggled in the past with sexual or anger issues, they may reemerge, and he may be prone to act out with peers. Increased parental supervision at this time will keep the child as well as others safe. In therapy, revisiting issues that had been moving toward resolution in the past may be helpful to the child because he is in a safe place to process their resurfacing.

Shame is ever present now, and the child cannot distinguish between "I am a mistake" and "I make mistakes." For the child, it is a fact that his birth parents "did not want" him, and he fears the same thing may happen in this permanent placement. Unstructured play and competition intensify the child's shame, unleashing dysregulated behavior that makes him feel even worse about himself. Close parent-child time is both the preventative and the elixir for this problem. Giving voice to the child's underlying feelings and mirroring his confusion and pain can help dissipate his shame and anxiety, thus decreasing negative behavior. "It is so hard for you right now because everything feels like it is colliding inside of you: 'Birth family or permanent family? Will my badness wreck everything?—it always has.' It's hard for you to make sense of it all, and that's making you feel out of control. I'm here with you, and I'm not going anywhere. Together, we'll get through this and come out the other side in a better place."

The Parents' Feelings. It is difficult to be around a person who is sunk into deep shame, especially if it is your own child, because feelings of helplessness to change the child's opinion of himself can be engulfing. Therefore, focusing on acceptance rather than trying to change the child's outlook is a way to stay lifted out of the emotional mire. It is helpful for parents consciously to look at their child's behavior differently, especially at this time

As your child is working through what it means to belong to your family, he may feel increasingly vulnerable and afraid; try to say "yes" as much as possible within this phase and be alert to your child's painful feelings

in the process. Becoming curious instead of angry and seeing the unpleasant behaviors as part of a birthing process, in a sense, can help parents see that they are in the middle of change, not at the end.

The child is testing parents determinedly to see if they are worthy of his trust. In addition to being taxing to parents' already strained stamina, this process can go on intensely for months. Outside support can help parents stay focused on the underlying issues instead of behaviors as well as provide respite for them in this seemingly endless battle to win the child's trust. Again, this is the time when many disruptions happen, and recognizing the telltale dynamics is essential for parents so they can hold on and get through it.

Saying "yes" to the child as much as possible during this fragile point in the process is another tool that can help parents feel they can make a positive difference. A keen eye for the positive things the child is doing and a willingness to affirm the child even as he attempts to put you in the "bad" role does nurture and strengthen the relationship. "Thanks for setting the table so nicely," a specific, genuine compliment, can help the child "feel the present" and momentarily pull him out of the automatic shame state he lives in. Remembering that the child cannot sustain this moment of temporary relief helps parents continue to call out the positives they see, no matter how small they may seem. Parents also tend to feel better about themselves, as well as more successful, as they string the beads of positivity together one at a time, over time.

Paying attention to their feelings helps parents track their own inner processes and gives them a clue to what their child may be feeling, making it easier to empathize and mirror him. If parents notice they are feeling inadequate, guilty, or angry, they can ask themselves if their child may also be feeling these things, which can help them identify his underlying need. Grasping onto any and all empowering actions can be a parent's life preserver in this phase of working through, which can begin to feel unending and less likely to be successful with each passing day.

Fear around disruption often causes parents to return to their fantasy about how this placement is going to turn out and thus to try harder to make it a reality. Staying aware of this tendency and nipping it in the bud will help parents focus on meeting the child's needs in the present, which will actually help them achieve the success they want. Revisiting their realistic expectations list prevents parents from wanting something from their child that he cannot give at this moment and helps them avoid a relational implosion. Remembering that their child's templates of what "Mom," "Dad," and "family" look like is different from theirs can ground parents in the present, which is the place everyone must strive to occupy to maximize forward movement.

The inner personal growth spiral does not take a holiday for parents at this time. As placement anxiety increases, parents may discover pieces of themselves they were unaware of or could not accept before. They may experience reengagement of past grief or trauma and feel overwhelmed by their child's feelings and needs, which leads them to feel unable to see and meet them. Parents then can feel guilty about their own inadequacy, which if left unacknowledged can negatively influence the whole family. Rather than allowing themselves to question, "Is anything I'm doing making a difference?" parents must proactively counter that question with this: "These are the things, no matter how small they may seem, that I am doing that are making a difference in this difficult time."

At this point in the working through process, the family is in a dance they must cycle through over and over again. The reoccurrence of grief, anger, and sadness begins to feel endlessly repetitive: parents try to get the child up to dance and the child stays down; the child is up and energetic and the parents are tired; and occasionally, the dance enters a synchrony that reminds everyone why they are doing what they are doing.

Family Integration and Reformation

Now that you and your child have formed an attached relationship, he can move on to becoming a real member of your family. This will involve sibling relationships and relationships with grandparents, aunts, and uncles, all of whom may have their own feelings about this expansion.

FAMILY INTEGRATION AND REFORMATION: TRUST IN CARE

The last part of "Second Steps: Working Through" is family integration and reformation, which is to say it is the time when the family configuration makes its definitive shift reflecting that the emotionally distressed child is becoming a true member of the family in all respects. This is both a hopeful time as well as a time for a reality check in terms of conscious or unconsciously held long-term expectations for what the family will "look like" when the child is "absorbed." No longer can parents live with fantasies about what things will be like when the emotionally distressed child completely enters the fold. At this point, that cake has been baked, and any expectations that are not in line with the reality of the extant nature of the family reformation need to be reckoned with.

Several important milestones have been reached by this time in the permanency process by the child, the parents, and the family as a whole. An outside observer would notice that the emotionally distressed child is now seeking care and nurture from his parents and that he is starting to like and feel comfortable around dad, no longer fearing him as the aggressor. The observer would also notice, however, that the child's more secure attachment and preference for one parent over the other has created the opening for the child to split the parents apart in their team approach. Parents' ongoing awareness of this possibility should be sufficient to stave off the child's ability to succeed in splitting them.

The child no longer needs or seeks to be constantly the center of attention in the family's world, seemingly having relinquished that role to whomever is in greatest need. The observer would notice that the child is more aware, more present, and more responsive to his parents. The child will appear to have largely internalized the elements of conscience that were once "held until" by his parents. Longer periods of normalized behaviors have begun to be the status quo as the child now has the desire not to disappoint his parents. This is good news and a long-awaited status for the child to have achieved; however, it does have a downside. When the child does succumb to dysregulation, it can feel like and become a bigger crisis than it is because normalcy has come to be expected by all.

Parents have shifted into a more normalized and less therapeutic parenting pattern and have become more skilled at responding from a cognitive rather than an emotional stance, recognizing when they are feeling hooked. They have come to understand the child's push-pull dynamics and incorporate this knowledge into what they do, allowing them to have

Family integration is a more "normal" time, as parents now can clearly see the needs beneath their child's behavior

more flexible expectations around care and control. Parents are now able to see the child's needs beneath his behavior and have become more accepting of the child's "crazy" behavior because they now have the confidence to handle it well. Mom begins to "get a life" again as the parents are now able to plan their breaks around more accurate predictions of when hard times are likely to occur. Getting treatment support becomes less of a priority for parents now that they have integrated so many of the skills, including the capacity for "therapeutic thinking," that have been provided for them in the past.

FAMILY INTEGRATION AND REFORMATION: TRUST IN CONTROL

As the family integration proceeds and professional supports and services decrease, the child's anxiety can skyrocket, even though he has achieved a substantial degree of trust in control of his parents. The child has been aware on some level all along that his parents' strength has been fueled by the treatment team, so when the treatment providers begin to pull back as the parents need them less, the child's perception of his parents' power can crumble. This can set in motion a reactivity in the parents that is brought on by their desire to be the "competent parents" they see themselves as at this point, causing them to over-respond to their child's anxiety, which actually increases his anxiety as he interprets their intervention to be a sign they fear they are faltering. Such action-reaction cycles have been common all along in the permanency process, but they may seem more pronounced now that the treatment team has pulled back.

FAMILY INTEGRATION AND REFORMATION: TRUST IN SELF

The child's sense of self-acceptance has increased alongside his parents' ongoing demonstrative acceptance of him to the point of it having a palpable critical mass. The external and internal acceptance of the child's "crazy" self has had the effect of calming the child's anxiety because he is more confident that whatever arises in him can be dealt with and contained within the family. Although he may tend to act out more now in a bid to keep treatment team services in place to maintain his sense of security in his parents' care, the child actually feels more trust in his own capacity to persevere. Now the changing external circumstances have become the variable to focus on instead of solely on the child's internally derived whirlwind, for both parents and child.

The "self" of the family has become dependent upon treatment services and now feels the weight of the change brought on by withdrawal of services. Therefore, although the child is more capable of having success in community settings, the family's confidence is in a transitional state, and any conflicts that occur in the community arena can feel more intense. At the same time for the parents, a paradigm shift from denial to acceptance of the "emotionally distressed" aspect of their child has occurred and been integrated. There is now a sense that the family is recommitting to the endeavor they have been undertaking, but this time the commitment feels more grounded in reality. The family's reformation is solidifying as the parents are now more capable of making a distinction between their emotional issues and the child's issues. The parents recognize that all they can truly control is their own responsiveness, thereby creating the emotional boundaries necessary for effectively corralling the child.

FAMILY INTEGRATION AND REFORMATION: INTEGRATION OF PAST TRAUMA

The child is becoming capable of distinguishing past trauma from current situations and now has a working "switch" that allows him to shift from now to then and back again. This allows him to feel intermittent relief from his past trauma and to pay attention to the here and now, wherein he is finding more and more enjoyment. Although he is still working through anxiety and safety issues, the child experiences less intense and shorter periods of acting out. He does not get stuck as often in the whirlwind of unregulated emotion and is easier to live with. The child's defenses are more recognizable to his parents and to himself, making it possible for the family to acknowledge, act, and move on when defenses arrest the present in service of flagging an unrequited need of the child.

Parents have become more proficient at recognizing their own tendency toward reactive reenactment of their own issues and at arresting and stepping out of transference when it erupts from difficult encounters with their child. Mom and dad are more capable of using one another for balance and to tag team when one needs a break. Past issues that reverberate in the present at challenging times are more transparent to parents, and they are more comfortable with their own issues as they get closer to resolution. The parallels between the child's and the parents' processes in

---

The child comes into the family
to heal the parents as much as to be healed himself

resolution of issues are uncanny at times, which serves as more evidence that the child comes into the family to heal the parents as much as to be healed himself.

FAMILY INTEGRATION AND REFORMATION:
ADAPTIVE FUNCTIONING/SOCIAL SKILLS/BENEFIT OF FUN

The child is decidedly more self-contained, and his ability to self-soothe is becoming more noticeable as his adaptive functioning increases. He can be seen using his parents as a safe base from which he can go out and be independent for short times, then to which he can return and touch into the security he needs. The child's shame is beginning to lift, and he now feels more balanced and begins to realize that success in competition is not all-important. The child has accepted and is identifying with family norms, traditions, and values, and is beginning to participate in related activities and hobbies when and where it is appropriate.

Having fun is now a motivating factor for the child, and he is discovering that his desire is to have fun within the context of relationship more than it is to have material gratification. Success with enjoyable activities and in relationships is self-reinforcing as the child continues to improve his social skills and reap the feel-good benefits of having fun. As the child becomes more able to succeed in the community and in interactions with peers, the family can find itself becoming over-committed to activities outside the home environment. Parents are therefore faced with having to address the home/community balance for the child as well as for themselves. In choosing out-of-the-home activities for their child, parents are now able to capitalize on their ability to identify accurately the child's strengths, which makes the likelihood of success more reliable.

FAMILY INTEGRATION AND REFORMATION: QUALITY OF RELATIONSHIPS

At this point, the child is starting to be able to identify his wish that he had been born into this family. He is more capable of navigating feelings of loss as he mourns the split he has made with his birth family. More than ever, the child is becoming able to distinguish past relationships from present ones and episodes of transference are less frequent. Caregivers have become "real people" to the child, who is now able to see that they have their own thoughts, perceptions, experiences, and feelings that do not necessarily revolve around him or the birth family. The child is accepting his "role as child" and now can identify with his same-sex parent.

A major milestone of this time of integration and reformation is that the child can now delay gratification, which makes him much more pleasant and desirable to be around.

Parents can accept their parenting abilities as "good enough" now and not berate themselves or feel inadequate so much of the time. The roles in the family become more balanced, and dad steps more clearly into a support role and out of the protect mode. Rather than being seen as "special needs," in this phase of reformation the child becomes a "regular" member of his family. The child's propensity to be the one who has "the right to have pain" has dissipated, and it has become okay for other family members to have pain—even that related to raising the child.

Yet with so much of the hard work of the family now coming to fruition at this point, there remain pieces of reality that cannot be overcome. The parents are coming to terms with the fact that their child does not measure up to their portrait of the idealized child, which they may not have even known they were still holding in their thoughts. Perhaps the actual child will not be able to be as close to the parents as they would like, and this reality has become much more apparent. The parents may have to work to redefine their ideal parent-child relationship to match the capacity of their particular child to be close. The concept of what a healthy parent-child relationship is must now incorporate and fit the needs of the child the parents actually *have* and have grown to love. Parents must mourn the loss of the idealized child and accept the reality of who their child is and will be.

FAMILY INTEGRATION AND REFORMATION: EMOTIONAL AWARENESS AND REGULATION

Increased emotional awareness and the ability to better self-regulate necessarily come with improved cognitive functioning. The child's growth in terms of his *understanding* of his situation has brought him to the place where he can start putting his birth family experiences in perspective instead of being blindly thrown off base by related triggering events. The child now has more accurate expectations of his birth family as his idealism becomes tempered by reality. He can also begin to realize that he is not "bad," but rather that he has some limitations related to actions of his birth family.

Still needing parents' help to maintain congruency between his feelings and behaviors, the child is beginning to be able to manage matching his inner state with his outer state on his own. The child's emotional vocabulary expands outside of the core five emotions—mad, sad, happy, afraid, and shame.

"Sad" becomes "lonely" and "mad" becomes "frustrated." This blossoming lexicon allows the child to be more accurate and succinct in voicing his inner process, making communication more effective and mirroring more meaningful for him. The child is more easily redirected because his defenses have decreased. Fewer, shorter, and less-intense mood swings allow the child to feel more peaceful inside and make him more enjoyable to be around.

Parents are also getting better at identifying what is going on emotionally for their child and can read the red flags that precede a crisis so they can intervene before the situation gets out of hand. Parent roles continue to become more emotionally balanced, and dad feels the need to start taking a more active role. This has a ripple effect, allowing mom to be more relaxed because she has more time for herself to renew her energy and pursue an interest outside the constant needs of her child.

FAMILY INTEGRATION AND REFORMATION: PROGRESS TOWARD PERMANENCY

Progress toward permanency becomes more visible in many ways that seem to reverberate more deeply for both child and parents. Having now consciously chosen his permanent family, the child can integrate pieces of himself that are in kinship with both his permanent and birth family. The loyalty binds that once constricted the child's choices, forcing him to select all or nothing when claiming a family, have now loosened to the point that the child no longer feels he must choose.

He can accept who his birth family is without completely dismissing them or his permanent family. The child is more able to hold both families in his mind at the same time without being overwhelmed with anxiety. The parents now begin to realize that for the child to have changed this much, they needed to have led the way by giving up their long-held vision of what "family" is to transform themselves in order to transform the family into one that could integrate the child.

The child still feels at times that he is unworthy and cannot understand why this family would want to love or care for him. He may still say that he wants out of the family on and off and accordingly will increase or decrease demands for attention with distancing or clinginess. Parents are wise to allow the child to wrestle with this inner struggle, yet help reassure him of their commitment to him by mirroring his thoughts and feelings and meeting them with acceptance and curiosity. Keeping the child physically close and smothering him with attention at this time is the goal, even if the child often seems he does not really want this closeness on his parents' terms. On some level, the child will soak up this attention he needs so desperately, and since his tolerance for care and nurture has increased substantially, he may not be so quick to push it away.

The dance continues to be one of incongruence, but as the graphic chart on page 282 illustrates, the partners are coming closer together and becoming more vulnerable with one another as the second steps of the permanency process draw to a close. Integration and reformation have occurred, but there is more growth to come within the new family paradigm for each and every family member. Getting used to the "new normal" the reformed family has achieved will take time, and time will be necessary to firm up the foundation the child will need to complete his identity formation and move toward increased autonomy.

Third Steps: Relationship Resolution

Identity Development and Increased Autonomy (placement months 18–21)

All attachment is in the service of individuation. Attachment allows us to carry the internal model of our attachment figure with us while we move on to become our unique selves. As your child experiences the safety and consistency of your care and control, he is capable of moving a bit further away from your immediate care, but he can still have times of emotional instability when he'll need you right by his side.

IDENTITY DEVELOPMENT AND INCREASED AUTONOMY: TRUST IN CARE

The child's growth toward identity development has turned a corner where his relationship with his parents is concerned. He is now confiding in his parents, reporting problems he is having rather than keeping them to himself or acting out as often. The child's fear of abandonment has decreased, and he is now having fewer triggering events that lead him to believe he will have to leave this family. Whereas respite and therapeutic intervention from the outside used to feel punitive to the child, now he is relatively good at accepting these integral aspects of the permanency process.

There are fewer disruptive incidents, and the parents are more often able to read the red flags signaling the buildup to them so they can intervene before the behavior goes beyond simple prevention. The parents

**While many of the biggest losses, traumas, fears, and anxieties
have been worked through, keeping structure high,
but more flexible, and remaining responsive to the child's needs
sustain parents' hard-earned success**

also now know which interventions work best with their child and how to implement them successfully. No longer is treatment prescribed by the therapeutic team as the parents now initiate any contacts, meetings, and support when they need it. Still invaluable, the treatment team becomes more of a third-party sounding board for the family.

Parents can now confidently sit with their child and support him in figuring out his problems and handling his issues. With each other's support, parents are now adept at discerning what is going on and unhooking themselves when they get triggered by their child's behaviors. Parents are more spontaneous and emotionally vulnerable with their child because they have learned to put his (less-frequent) rejection in perspective. In this stage of the process, both parents and child are developing a more solid sense of identity within the family. The family has arrived at the point where trust in care extends not just from the child to the parents but from the child to himself and from the parents to each other in the parallel manner that has characterized the journey from the start.

IDENTITY DEVELOPMENT AND INCREASED AUTONOMY: TRUST IN CONTROL

Although the child is working his way toward increased autonomy, he still requires external control much of the time to keep him on track. That the child now knows what gets him into trouble and is aware of how to stay out of trouble is more evident as the parents see their child begin to make better choices and his capacity for internalized control expand. Parents encourage the child's growth toward being more in charge of himself as they witness his greater confidence and more frequent success. The parents' interventions do not feel as punitive to the child because he has grown to expect them and has become less shame based in his view of himself. The child is more likely to have success in the community at this point, and the parents are getting better at discerning when their child will be able to enjoy the experience and take pride in his social accomplishments.

IDENTITY DEVELOPMENT AND INCREASED AUTONOMY: TRUST IN SELF

The child can now sustain autonomous functioning for longer periods of time, and he is more accepting of the fact that he lacks some age-appropriate problem-solving skills. His greater self-acceptance allows him to try out new ideas and new ways of doing things without the constant fear of failure he was once consumed by that emanated from his shame-based core. Parents, too, are beginning to enjoy the child's increasing autonomy, and their expectations for normalcy become more warranted.

IDENTITY DEVELOPMENT AND INCREASED AUTONOMY: INTEGRATION OF PAST TRAUMA

In the realm of therapy, the child now will fight with the therapist as he feels he does not need help anymore because he is "normal." The child must hold on tightly to this vision of himself as he makes the transition from "identified patient" in the family to an integrated part of the family because he is still unable to hold these two "selves" in his mind simultaneously. Anyone who reminds him of his "former" self is bad; thus, contact with members of the treatment team can trigger a reaction. At the same time, the child continues to make advances in his ability to "hold" both birth and permanent families in his consciousness and distinguish between past and present reality.

Parents experience relief as the child's transference of birth parents onto them begins to dissolve substantially, and they now feel more like themselves—less guarded and crazy. The parents are better able to examine their own historic issues without being as reactive. Due to increased self-confidence in their abilities to handle the dynamics created by bringing an emotionally distressed child into their home, the parents now want to share their experiences with other families to help them.

IDENTITY DEVELOPMENT AND INCREASED AUTONOMY:
ADAPTIVE FUNCTIONING/SOCIAL SKILLS/BENEFIT OF FUN

Now, the child is more capable of sustaining friendships, and he may have a few friends he plays with regularly. No longer identifying as a loner, the child feels like he is a part of something, that he belongs more to the community at large. The increased confidence the feeling of belonging brings activates the child's desire to self-monitor his anxiety and emotions; thus, he becomes more capable of doing so. The child can engage in competitive games more successfully without always having to win in order to avoid being overcome with shame.

Although more adept at managing himself within peer relationships, the child is still reliant upon adults to solve peer problems. The way the adults handle intervention, however, can make all the difference between the child remaining dependent upon them to solve these problems and the child learning how to do so by himself. Using an alliance approach, parents can both oversee and engage their child in the resolution process at the same time: "Let's see if we can figure out together what the problem is and how to solve it."

Increased capacity for socialization also brings with it the possibility of the child indulging in peer relationships as a way to distract himself from the bonding work he still needs to do with his parents. Fortunately, the child's ability to be more spontaneous and to have unguarded fun assists his parents with keeping him on the road to relationship resolution. The family is now able to enjoy having fun together as a unit, and family life feels more normalized because it now revolves around activities instead of acute needs of the child and therapeutic intervention. The child is capable at this point of more reciprocity, which makes parents feel confident about moving forward into adoption.

IDENTITY DEVELOPMENT AND INCREASED AUTONOMY: QUALITY OF RELATIONSHIPS
The child is developing more empathy for the parents at this point, but he still is not often able to extend this capacity to others outside immediate family. Decreasing core shame allows the child to be more accountable within his relationship with his parents. The child also trusts more in his parents' ability to handle anything that comes their way and is confident that if they need support, his parents will reach out for it. Likewise, the child trusts more in his ability to meet his own needs appropriately, and he can better compartmentalize and delay gratification. As the strength of the family increases, the child's ego strength also rises as he truly sees himself as part of a family, which he can now carry as an internalized entity within himself.

The quality of the parent-child relationship has become more mutually gratifying because the focus is not as much directed at the child's pathology, but rather at normalized family activities. Parents begin to feel a significant sense of relief and comfort because they are able to be more spontaneous with their child as he becomes more adaptive and they gain more confidence in their autonomy and skills. There is a clearer picture in the parents' minds about how to handle birth family issues as well as making decisions regarding respite.

IDENTITY DEVELOPMENT AND INCREASED AUTONOMY:
EMOTIONAL AWARENESS AND REGULATION

The child's ability to compartmentalize has become a more reliable and adaptive defense to his still sometimes overwhelming emotions. Feelings no longer are considered the "f" word by the child because he now can hold in his mind that both he and his placement will survive anything he may feel or express. The child's generalized and sexual aggression becomes more and more easily subsumed as he is now able to sublimate and redirect it into more socially appropriate activities. More aware of and less gratified by impulses to act out feelings, the child realizes he has an ability to make a conscious choice between expressing feelings in "old," potentially damaging ways or more healthy, pro-social ways.

The parents also realize they have the choice to act in "old" or healthier ways as they get stronger emotionally and find they can improve their own social boundaries. No longer does the family operate by the drive to "look good," so they are able to communicate openly that they have less of a need for therapeutic services. As an improved and more balanced system, the family can now regulate itself for the most part and ask for support when they need it.

IDENTITY DEVELOPMENT AND INCREASED AUTONOMY: PROGRESS TOWARD PERMANENCY

Knowing all about the child at this point, the parents make a meaningful, conscious choice that they truly want the child to be part of their family. At the same time, the child makes a conscious choice that these parents, although not his birth or even his ideal parents, are *his* and that he wants to be in this family. The child needs his parents to continue to help him discover the whole person that he is, to help him integrate his associations with his birth family, and to help him achieve a balanced perspective. Parents must still be careful about how they talk about the child's birth family because, more than ever, he is allowing himself to identify parts of himself that he has in common with them. "I know that your mom worked two jobs, which means she was a hard worker. That's where you must have gotten the ability to work so hard."

The child interprets parental negativity about his birth parents as his parents feeling negatively about *him*. Although honest anger about what the birth parents *did* can be appropriate, because their choices have, indeed, made it more difficult for the child, birth parents are multidimensional and their positives also reside within the child. The child's ambivalence and pressure to feel loyal are diminishing and will continue to diminish if his parents can help him embrace the parts of his heritage that have contributed positively to his identity. Integration is the goal as the child brings together aspects of both families that have helped make him who he is.

Rite of Passage—Mastery and Control (permanency months 21–24)

As with other parts in the dance of attachment, during mastery and control the child continues to have some minor missteps. Because of the relative peace of this and the preceding period, the behaviors may seem more major and troublesome than they really are. The great news is that you and your child now have the ability to talk through the meanings beneath the behavior and resolve them.

RITE OF PASSAGE—MASTERY AND CONTROL: TRUST IN CARE

Just when everyone thought they were home free, fear cycles back for the child, unleashing a return of regressive behaviors. All issues surrounding adoption resurface for the child, and thus for the parents. All the while, identity integration continues as a theme running in the background for both the child and the family. As the child slips back into regressions temporarily, the parents wrestle with their fear of loss of services. This regressive slippage momentarily shakes the confidence of the whole family system, but with the realization that the regression is temporary, the system can relatively quickly right itself.

RITE OF PASSAGE—MASTERY AND CONTROL: TRUST IN CONTROL

Depth issues reemerge for the child, and to process these issues he needs the external support of his parents, support which he more readily accepts due to his trust in their control of him. However, because he now intellectualizes issues, the child will not always find relief in the processing as he is stuck in his head. Eventually, the child will be able to touch the emotional depth of each reemerging issue, but he will do so in his own time and at his own rate. The parents are more accepting of the child's cycling, but they begin to question again if their child will ever be "normal."

With the realization that regression is temporary, the family system can relatively quickly right itself

Reassurance from the treatment team that they are still there for the parents to call on helps the parents reconnect with the trust they have in themselves that they can handle whatever comes.

RITE OF PASSAGE—MASTERY AND CONTROL: TRUST IN SELF

The child's trust in himself is shaky during the rite of passage. Although he experiences longer periods of being "really on," when he bottoms out, he retreats into a state of learned helplessness and his behavior can quickly spiral down. The child worries about what contact with birth family will look like and if and how they will be involved in his new life. If he does have contact with his birth family, the child wonders if he will be able to hold on to the new parts of himself. The child can be ambivalent and adult-pleasing around the adoption issue, but if his parents look closely, they will be able to see their child's lack of genuineness, underneath which is the reemergence of his mourning.

Again, parents go through a parallel process of losing trust in themselves as their child loses trust in himself, and again they question their ability to be successful. During this time when they fail at an intervention with their child, the parents feel ineffective, and visions of their fantasy family in which their child is no longer distressed once again emerge only to result in disappointment. The parents cycle back around, trying to get the child to reengage in their attachment patterns because they fear that the problems that existed in the beginning have returned. Parents' insecurities beget insecurity in the child, and the whole system is vulnerable to spiraling down, albeit temporarily.

RITE OF PASSAGE—MASTERY AND CONTROL: INTEGRATION OF PAST TRAUMA

After the adoption is finalized, the child's drive for birth family contact revs up, and if contact is allowed, it may cause disorganization and disintegration of the child's equilibrium. Reactivity to triggers relating to past trauma can increase for the child, and the parents can get hooked back into a reenactment cycle with him. Still holding on to a fantasy of normalcy, the parents can feel that the child is deliberately hurting them by acting out and is consciously choosing to cause chaos and pain within the family. Much careful thought and planning must be put into any consideration of birth family contact, not just at this point in the process but also in the future.

RITE OF PASSAGE—MASTERY AND CONTROL:
ADAPTIVE FUNCTIONING/SOCIAL SKILLS/BENEFIT OF FUN

On his more stable days, the child feels better about himself and thus becomes more confident in his ability to socialize successfully. The child now feels like he does not stick out as much, and he is more comfortable "wearing" his chronological age than he is in returning to a previous adult-like or regressed state. He can identify his interests and gain a sense of his identity through successful activities. The child's parents are less troubled when they allow natural consequences to prevail, and they feel more comfortable letting others see into their family.

RITE OF PASSAGE—MASTERY AND CONTROL: QUALITY OF RELATIONSHIPS

Both child and family have a greater capacity to "look normal" because the number of incidents of extreme behavior has greatly diminished. The child feels more a part of his permanent family than ever, and his parents feel a greater acceptance of the child as he is. The child's relational limitations have not faded away, but the parents' understanding of and confidence in working within these limits have increased so that the relationship is nevertheless more functional.

RITE OF PASSAGE—MASTERY AND CONTROL: EMOTIONAL AWARENESS
AND REGULATION

Entering this final stage of relationship resolution, both family and child are able to bounce back more quickly after a crisis if it is dealt with in a conscious manner, which parents are now more proficient at doing. The emotional balance within the family is now directed from within by the parents instead of from the outside by the treatment team. Yet when they do need assistance, the family is able to recognize and act on the need more quickly. That objective capacity, so necessary to steer clear of personalizing the child's negative behaviors, is well honed at this point and allows parents to feel a sense of confidence they lacked earlier on in the process.

At this point, the parents may be experiencing . . .
➤ acceptance of who the child is
➤ a sense of feeling less crazy and guarded as their more secure and steady attachment manifests
➤ raised expectations and lower defenses, which can make slight regressions feel catastrophic

➤ more normalcy because life revolves around activities versus therapy and the child's disturbance, and the family can bounce back more quickly

➤ some reciprocity and success in the relationship

➤ increased confidence in use of treatment principles and the capacity to intervene before a crisis occurs

➤ a better clue to when their child is in a regressed mode and needs extra help

➤ the ability to make distinctions between their emotional issues and the child's, recognizing that all they can control is their own response

While the child may be experiencing . . .

➤ less fear of those who have hurt him in the past

➤ that his true self is more accepted and can be contained in the family

➤ a feeling of normalcy because, increasingly, life revolves around activities versus therapy and the child's disturbance

➤ lower anxiety and more empathy for parents

➤ a broader range of emotions within himself, such as confusion, loneliness, or aggravation, as well as ability to name those feelings

➤ less defensiveness in seeking care and nurture

➤ some fun within parental and social relationships without having to be the center of attention

➤ internalization of conscience as he can now hold the question, "What would my parents say?" more in the foreground of his thought process

➤ increased capacity to be more accountable as his core shame is diminishing

RITE OF PASSAGE—MASTERY AND CONTROL: PROGRESS TOWARD PERMANENCY

Permanency is achieved in the form of adoption or through other legal means, and the family members now have a sense they have "arrived." This does not mean there cease to be issues related to identity, growth, and adjustment the family must traverse, but being on the other side of the mountain they just climbed together allows the family the momentum it needs to stay on a more successful track. The family shift toward competency is palpable in the way in which parents more confidently negotiate

Adoption is also about loss—loss for the child in dreams of living with his birth family; loss for you in having a "normal" family

difficulties that arise and in the speed at which the child processes upsets and returns to a state of equilibrium.

Ongoing feelings and experiences include those that all families undergo as the child meets subsequent developmental milestones on the way toward adulthood as well as those particular to families who have taken on an emotionally distressed child. The child still feels different from both family members and peers but wants to be "normal." As a result, the child may amplify, try to deny, or fight things that may indicate to others or signify to him that he is different, such as being of a different race, taking medication, going to therapy, or needing help in school.

Parents need to listen to what the child thinks is "normal" as far as identity is concerned and empathically allow him to have his feelings about how he sees himself in the world instead of trying to convince him otherwise. "It must be really hard to feel like you're so different from everyone else, like you don't belong" is a more helpful response than, "No, you're not different, you're one of us!" because the former mirrors the child's self and world views, whereas the latter negates them, which in effect negates the child. A child can only get from where he is to where parents might want him to be if they are willing genuinely to be with him where he is as long as he needs to be there.

This is the time when parents turn to helping their child cement trust in himself through merging accountability with responsibility. The more accountable the child is, the more freedom and responsibility he is given. Parents can build their child's confidence through statements such as, "You know how to make this decision in a way that's going to be helpful for you." They can put their child in an environment in which he is capable of successfully demonstrating that trust in himself. Parents can do some role-playing to prepare their child for new social situations in order to increase his confidence in those events. They are able to give their child more positive feedback and praise as he racks up more and more successes. Parents reinforce to their child that no matter what anyone does or says, it is *his* decision about how to respond that counts.

Parents come to accept the whole child for who he is, and the child comes to feel his parents' acceptance. The child also has accepted his

Forming the permanent relationship is ultimately about acceptance: the child accepting his parents as "good enough," and the parents accepting the child for who he is, not who they want him to be

parents as "good enough," and the parents feel their child's acceptance of them. Although they know they will never be "normal" or perfect, the parents and child have become a true family and can now see themselves and their ongoing struggles as more like those in other families. The family's acceptance of itself is the final achievement in a process that has been possibly the most difficult journey the family has ever taken, and yet, the most rewarding.

A Picture Is Worth a Thousand Words

After this close examination of the stages and aspects of the working through process, visualizing the overall process of permanency can be difficult. You have been immersed in detailed descriptions of each segment of the road to permanency in this lengthy chapter. Now, you need an image of the process that summarizes it visually to give you a feel for the permanency dance in a way reading about it cannot provide. The diagram below is a representation of this dance of belonging, which ultimately is about acceptance.

Stages of Treatment and Process of Permanency for Emotionally Distressed Children over Time

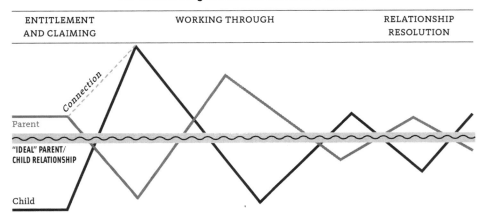

As you can see in the diagram, at first new parents are vulnerable and the child is not. As the dance continues, both parents and child go back and forth, often in different directions in terms of vulnerability, with an occasional meeting of shared vulnerability and shared hopes and dreams. As the child begins to work through and integrate his past into his present and as the parents come to accept the child for who he is, not who they want him to be, the cycles become closer and more coordinated. As the relationship evolves and resolves into a permanent sense of belonging, there can still be times of "not getting" each other, but those are fewer and less extreme.

Key Points for Chapter 11

1. It is the child who leads the dance steps of relationship while it is you, the parent, who determines the path across the floor. You are the dance partner as well as the coach.

2. The honeymoon period is the tender time full of hopes, worries, and newness. Your child may be on his best behavior or at his worst, as his anxiety about being acceptable is high.

3. Engagement is a more realistic time in which your child's issues may begin to come to the surface. Keeping structure high creates safety for this unfolding.

4. Working through is the time in which the child begins to feel safe enough to show you and himself who he really is. Traumas, fears, losses, and anxieties all can come into the relationship, and the child seeks a different outcome than he had before. This is the hardest work!

5. As your child is working through what it means to belong to your family, he may feel increasingly vulnerable and afraid; try to say "yes" as much as possible within this phase and be alert to your child's painful feelings.

6. Family integration is a more "normal" time as you—now your child's attuned parents—can clearly see the needs beneath his behavior.

7. In relationship resolution, many of the biggest losses, traumas, fears, and anxieties have been worked through and everyone just wants to be "normal." Keeping the structure high, but being more flexible, and keeping yourself responsive to your child's needs when big feelings emerge facilitates this resolution.

8. Remember that adoption is also about loss—loss for the child in dreams of living with his birth family and loss for you in having a "normal" family.
9. Forming the permanent relationship is ultimately about acceptance: the child accepting his parents as "good enough," and the parents accepting the child for who he is, not who they want him to be.

12.
Nobody Really Wants Me

Impact of Core Issues—Shame, Loss, Identity, Sexual Reactivity, and Psychiatric Disorders

Shame, blame, disrespect, betrayal, and the withholding of affection damage the roots from which love grows. Love can only survive these injuries if they are acknowledged, healed, and rare.

BRENÉ BROWN

 THE COACH WATCHED DeShane sink several baskets in a row in practice. When the coach enthusiastically said, "DeShane, you are a great basketball player!" DeShane responded angrily, "No, I'm not. I suck!" The more the coach insisted, the more frustrated and dejected DeShane became, until finally he threw the basketball as hard as he could and stormed out of the gym. Later, when DeShane had calmed down, the coach listened intently as DeShane proclaimed: "I'm just nothing, less than a pile of s**t under the bed. I mean, what kind of kid has a mother who chooses drugs over her kid, and gets rid of the kid? Every time you say I'm good, I know deep down I'm not, so it just makes me mad!" DeShane continued, now in an almost inaudible voice, "I get scared that you'll expect too much and that I'll fail. I really am just worthless."

At the Heart of the Matter

Every child working toward having a permanent home struggles with core shame, grief and loss, and identity issues. Additionally, the child may be struggling with other problems related to sexual abuse, genetics, developmental gaps, or early life experiences, both pre- and post-birth. Often, parents are not oriented toward sustaining awareness of the depth and scope of their child's problems and instead slip into their preformed, unrealistic expectations of their child and their desire for him to be okay. Thus, it is necessary that parents accept and maintain awareness of these factors as they work with their child. To stay open to and mindful of a child's core challenges and their origins may not be something parents desire to do, but it is essential. In each moment, the child is living out the manifestations of his difficult history, and to help the child heal, parents must attune to this reality as well.

Guilt, Shame, and Core Shame

There is a distinct difference between guilt and shame, and between shame and core shame. This distinction is a hierarchy of sorts: guilt is a sense of knowing we have *done* something wrong; shame is a temporary feeling that there is something wrong *about us*; and core shame is the chronic feeling that *we are bad, worthless beings*. In the story above, DeShane clearly experiences core shame, no matter how successful his actions are.

Feeling guilt is a ubiquitous human experience, one that we all know to some degree. For example, if we drive forty miles per hour in a zone where the posted speed limit is twenty-five miles per hour, we may feel guilty for doing so, even if we do not get a ticket for speeding. Guilt serves the purpose of correcting our behavior by aligning our moral compass so that we remain on the right side of the law and act according to the social mores of our culture. Guilt is a *necessary* feeling that allows any society to function without undo chaos or anarchy, whether that society is a primitive one or a modern one. Therefore, guilt is a useful feeling that allows human groups, large and small, to keep the order necessary to sustain our species' existence. Guilt requires that we experience the presence and importance of another human being.

Shame, on the other hand, is an undesirable, *unuseful* but *temporary* feeling that something is *wrong about us*—that we are deficient in some way. Unlike guilt, where the feeling has to do with a transgression or something that *we did* that was wrong, shame is a feeling that flushes over and through us, leaving us with a transient sense that something is wrong *with us* as individuals. Shame can be triggered by any event or action that temporarily renders us feeling "less than." The event may be something we or even someone else did that was wrong or incorrect, but instead of, or in addition to, feeling guilt—which is knowing we *did* something wrong—we feel like *something is wrong with us*. For instance, if we take a bottle of juice off the shelf in the store to purchase it and it slips out

---

Guilt is feeling bad for something we did, *shame* is temporarily feeling bad about who we are, and *core shame* is persistently feeling worthless no matter what successes we may have achieved

of our hands and shatters on the floor, we may feel a wave of shame flood over us when we tell the clerk about it so it can get cleaned up. Shame is an impermanent feeling that, unfortunately, most of us feel at times, but which passes relatively quickly and life goes on.

Core shame is the *engulfing* sense of worthlessness, a chronic feeling of being bad that is pervasive and persistent. Its origins lie in insufficient or abusive caregiving experience during infancy. At this crucial developmental time, if an infant does not get his needs met, does not get positive, accurate reflection on a regular basis from his primary caregiver, and/or suffers abuse and neglect, he develops a negative sense of self, which will color how he sees himself and the whole world as he grows. Although an infant cannot actually *think* the thought, "I am worthless," the *experience* of being neglected or given away by his birth mother implants that knowing at such a deep level that it becomes the child's core self-concept.

The way an infant comes to know he is valuable, loveable, and wanted is through his mother's loving eyes and through getting his needs met by her as they arise. Emotionally distressed children have not had this experience. Instead, they have been neglected, abused, or abandoned and/or have experienced too many transitions and caregivers. If a child is to come to feel he is worthwhile, he must experience consistent care and positive attention from his primary caregiver throughout his first few years. Developing self-worth goes hand in hand with forming a secure attachment with the primary caregiver, which is a process that takes place over time; it is not a one-time event.

When a child has core shame, it is always present to some degree and is seemingly "lying in wait" for an action or experience to trip the switch. Core shame can be flash-triggered by almost anything at anytime. This triggering may fly below or within the adult's radar, depending upon the distinctiveness of the child's behavior and/or the parent's empathic acuity. Sometimes the trigger can be a singular event, something that may create momentary guilt or shame in any of us—but results in the complete dysregulation of the emotionally distressed child because of his plummet into his core shame. Fortunately, few of us know this experience firsthand; thus, we need to learn about it to better understand the world from the emotionally distressed child's point of view.

Classic signs of a child tapping into core shame include enduring loss of eye contact, head turned down or away, painful blushing when given attention, slumping posture, markedly slowed body movement, succumbing to feelings of powerlessness and despair, and/or instant dysregulation into rage. Core shame taints the emotionally distressed child's world so that everything he sees, hears, smells, touches, and tastes is fouled, as if in just being who he is contaminates everything around him. It is not difficult for parents to identify the arousal of core shame if they know how it manifests in their unique child, if they are keenly attuned and are on the lookout for it. When parents keep part of their awareness tuned in to their distressed child's ever-present "shame channel," they can more effectively manage his fluctuating emotional states. So much of a child's reactivity is triggered by touching into his core shame, which is ever present and lies just under the surface.

Common Triggers for a Distressed Child's Core Shame

➤ Experiences or dynamics that remind the child of his abuse or abandonment
➤ Forced eye contact ("Don't look at me because you will see my awfulness.")
➤ Genuine or felt inability to do what is being asked ("I can't, so I am worthless.")
➤ Generalized praise (e.g., "You are such a good boy!") because it is the opposite of how the child feels about himself
➤ An adult saying "no" to something the child wants (The child takes it as personal rejection)
➤ Behavioral correction or consequences (The child experiences both as "I am bad.")
➤ Perceived or actual criticism
➤ Grades, ratings, comparisons, judgments, contests, competitive sports, and so on

Parents sometimes feel, and often it is true, that there is nothing they can do or say that will *not* trigger their child's core shame. When a child is consumed by core shame, parents cannot talk him out of it. A child engulfed in shame is dysregulated and is actually in an altered physiological state; therefore, shifting out of this state takes a physiological change. If the child can tolerate touch, parents can put a hand on or around his shoulder, hug him, or bring him next to them to sit as a gesture of acceptance. This provides the child with reregulation from the outside as his parents' touch shifts him into their own more regulated physiological state.

Changing location, activity, or environment may temporarily alleviate core shame, but only consistent acceptance and attachment can begin to heal core shame

If the child is in a place within himself where he cannot accept touch, parents can feel powerless in the face of their child's core shame because it is such an immobilizing state. However, if parents can remind themselves that the solution for physiological immobilization is mobilization, they can help their child begin to shift by changing his location, activity, or environment, getting the child something to eat or drink, having him take a bath or shower, or shifting the social mix. Although these momentary changes do not "cure" core shame, they can be helpful in remobilizing and shifting the child out of the depths of his shame for the time being.

To complicate matters, shame in one person often triggers shame in another, and parents are vulnerable to falling into their own unhealed shame each time their child is overcome by his. Therefore, parents need to be very familiar with the particulars of their own unfinished business so they can remain objective and untouched personally when their child becomes enveloped in his own shame.

Healing core shame in a child can seem like an impossible feat to parents because it is as if every cell in the child's body is infused with it. Parents can also feel disconnected because the enduring nature of a child's core shame is not something they can relate to, which can prevent them from truly seeing or attuning to their child. In addition, parents' true acceptance of the child precedes the child's acceptance of himself, often by a substantial margin of time, so patience can wear thin while parents wait for the child to catch up to their positive view of him.

If parents can remember that lack of attachment is also the correlate of core shame, they can hold on to the fact that along with the secure attachment they are cultivating with their child will come the development of his sense of self-worth. This knowledge can help parents sustain the hope they need in order to ride out their child's seemingly endless bouts of feeling worthless during the journey toward permanency. In the meantime, along the way, parents can sustain accurate empathy and mirroring to help their child see himself, to help him learn who he is and what he thinks and feels, and to let him know they really "get" him.

Accurate empathy and mirroring are carried out by reflecting back to the child his true feelings and thoughts in any given moment. When a child is engulfed in core shame, what he needs to hear is, "Wow . . . you are really feeling like you are a bad kid right now, and you can't understand how anyone can love or even like you." However, parents want so much for their child not to feel this way about himself that they are usually tempted to say something more like, "Don't feel bad about yourself. We love you and care about you, and you are a good kid." Unfortunately, a misattuned response like this only convinces the child that his parents just do not "get" him, and forces him to retreat further into his independent and closed-off world.

Parents do not have to *like* that their child is stuck in the revolving door of unworthiness and feeling like he is a bad kid, but they do need to *accept* him wherever he is in the moment. Parental patience and acceptance are the most powerful elixirs for the problem of core shame and are crucial elements of the relational developmental experience the child has been missing from the beginning. Consistent, *long-term use* of PLACE (playfulness, love, acceptance, curiosity, and empathy) and/or Language of Supportive Control will, over time, begin to create new neural pathways in the child's brain for the feeling of being valued and thus valuable. Eventually, this new network of neurons will become stronger and more used than that created by early neglect and abuse, and therefore able to preempt the child's habitual plunge into the rut of core shame.

Grief and Loss

When parents think of adoption, they usually think of gains: a family enlarges by adding another child or by welcoming its first; a child finds a forever family; a community grows in its comprehension of what true family is; and longings are fulfilled and dreams are actualized. While blood and chromosomes naturally generate familial connections, securing permanency for a child links hearts, hands, and lives to create family. Yet aside from all of the positives associated with finding a permanent home for a child, there are numerous losses experienced for all involved—adoptive parents, birth parents, and the child. Infertility or physical limitations may have interrupted plans to have a biological family, and personal circumstances or conditions beyond the birth parents' control may have forced them to give up their child. The result inevitably is unavoidable loss and pain for all, especially for the adoptive child.

Adoption is also about grief and loss, both for your child and for you

Grief and loss are two of the most crucial core issues children and families face when an emotionally distressed child is brought into the family with the goal of adoption. However, for the majority of children and families, feelings and issues of grief and loss, as such, run under the radar because they are often disguised as rage, aggression, anger, frustration, anxiety, regression, or withdrawal. If left unidentified, thus unaddressed, grief and loss issues do not lay dormant: they fester and swell into the vulnerable emotional space that exists between the child and his permanent parents, at the same time the parents are working to fill this gap with bonding experiences that will lead to attachment.

Emotional pain is no different from physical pain in that it is a signal something is wrong. Yet our culture tells us to avoid emotional pain or fix the problem causing the upset right away and put it behind us. This avoidant approach does not heal grief and loss, especially if the cause is abandonment by birth mother or removal from birth family, because when a child has these experiences, grief and loss become lifetime issues. *Permanent separation from birth mother sears a primal wound into a child's heart that cannot be excised.* It can be hard to comprehend that when a child is getting his needs fully met in a loving, permanent home that separation from birth mother could continue to leave such a deep wound. However, if we consider the fact that birth mother's womb was the sole environment in which the child began and lived life for nine months, we can see that being removed from birth mother feels like leaving Earth to live in space. We can live in space for a period of time if tethered to artificial life supports, but we feel ungrounded, alienated, and foundationally insecure until we arrive back on Earth. While there is no real substitute for birth mother, becoming a part of a permanent family can give a child the stability and quality of ongoing relationships necessary for a successful, connected life.

As much as parents would like to, they cannot take away their child's grief and loss to relieve his suffering, although they are not powerless in

Permanent separation from birth mother sears a primal wound into a child's heart that cannot be excised

helping their child navigate his painful issues. Right from the beginning, before their child enters their home, parents can remind themselves of the child's primal wound and seek information about their child's history and losses in order to prepare themselves to see through their child's surface emotions. The child will not be able to identify his feelings for himself and will need his parents not only to be aware that he has issues, but also to lead the way in identifying the true feelings associated with his losses that show up as negative behaviors. The following are areas of inquiry parents can explore regarding their child's history.

Gather Your Child's Background Information to Help Him Transition

➤ circumstances and information surrounding removal from the birth mother, especially the child's age and developmental status
➤ relationship history with subsequent caregiver(s)
➤ present status of the birth family and the child's contact with them
➤ whether there are siblings, and information about the child's past and current relationship with siblings
➤ abusive events and what is known about the gender/role/physique of abuser
➤ known trauma triggers (sounds, smells, sights, anniversaries, etc.)
➤ comfort items
➤ cultural losses
➤ availability of positive birth family contacts
➤ whether the child tends to internalize or externalize emotions

Parents also need to keep in mind that grief and loss are harder on children because children have a tendency to blame themselves. "There must be something wrong or bad about me, or she wouldn't have gotten rid of me" is the conclusion a child makes when removed from his birth mother. Children have no cognitive tools to make sense of their losses any other way, nor are they able to identify, cope with, or regulate the overwhelming emotions they feel. When parents have the information they need to begin to understand some of what their child has experienced, they can prepare themselves to handle the emergence of their child's related feelings. Remaining clear about the way in which each experience of loss has come about in their child's life, parents can be more objective in the way they interpret his behavior and respond.

The experience of loss has three parts: separation—the change that occurs when there is a relationship disruption; loss—the effect of that separation; and grief—the process through which the pain of loss is healed. If parents can identify the exact nature of these three aspects of each of the losses in their child's life, they have the information they need to guide their child through his grief. For example, looking at the child's separation from his birth mother, parents need to find out when, how, and why the separation occurred; how the child understands what happened and the effect this loss had on their child at the time and in the time since then; and their child's progress in the process of grieving.

For all of us, *grieving loss requires being in a trusting relationship*, which supplies us with the co-regulation of affect we need to process the traumatic experience, especially when that experience has been profound. Your relationship with your child is the safe holding environment he needs to fully let go/let down all of his feelings and to come to terms with his experience both cognitively and emotionally. Your ability to help your child make sense of his experience, *without blaming his birth parents*, is crucial, because the child does not have the perspective or cognitive ability to create context for events. Loss can seem incomprehensible, so to learn to live with a loss, your child needs to make some kind of sense of it in the manner of a story that includes a beginning, a middle, and an end.

Parents do not necessarily need to create the entire context for a child's loss: through co-creation, parents and child can develop a story that fits for him in meaning and is cognitively understandable for his current stage of development. The story they create is one that can be retold whenever the child needs to have a connection point for his feelings or when he needs to hear the story again for comfort. Even an experience of loss, if it is put into a narrative context, can be of comfort to a grieving child because it gives him something palpable he can hold on to when the object of the loss is absent.

Each broken attachment that is negatively affecting a child's development is a loss that needs to be grieved in all of grief's stages. Grieving is a nonlinear phenomenon, and grief comes in waves that are triggered by memory, circumstances, meeting developmental milestones, and experiencing progress in relationship growth between the child and his

---

Grieving loss requires being in a trusting relationship

permanent parents. Loss occurs not just when a child loses someone in death or through being abandoned. For a child, loss occurs each time he is moved on his way toward permanent placement, it occurs when he is separated from his siblings, and it occurs when the simplest of objects gets taken away, for example, an old shirt he may have had prior to permanency. Sensitivity to the need a child has for knowledge of his history, for ties to his culture of origin, for maintaining relationships from his past, and even for fantasies about birth family will help parents empathize with their child and provide him with what he must have to feel he belongs in the world.

Parents can identify and remain alert for current events that trigger their child's grief, and they can anticipate events that potentially may arouse feelings of loss in him; not for the purpose of suppressing them, but rather to prepare themselves to support their child when those feelings arise. *A child's ability to attach depends upon him having the opportunity to thoroughly grieve his losses.* If a child has not adequately grieved, compounded grief can develop and become a barrier to attachment with his permanent parents. Waiting until the child's feelings of loss erupt in dysregulated behavior is not in the best interest of the child or the family. Rather than allowing themselves to feel threatened by their child's allegiance to and love for his birth family, parents can take a proactive stance and sit with their child regularly to address his grief.

Even if a child does not remember his birth parents and birth family members, he still will want to know and to hear about them. The child's love and loyalty continue even if he was abused by those who were supposed to love him, and he must sense that his permanent parents have respect for his roots in order to trust and get close to his new family. Accepting the child's grief over the loss of his biological family may be one of the hardest things parents have to do, especially if their child was abused by members of that family. An open attitude on the parents' part is crucial and over time will, in fact, foster their child's respect and love for them.

Parents must be at least somewhat objective during times their child

---

Grief occurs in waves, and each new loss brings with it the sadness of prior losses. Your child's ability to attach to you depends on him grieving all of his prior losses.

is grieving, particularly at the beginning of placement. If parents get too close to the child too fast, it will be extremely hard for them to treat those who have hurt the child with any modicum of respect. Additionally, the child will likely not attach as quickly to his parents as they will to him because he is coming from a place of grief, shame, and deep hurt, whereas the parents are beginning with open and willing hearts. However, parents need not sit idly by while their child suffers; instead, they can maintain consistent awareness, be honest about facts, and translate their knowledge of the child's need to grieve into action.

Proactive Parenting for Handling Grief
➤ drawing out his feelings and thoughts consistently
➤ remembering his layered history
➤ journaling for/with child
➤ co-creating the child's life book
➤ reading storybooks about grief and loss
➤ being patient with child's need for repetition of his loss history
➤ determining when grief is productive or perseverative

Response to Loss at Various Developmental Stages

The effects of grief and loss are not necessarily greater or lesser at any particular age, but the developmental stage a child is in at the time of the loss tremendously affects his ability to process the loss. Refer back to Chapter 4 to review relational and psychosocial stages so you can understand the developmental level from which your child's grief arises. Suffering a loss at any stage of development usually leads to the child's regression to a previous stage and results in a temporary reversal of his most recently acquired skill(s). The blow to a child's psyche when he experiences loss shifts the child into survival mode, particularly when the loss is of the child's primary caregiver. Longing for his loved one, having to adapt to a new situation, learning new rules, and trying to get used to new people

---

Considering their child's age and maturity, parents will need to help him find developmentally appropriate ways to understand and cope with his losses

takes all of the child's energy, leaving none for the normal process of development. Even years later, a child can remain stuck at the developmental stage he was working through at the time the serious loss occurred.

Knowing more about how a child at a particular age generally experiences loss can help parents discover the best way to help their child. For example, if the loss occurred in infancy when the developmental task is resolution of the trust versus mistrust dilemma, the child may never have learned to trust anyone but himself. If the loss occurred when the child was eighteen months, just as he was beginning to separate psychologically from his mother, he may be terrified of separation or avoid relationships completely for fear of loss. Development and structure of a child's personality are endangered when a child experiences significant loss, and parents need to remember this when they realize their child is developmentally behind his peers. The child can catch up if parents persist in forming a new relationship with him at the same time they accept and support him in processing his grief.

Grief and Loss: Ages 0–4

Between the ages of zero and four, a child who has experienced significant loss

➤ may exhibit strong attachment to present primary caregiver and excessive fear when separated or may seem unaffected
➤ may be excessively fussy or need to be cuddled more than usual
➤ cannot understand the concept of forever
➤ may be sensitive to changes in routine
➤ may display regressive behaviors
➤ may understand something major is going on and feel like the cause of it
➤ may respond intensely but briefly and frequently
➤ may wonder what will happen and who will take care of him
➤ may remain very present-oriented
➤ may engage in magical thinking and mistake fantasy for reality
➤ will have minimal or no knowledge or understanding of the concept of permanent loss

Parents can respond supportively by

➤ being comforting
➤ holding
➤ playing with and reassuring

➤ maintaining regular routines
➤ using simple, honest words and phrases
➤ maintaining a secure, loving environment
➤ creating stories that mirror the child's actual loss experience
➤ including the child in grieving rituals

Grief and Loss: Ages 4–7
Between the ages of four and seven, a child who has experienced significant loss may
➤ engage in fantasy and magical thinking
➤ feel responsible for the loss
➤ continue to see the loss as reversible ("If I am better, mommy will return")
➤ feel confusion, general distress, and disorientation
➤ display regressive behaviors
➤ have the need to understand the loss in a concrete way
➤ express denial, anger, and sorrow
➤ behave as though nothing has happened
➤ need extra physical activity
➤ ask questions repeatedly
➤ be agitated at night
➤ have frightening dreams or perseverate on boogiemen, ghosts, and monsters
Parents can respond supportively by
➤ using comforting words
➤ answering questions directly and honestly
➤ giving reassurance about the future
➤ creating times to talk about feelings
➤ offering physical outlets
➤ reading to the child
➤ co-creating a narrative of the child's actual loss experience
➤ including the child in grief and loss rituals

Grief and Loss: Ages 7–11
Between the ages of seven and eleven, a child who has experienced significant loss may
➤ see loss as a punishment
➤ begin to seek peer conformity

➤ become stuck on everything being "fair," and loss is never fair
➤ start to ask questions that are very specific and detail-oriented
➤ begin to explore the concept of forever
➤ no longer see death as reversible
➤ experience shock, denial, anxiety, and distress
➤ wear a facade of coping
➤ have morbid curiosity
➤ struggle to develop a philosophy that accepts reality but still defends against daily vulnerability

Parents can respond supportively by
➤ allowing the child to express secret fears and desires
➤ letting the child know that he did not cause the loss, nor can he change it
➤ giving simple and honest explanations and answers
➤ looking for and addressing confused thinking
➤ reassuring the child about the future
➤ playing together with the child
➤ co-creating stories that mirror the child's actual loss experience
➤ including the child in grieving rituals

Grief and Loss: Ages 11 and up

An adolescent who has experienced significant loss may
➤ increase his struggle for independence
➤ be tempted to take risks in response to pain of loss
➤ find it difficult to listen to adults, especially parents
➤ feel shock, anxiety, distress, denial, anger, depression, withdrawal, and/or aggression
➤ respond like an adult but have fewer coping mechanisms
➤ feel younger and therefore more vulnerable
➤ feel a need to try to defy death

Parents can respond supportively by
➤ allowing and encouraging the teen to vent feelings
➤ encouraging peer support
➤ helping him find a structured teen group that is dealing with loss issues
➤ giving him appropriate reading, or by reading to him
➤ involving supportive adults
➤ maintaining a consistent environment

➤ co-creating a narrative of the child's actual loss experience
➤ including him in grief and loss rituals
➤ encouraging involvement with the family
➤ being extra-sensitive to his struggles with identity

For children of all ages, two major global issues related to loss are fear of attachment and a need to be in control. In general, the grieving child may have temper outbursts, become unusually loud and noisy, initiate fights with others, defy authority, or simply rebel against everything and everybody. Somatic complaints, irritability, crankiness, and social withdrawal are particularly common in a grieving child. The child may often have low self-esteem, have poor social skills, be pessimistic, and be dealing with some degree of depression, which may display as sadness, anxiety, and restless irritability, as well as have eating or sleeping problems. Since children are rarely able to articulate their grief verbally without adult assistance, they may show their grief in feelings or behaviors.

Behaviors Associated with Grief
➤ insecurity
➤ fear of abandonment
➤ trying to provoke being punished
➤ becoming self-protective against future losses
➤ externalizing or internalizing a variety of feelings

Parents have to be in the right place within themselves to provide supportive responses to their child's grief. Personal issues of grief must be resolved enough to be set aside in order to see the child's issues clearly. Parents must also create an atmosphere conducive to personal interaction and then take the right tact in order to offer the level of safety and availability the child needs to process his grief. The following are some general guidelines parents can follow when they intend to address their child's feelings of loss.

Parent Guidelines for Addressing Loss
➤ Stop, regulate your own breathing, and calm yourself
➤ Be patient
➤ Think about what you want to say and be honest with the child about your thoughts, concerns, and feelings

➤ Think about how the child may hear your words

➤ Ask questions when you are in doubt (i.e., "How is that for you?" "How do you feel right now?" "Can you tell me more about that?" "What do you think you might need?")

➤ Use "I" statements such as, "I feel . . . ," "I believe . . . ," "I would want . . ." instead of statements such as, "You should," "That's wrong," or "Everything will be okay"

➤ Stay in the present as much as possible (e.g., "Right now, what might you need?" or "How do you feel right now?")

➤ Use concrete words to define loss (e.g., "death" instead of "gone away")

➤ Use short sentences and age-appropriate vocabulary

Parents do not have to always be blindsided by their child's bouts of grief. They can adjust their expectations and prepare themselves to identify times when their child may be triggered into feeling the grief of losses he has survived. Also, parents can proactively create opportunities for their child to process the grief about his losses at times he is most likely to feel it so that he does not have to unnecessarily experience loss of control or emotional meltdowns every time he needs to mourn. Honoring the fact that an adoptive child has losses he will need to mourn and preparing to be there for him when he grieves is a powerful way to increase the depth of trust a child feels because it gives the child the sense that his parents are competent and capable of handling anything he may need them to.

Each adopted child will experience the gains and losses of adoption differently. Some will frequently return to the losses and need to process them repeatedly. Others will walk through life with resilience and confidence and have a limited number of questions related to the adoption journey. No matter what the adopted child's experience is, it can be a parent's joy and privilege to be a sojourner with him, a guide helping answer his questions that can be answered, a catalyst for him to actualize his future, and a collector of tears that he may shed along the way.

Identity

Identity is the sense of self that allows for consistency and continuity in personality over time. When a child is born into his birth family, his sense of identity is contiguous from conception through birth and throughout

Recognizing and Honoring Your Child's Loss

Rosemary Miller (2011) has proposed the following ways for parents to recognize and honor their adoptive child's loss. The elaboration for each of Miller's points is ours.

1. *Expect adoption-related losses to surface during particular rites of passage.* For example, it is quite common for adopted children to think of their birth families around the time of birthdays, at graduations from elementary school or high school, on wedding days, on Mother's/Father's Days, or other celebratory occasions. Recall Juli's meltdown in Chapter 9. Parents can avoid being caught off guard if their adopted child seems moody, irritable, or uncharacteristically agitated on days like these.

2. *Plan ahead; give yourself and your adopted child time to process and grieve losses.*
If parents notice that their child is sad due to a loss related to adoption, or if parents anticipate that emotions related to adoption may be brewing, they can create time and space to process these emotions. For example, parents might plan a special tea for a few days before their child's birthday. During the tea, they can sit together with cups of tea and the child's favorite cookies and have an extra, special teacup on the table in honor of the child's birth mother. Sometimes this type of ceremony can elicit conversation, while at other times the symbolic acknowledging of birth family can be a healing gesture without words.

3. *Encourage your child's tears.*
A child's resilience can be fostered by parents supporting the child's expression of emotions. Sometimes it can be uncomfortable for parents when their child is expressing deep emotions, especially sadness and anger, but adopted children need to have the freedom to grieve the losses they have suffered, so parents must discover a way for themselves to be there for the child.

4. *Help your child find words for his deep inner sadness and help him discover the root of his feelings.*
For instance, "You seem a little sad today—maybe you would want to take a walk and talk," or "It seemed like you were feeling upset when we were looking at your baby book. I wonder which of the pictures or stories made you start to feel that way." As long as exploration is not done in a demanding way, it does not hurt for parents to explore and to open a door for sharing and healing. By maintaining openness, parents will ultimately offer a safe place for their child to process his feelings and heal.

◆ *continued next page*

◆ *continued from previous page*

5. *Honor the journey-like nature of the adoption process.*
Often the easiest answer, word, or story can help heal the heart of a hurting child. At first, parents can give little bits of information and small details to satisfy their child's questions about his adoption journey. Then, as the journey progresses and as the child ages and matures, more details can be added to fill out the adoptive story and give the child a fuller understanding. As the child is ready for details, parents can talk about his birth family and the details surrounding the placement for adoption.

6. *Help your child create his life book and/or help him keep a running journal.*
Even if there are no photos of the child before he was adopted or of the birth family, there is still a history that can be fleshed out with drawings or pictures cut out of magazines to represent the child as an infant or toddler. Whenever the child has questions about his life prior to adoption, parents then get out his life book and tell the story they have created in there, filling in the blank spaces by asking questions such as, "What do you imagine the house you lived in when you were a baby looked like?" Children love to hear their own stories over and over, even if the information is not accurate in every detail, and it can be a bonding experience between adoptive parents and child as well.

7. *Encourage and help your child to write letters to his or her birth parents—ones he may or may not actually send.*
The child can write anything expressing anger or love, regrets or joy, or lists of questions, updates about his life—nothing is off-limits. Parents can emphasize that no one, including them, ever has to read the letters and that it is up to the child whether he wants to mail those letters.

8. *Visit your adoptive child's place of birth.*
In circumstances where this cannot be done right away or at all, parents can help their child find and study information about his place of birth or culture. In taking an active role in embracing the homeland and culture of the child, parents can affirm their acceptance of him, which increases his feelings of worthiness.

9. *Celebrate your adoptive child's unique cultural background.*
Reflect positives about the child and connect those positives with the child's birth parents. For example, an adoptive parent might say, "I bet one of the reasons you are so handsome and smart is because you have your birth parents' genes." If the child happens to enjoy a different cultural heritage than his adoptive parents, they may want to make an effort to discover and acknowledge holidays and other traditions unique to his place or culture of origin. ◆

his childhood development. Then in adolescence, from the foundation of belonging to his birth family, the teen explores his identity and tries on altered personas, which eventually leads him to embrace the attributes, ambitions, interests, and social standing he has discovered that define who he is. The child raised in his birth family remains tethered to his birth family when he becomes an adult, whether by active intent or passive fact. There is no deeper foundational affiliation that can become a part of one's identity than being related by blood.

However, when a child is taken away from his birth family for whatever reason, he loses that foundational affiliation, the wellspring of who he is, and he cannot get over the feeling of being untethered in the world at some level. This is the crux of the adopted child's dilemma, and the core issue he will struggle with his whole life to a greater or lesser degree depending on his temperament, developmental stage, and history before and after separation from his birth family. Even when separated at birth and taken immediately into a permanent family who raises him like one of their own, the child knows and feels deep within himself that he does not fully belong. Some children describe feeling like they just don't "fit." This knowing remains rooted in the child's cellular memory and cannot be expunged with time or circumstance.

A child's history, no matter how traumatic or pleasurable, is part of his identity, and knowing that history is essential for the child to be able to integrate all parts of himself. As the child develops, his parents help him flesh out his narrative through a life book and/or as a verbal story. As parents work through his issues with him, the child's life story grows and deepens. Discovery of self is one of the most important tasks in life, and for a child whose past is not wholly known, it is even more crucial.

Being separated from birth family is not the only source of loss there is for an adopted child. As a "transplant," the child carries with him a sense that he does not belong due to additional factors such as culture, race, ethnicity, and physical looks. It is essential that permanent parents make a wholehearted effort to discover, understand, and honor the history,

---

Some adopted children feel that they simply don't belong within the new family. Honoring your child's history helps him solidify his unique story and consolidate his identity.

values, and culture of the child's birth parents, no matter how similar or dissimilar these may be to their own. The more respectful and accepting parents are of their child's heritage, the more respected and accepted the child will feel. Embracing the whole child includes going the extra mile necessary to find out about his previous affiliations, even if the child does not consciously remember them himself.

When digging into a child's past, parents often find that some of their child's behaviors actually reflect the values and culture of his birth family. Becoming familiar with their child's cultural heritage, his birth family's native language, and his birth family's history gives parents important insights into who their child is, which allow them to truly embrace him as an individual. This enables the parents to distance themselves from their expectations for who they thought their child would be or who they needed him to be, freeing them up to actively support their child's individuality and his developing identity.

While racial, cultural, and ethnic differences between an adopted child and his parents may remain apparent to outsiders, parents can become blind to the importance of the issue of identity for their child because they tend not to see his dissimilarities as he is absorbed by the family. However, parents realizing and acknowledging that the need for their child to come to terms with his identity is the most central issue as he moves into adolescence can make all of the difference in his chances for success and in him becoming well adjusted. Already carrying core shame due to the feeling of being rejected by the birth mother, a child with obvious racial and cultural differences can feel like an outcast in his permanent family and community, leaving him no place to feel like he belongs.

Integrating a child's uniqueness into family life is not an optional part of creating permanency for a child. Bringing a child of another race or culture into the family changes that family forever. This is true for a child with "invisible" differences as well. An adoptive family is actually a blended family in the sense of the term that is commonly used for stepfamilies— the union of members of two different families who bring separate and

---

**An adoptive family is actually the union of members
of two different families who bring separate and unique experiences,
world views, interests, values, and norms with them**

unique experiences, world views, interests, values, and norms with them, all of which must be equally valued and honored. Diminishing the importance of these contributions when it is the addition of "only" a single child to the family is a mistake that will eventually lead to unrest within the family because the "two sides" have not reconciled their differences to become one.

Unfortunately, a single child cannot advocate directly for his set of unique contributions to the creation of the new, third entity—the family created by the merging of two disparate worlds—so either he and his history of previous affiliations are recognized and valued as an equal part of the newly blended family, or they are not. It is up to the child's permanent parents to make this happen, and it behooves them to do so if they are to create a harmonious blended family. Too often, the child's contributions to his permanent family are overlooked, undervalued, or not recognized at all.

Even if the child were to come from a birth family whose racial and cultural differences from his new family seem minimal, those differences largely define who the child is and must be acknowledged. The difference it makes for parents to pursue and hold this level of respect for the child as the whole, separate entity he is and for his unique and valuable contributions to the family is tremendous. The uniqueness of a child can be both the source of family discord and the solution to it.

Other Specific Issues of Concern

For you to help your child in every way possible, identifying deficits is essential and provides a starting point for the pursuit of intervention, accommodation, and healing. Being able to pinpoint the child's present handicaps gives parents an explanation for the difficulties their child may be experiencing, a source of empathy, and a path to follow toward hope and healing. Keeping an open mind, knowing the scope of possibilities, and becoming familiar with the range of interventions available allow parents to shift out of helplessness and take what action they can to help their child maximize his capacity for eventual independence.

Genetic Disorders

Genes determine everything from eye color to basic intellectual capacity to potential for longevity. Some genetic traits are more "fixed" than others, in that environmental influences can act to switch on or switch off the mechanism of some genes, while other traits cannot be influenced at all. In some areas, a child's genetic makeup can be as influential as are his life experiences in determining who he is, while for other genetic traits there may be no potential for change. For example, a child might be born with a potential for a high IQ, but if he does not receive adequate attention and mental stimulation, he will not reach that potential, whereas there are no environmental influences that can alter his eye color.

Genetic disorders such as Down syndrome, cystic fibrosis, and sickle cell anemia are fixed problems that environment cannot change. As we noted in Chapter 2, a child's temperament is genetically defined and fixed, and it can affect his parents' ability to raise him if it conflicts with their own temperament or presents challenges the parents cannot or do not know how to handle. For fixed problems, parents focus on helping the child cope with life's challenges and to "learn to live with it" because they cannot repair or change the problem. Identifying exactly what genetically fixed disorder or temperamental challenges their child may have can help parents seek the optimal compensatory interventions that can improve and maximize his functionality.

There are brain-based disorders that may be genetic and/or environmentally induced, including mental retardation, schizophrenic disorders, autistic-spectrum disorders, sensory integration/sensitivity problems, and alcohol/drug–related neurodevelopmental disorder. Ongoing research is examining the origins of many of these permanent problems to determine their nature/nurture etiologies in order to develop preventative and therapeutic interventions that will improve prognosis.

Unfortunately, where potentiated genetic changes are concerned, children affected by early trauma have already had the negative experiences that have either activated or not activated some of their genes. For example, the genetic predisposition for a mood or anxiety disorder can become an actual disorder if the "right" environmental conditions have acted upon the set of genes that hold the potential for that disorder to develop. Stress, which can be defined as the deleterious effects that certain experiences

**Genetic disorders can be activated or intensified
by early life stressors for your child**

have on one's biochemistry, is one of the most powerful agents responsible for "switching on" latent genes which are coded for, say, a mood disorder. Environmental toxins, in utero exposure to substances consumed by the birth mother, and maternal stress caused by ongoing abuse or anxiety are all experiences that can be responsible for affecting gene potentiation in the preborn child. During and after birth, trauma, abuse, and neglect as well as environmental toxins can prevent or potentiate genetic unfolding.

Generally, children come into permanent homes after experiential and environmental damages have taken their toll, so parents are in the position of having to deal with the effects past experiences have had on their child. For the most part, parents cannot fully undo the damage, but if they can assemble as detailed a history of their child as possible, they can both anticipate and recognize symptoms of the problems that have resulted from prior negative environmental experiences so they can address them more effectively. For example, if a child was moved multiple times prior to his permanent placement and, over time, the resultant pattern of stress developed into selective mutism, any change in his present daily routine may trigger a return of this stress-induced silence. However, the child's parents can begin to work with him each time he is triggered to rewire his anxiety reaction via consistent, supportive emotional co-regulation.

Associated with either traumatic experience or lack of necessary experience, the development of the frontal cortex—the area of the brain crucial to executive functioning and overall self-control—can be responsible for behavioral disorders, including attachment disorder, attention-deficit/hyperactivity disorder (ADHD), oppositional defiant disorder, conduct disorder, and intermittent explosive disorder. Prior to intervention, expecting a child with one of these behavioral deficits to be able to handle himself in a better way is unrealistic because he is doing the best he can with the brain structure he has. With relational intervention that focuses on helping the child regulate himself, however, it is often possible to promote change at the structural level of the brain that largely heals these deficits.

Related to the capacity of the brain to process information are problems such as speech and language disorders, mathematics disorder, learning disabilities, memory impairment (acquisition, encoding, storage, and retrieval of information), sensory integration/sensitivity problems, and motor (body movement) disorders. Myriad causes exist for these challenges, some related to genetics, some to in utero or environmental toxins, and some to trauma. If the cause is not one of fixed genetics, interventions facilitated through relationship can be effective in improving these conditions. The influence of repetitive, supportive co-regulation of experience can create new neural pathways that solidify a new ability in the brain's structure.

Psychiatric Disorders

As genetics interact with developmental traumas and losses, the resulting behaviors can look like a psychiatric illness, and indeed may be. The emotional disturbance may be a normal response to what was an abnormal environment—your child's life before he arrived in your care—rather than an abnormal response to a normal environment—an inherited psychiatric illness—or may be a combination. In treating behavioral and emotional manifestations of early distress, parents and physicians must understand that medication is not a cure but a useful adjunct that can help regulate the child as the relationship takes over.

Mood disorders can sometimes impair a child's overall functioning, as if there were an opaque veil between the child and the world. Mood disorders include dysthymic disorder (mild, but prolonged depression), seasonal affective disorder (seasonal depression), major depressive disorders, and bipolar (manic-depressive) disorders. Additionally, abandonment depression and deep grief and loss issues can be a burden to a child's overall functioning, complicating the picture. These grief issues can stand alone, add to temperamental problems, or accompany other disorders. A prime example of coexisting disorders for a child working toward permanency is abandonment depression intermingled with attachment disorder. Depressed children don't always look depressed; they may appear angry, agitated, and easily triggered into rage.

Anxiety disorders can be present as a result of early trauma by way of an inherited genetic predisposition or through trauma taxing the body's stress mechanism. These include post-traumatic stress disorder (PTSD), panic disorder, generalized anxiety disorder, separation anxiety disorder, and others. Major psychiatric disorders such as schizophrenia, schizoaffective disorder, delusional disorders, and autism spectrum disorder have been shown to be heritable as well as possibly environmentally inducible. Again, these disorders can stand alone, be an integral aspect of temperament, or accompany other problems.

Unfortunately, there are still societal stigmas that brand a child's mental disorder either as a parent's failure or as a "weakness," so parents may not feel comfortable admitting that their child is struggling. These stigmas set up unfortunate roadblocks to individuals and families getting treatment and help. The truth is that most brain-based ("mental") problems are no different from body-based ("physical") problems such as diabetes or high blood pressure when it comes to treatment because most can be effectively treated with medication, behaviorally targeted interventions, and/or individual or family therapy. Getting past the stigma in order to get help can be the most difficult part of the process for some parents.

The importance of seeking medical assistance cannot be overstated because some problems cannot be fixed with behavioral or therapeutic interventions alone. When early experience "has become flesh"—that is, has become part of the neural functioning of the brain—treatment has to include the modifying neurochemical responses as well as understanding and modifying the emotions and relationship. Research has shown that the most effective treatment involves a combination of both medication and behavioral/therapeutic interventions.

Indeed, this dual approach may well prove to be the most efficacious way to treat most brain-based or body-based disorders. For example, there are numerous books, methods, and therapeutic interventions that address the problematic behaviors associated with ADHD. Many of the ideas espoused in these approaches can be very useful, although they may only prove to be partially effective because the biochemical aspect of ADHD also may need to be addressed to fully alleviate the problem. Dietary alteration may be a place parents feel comfortable starting to intervene biochemically when their child is struggling with an identified disorder. Parents may decide to look into vitamin and amino acid therapy, or they may want to try what alternative medicine has to offer.

If parents receive a diagnosis for their child that has been proven to respond to pharmaceutical intervention, they nevertheless may be leery of starting their child on a psychotropic medication. To become clear and objective about what to do, parents can turn to recent literature about the particular medication to get a better understanding of the drug's biochemical action, its effectiveness, and its safety track record. Parents can also

---

Psychotropic medication may be a useful aid in helping regulate your child. The addition of psychiatric medication to therapy interventions can make all interventions more effective.

gain information and peace of mind by joining an Internet forum that focuses on the topic of their child's disorder or do web searches regarding the proposed medication.

After researching, parents may agree to a medication trial overseen by their medical provider, which begins with establishing a formal or informal baseline—basically a "snapshot" of the child's present functioning. Next, parents along with their provider would agree on a timeline that would allow them to see if the medication might work for the child and would discuss any possible side effects the parents should watch for. At the end of the trial period, when the parents bring the child back to the provider, they would take another "snapshot" of the child's functioning on the medication. Then, comparing the before and after profiles and discussing the pros and cons of the child continuing the medication, the parents decide whether to continue the medication, change the medication or its dose, or discontinue it.

In dealing with challenging children, parents who assume that it is only the quality of their parenting that can make a difference often set themselves up to feel like failures. If a child truly has a brain-based condition that needs to be addressed medically, parents may not be doing all they can to help unless they seek medical intervention. Getting therapeutic support for parenting the challenging child, along with whatever medical support is called for, will ensure that parents are doing everything they can to help their child be the best that he can be. In keeping an open mind and a full toolbox, parents can succeed with their goal of helping heal their emotionally distressed child.

Alcohol-Related Neurodevelopmental Disorder (ARND) and Maternal Drug Abuse

Especially virulent to a child's brain development, in utero exposure to alcohol is responsible for permanent cognitive and emotional disabilities in increasing numbers of children who are being integrated into permanent families out of foster care and orphanages and via adoption agencies. Alcohol-related neurodevelopmental disorder (ARND), formerly referred to as fetal alcohol syndrome or disorder, is one of the most devastating problems a child can have because the damage is permanent. Throughout its development, a baby's brain passes through critical periods that are especially vulnerable to impairment. Each of these periods of development is unique in that each marks the unfolding of very specific parts of the brain. The brain's structures are interrelated and are meant to unfold in a particular sequence and with precise timing. The quality of neural architecture that is created will determine the level of functioning of the whole brain as well as its parts.

During the first trimester, as stem cells migrate to form brain tissue, their organization is particularly vulnerable to disruption in the presence of alcohol. This is the time when the brain stem and mid-brain—the areas responsible for autonomic regulation, sensorial capacity, motor abilities, and basic reflexes—begin to develop, as well as the time alcohol can cause the facial and limb abnormalities associated with the most severe type of ARND. The second trimester is the time where the presence of alcohol in the growing brain causes the majority of the clinical behavioral features of ARND due to disturbance in the allocation and differentiation of the migrating cells to various parts of the brain. In the third trimester, the presence of alcohol leads to cognitive problems such as deficiencies in encoding of visual and auditory information, which can affect the child's academic abilities in reading and math.

Parents who discover that their child has been affected by alcohol in utero—a determination that can be made by historical review (if the prenatal information is available), observation, and neuropsychological testing—can feel helpless and defeated even before they have begun parenting. Although for the most part brain damage caused by fetal exposure to alcohol cannot be ameliorated, parents can get specific support and interventions that accommodate the child's disabilities and can maximize his potential and success. The key is to find out what the child can and cannot do, adjust expectations accordingly, and employ the specific accommodations the child needs to succeed in whatever capacity he can.

Research continues to look at the effects of illegal and prescription drug abuse on the developing fetus, and it appears that there are various ways these substances in their numerous classes can negatively affect brain development during each of the three trimesters. We have not gone into detail about these effects here because it is often the case that illegal use of drugs is accompanied by alcohol abuse, and the possible combinations of

---

Exposure to alcohol in utero can cause permanent cognitive and emotional disabilities. The timing of exposure determines which systems are impacted.

various substances used at particular stages of fetal development are too numerous to make definitive conclusions regarding damage to the growing brain. Thus, we have focused here on the effects of alcohol use on fetal development and the ways alcohol permanently damages the growing brain because it is the most studied and most widely abused neurotoxin available.

Sensory Integration Issues

Parents may find that their child suffers from sensory integration deficits, again affirmed through observation and testing. Sensory issues range from those characterized by high oversensitivity to environmental and interactive stressors, known as sensory-avoidant, to those that are related to diminished sensitivity, known as sensory-seeking. Discovering that their child's challenging behaviors are related to sensory issues can be a relief for parents who may have tried a wide array of interventions to no avail. The highly anxious whiny or distracted (sensory-avoidant) child may be responding to relational stress and/or environmental stimuli that feel overwhelming to him, such as noise, bright light, touch, tastes, or smells. The sensory-avoidant child can be soothed by reducing or removing the offending stimuli in the moment and treated with occupational therapy, physical therapy, or neurofeedback for a more permanent solution.

A child who is highly accident-prone, does not have the ability to physically regulate himself, and has personal boundary issues where touch is concerned may be sensory-seeking because he does not register pain or touch as he should physiologically. This child, too, can be helped in the long run via the same class of interventions mentioned above, though through different exercises. More immediately, the sensory-seeking child can be given therapeutic substitutes to meet his need for physical contact, such as sitting on a ball chair at his desk, by wearing weighted clothing, or by wrestling with an adult who regulates the action. Sensory issues can be improved or, in some cases, eliminated if an accurate diagnosis is made as early as possible and effective intervention ensues.

Sensory integration issues may arise as a result of abuse or neglect. Hypersensitivity or insensitivity to touch, sound, or noise or difficulty reading or balancing may impact the child.

Cognitive and Learning Disorders

Cognitive and learning disorders can result from genetics, fetal exposure to toxins, environmental deprivation, or abuse. Hope for permanent improvement through therapeutic intervention depends upon the origin of a child's disorder and the area of the brain that has been affected, but in all cases accommodations can be employed that allow the child to function to some extent in most environments. Parents may discover their child's behavioral difficulties in school are rooted in cognitive and learning disorders. Discovering exactly which academic tasks are challenging for a child and pursuing appropriate intervention can diminish or eliminate the behavioral reactivity to school tasks. This is true for home tasks as well, especially those that involve memory or require more than one step for completion.

Abnormal Sexual Behavior

Children who have been molested or exposed to sexual material or sexual experiences may manifest abnormal sexual curiosity and behavior. Parents may be shocked when they see this, but it is critical that they understand that sexual behavior, like any other behavior, may be a result of early relational experiences. That gives hope for change through a patterned, repetitive healing relationship with you. Toni Cavanagh Johnson (2014) in her extensive clinical and research work has described nonnormative sexual behaviors exhibited by distressed children which may, but do not always, have their origin in early abuse. Children coming from orphanages may have engaged in self-stimulation or sexual contact with peers for comfort and connection. In addition, in some cultures, child-to-child sexual play is normative within social behavioral mores.

However, a child engaging in ongoing sexual behavior with adults (as opposed to within the context of initiation ceremonies in some cultures) is likely nonnormative for most cultures. Johnson has divided child sexual behavior into four categories (see below). For children in the Sexually Reactive and Mutual Engagement categories, specialized treatment is indicated, but it may be carried out while the child remains in the home with direction from trained therapists and vigilance from the parents.

Children who have been exposed to sexuality prematurely may engage in sexual acts in order to feel close, powerful, or soothed

Children who meet the criteria in Johnson's last two categories—Children Who Molest and Contact Offenses—may require specialized treatment outside of the home. Problematic and highly concerning, a child who molests other children has likely been physically and/or sexually abused by someone older, whether adult, teen, or child. This serious behavior marks the child's need to lash out reactively in response to his lack of control during his own abuse, and in some cases it is his attempt to "pass it on" as a way of trying to rid himself of the trauma he carries. As Johnson articulates, children who molest children have problems across the board in all aspects of their lives. Some nonnormative sexual behaviors are also legal offenses, the distinction being made by local, state, or federal statutes. Helping a distressed child who has crossed the legal boundary with his behavior may be further complicated by legal consequences for his actions. Commonly considered illegal are the behaviors in category IV.

Johnson's Categories of Child Sexual Behavior

I. Sexually Reactive Children
➤ engage in [excessive] self-stimulating behaviors
➤ engage in sexual behaviors with other children
➤ engage in sexual behaviors at times with adults
  • generally in response to things that are going on around them
  • in response to feelings which reawaken memories which are traumatic, painful, hard to understand

II. Children Who Mutually Engage in Full Range
of Adult Sexual Behaviors
➤ are distrustful of adults
➤ are often abandoned by adults
➤ are chronically hurt by adults
➤ relate best to other children
➤ use sexual behaviors as a way of making a connection to others
➤ use sex as a way of coping with feelings of hurt, sadness, and anxiety

III. Children Who Molest Other Children
➤ manifest sexual behaviors that are frequent and pervasive
➤ have evident history of sexual behavior problems
➤ closely link sexuality and aggression
➤ use some type of coercion, bribery, trickery, and manipulation

➤ select others who are vulnerable

➤ are impulsive and/or compulsive

➤ have problems in all areas of their lives

IV. Contact Offenses

➤ touching breasts or genitals

➤ rubbing and humping (either clothed or unclothed)

➤ penetration of vagina, anus, and mouth (by fingers, penis, tongue, or objects)

Noncontact Offenses

➤ exposing self

➤ voyeurism

➤ child pornography

➤ public masturbation

➤ forcing others to engage in sexual activity and watching sexual activity

Related Sexual Behaviors

➤ disrobing

➤ inappropriate or forced kissing

➤ viewing of pornography

➤ using sexual reference to demean and demoralize

➤ forcing others to get naked

Encopresis and Enuresis

Children who have been physically neglected or sexually or physically abused may have problems with toileting issues that increase as tension or anxiety increases. It is important to have medical/physical reasons for encopresis (fecal soiling) and enuresis (wetting) ruled out before assuming there is an emotional basis for them. Encopresis can result from chronic constipation from psychotropic medication or from avoidance of the bathroom that then results in insensitivity to full-bowel feeling and leakage. It can also result from sexual abuse, particularly for boys. Enuresis can result from lack of early toilet training or from slow developing systems. Both encopresis and enuresis are often triggered by tension or anxiety. Smearing and hiding of dirty underwear may also be a problem. The more matter-of-fact and non-shaming the parents can be, the better. These are simply behaviors that are concrete examples of your child's inner world of shame and anxiety.

Key Points for Chapter 12

1. *Guilt* is feeling bad for something we did, *shame* is temporarily feeling bad about who we are, and *core shame* is persistently feeling worthless no matter what successes we may have.

2. Changing location, activity, or environment may temporarily alleviate core shame, but only consistent acceptance and attachment can begin to heal core shame.

3. Adoption is also about loss for you and your child.

4. Grief occurs in waves and each new loss brings with it the sadness of prior losses. Your child's ability to attach to you depends on him grieving all of his prior losses.

5. Considering your child's age and maturity will give you developmentally appropriate ways to help him understand and cope with his losses.

6. Some adopted children feel that they simply do not belong within the new family. Honoring your child's history, both the joyful and painful parts, helps him solidify his unique story and consolidate his identity.

7. Genetic disorders can be activated or worsened by early life stressors for your child. These may include psychiatric disturbance, fetal alcohol effects, cognitive and learning disabilities, and sensory integration issues.

8. The addition of psychiatric medication to therapy interventions can make all interventions more effective.

9. Other special issues that may result from early history are abnormal sexual behaviors, encopresis, and enuresis. Treating them as behaviors, like any other behaviors that arise from early exposure to stress, can lessen the shame and fear your child experiences.

13.
Choosing Your Team
How to Form a Constellation of Support

Ora na azu nwa.

It takes the community/village to raise a child.

NIGERIAN IGBO PROVERB

〜 MICHAEL AND SANDRA JAMES at times felt that their home *was* a village, or maybe a fishbowl. They were finally ready to adopt seven-year-old Jenny, who had been in foster care in their home since she was eighteen months old. The Jameses' extended family lived in the same town and understood that Jenny was special and raising her took special skills. Michael and Sandra had been in therapy with Jenny since she was two for her episodic uncontrollable rages. There had been ups and downs, but their family therapist was skilled in attachment-focused therapy, and Jenny's adoptive-parents-to-be felt confident and encouraged due to their progress. The Jameses had professional family-based services workers who came into their home and helped them with specialized parenting techniques. The Department of Child and Family Services also had a social worker who worked closely with the whole foster parent/therapy team.

Additionally, Jenny had a court-appointed special advocate (CASA) who understood the importance of the attachment she had made to Michael and Sandra, and Jenny had her own court-appointed attorney. So when Jenny's birth father suddenly reappeared when Jenny was three years old, the Jameses had legal advocacy for Jenny in place. Though custody was not awarded to Jenny's birth dad, the Jameses knew that the connection between Jenny and her birth father was still important, so he would remain part of her life under their guidance. Michael and Sandra also had worked with Jenny's school to help her get special education services for her documented learning disabilities and sensory motor issues. Now, as they readied for Jenny's post-adoption party, Michael and Sandra James realized they would have a house full of family, friends, and professional team members to celebrate this official part of their journey. This was their village; these were their stars in heaven.

The Circle of Support

Parents who embark on the journey of foster care or adoption without the expectation that they will need the support of other caring adults and professionals or without a commitment to seeking this support often struggle needlessly and ultimately put the child's placement at risk. Raising an emotionally distressed child is a specialty occupation for which there is available training and plenty of "on-the-job" support. However, parents must first know they need the support, know the levels of support they will need, and seek to surround themselves at all levels with that support.

The diagram below illustrates the layers of support that are necessary to have in place to ensure the best chance for permanency success.

At the center of the circle is the emotionally distressed child, whose uniqueness, circumstances, needs, and healing are the prime concern for all of those in the graduated surrounding circles of support involved in the

Circles of Support

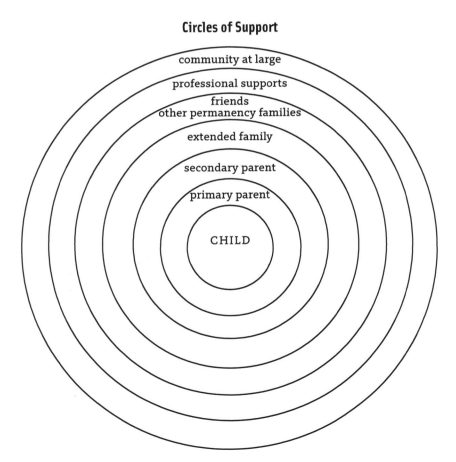

child's life. Immediately surrounding the child is his "primary" parent or caregiver—the person with whom he needs to form a solid attachment if he is to heal. Surrounding the primary parent is the "secondary" parent, or the person who supports the primary parent in the daily process of developing the primary relationship.

It is important to keep in mind that although both roles are crucial, the primary parent role is the first layer of connection for the child. It is within his relationship with the primary caregiver that the child learns how to connect with another human being, and it is the quality of that relationship that determines the child's capacity for connection. In the case of a single-parent family, the secondary parent role can be filled by a relative, a friend, a neighbor, a big brother or sister, or a combination of these. It is imperative that the primary parent has this layer of support in order to carry out the immense task of building a securely attached relationship with an emotionally distressed child.

Supporting the primary and secondary parents in their work with the child are extended family members, such as the parents' mothers, fathers, sisters, brothers, or cousins. In past generations, extended family members were readily available, perhaps even living next door. The need for this crucial support has not changed, yet the values and pace of current society have greatly lessened its accessibility. The norm now is for adult members of a nuclear family to live very separate and disparate lives alone with their own children, rarely in the same town or state with those in the immediate extended family. This unfortunate "modern" arrangement renders extended family support less available, less connected, and less helpful than it really needs to be, leaving a void in the circle of support that extended family members, nevertheless, still need to fill. Indeed, this societal shift may also be contributing to the problem of rising numbers of children who are in need of permanent families.

With the advent of the disintegrating extended family, the next circle of support—friends and other adoptive families—has become even more crucial to a family raising an emotionally distressed child. The emotional support friends and those who have "been there" can lend to a struggling family is immeasurable and can be fostered by those in the subsequent circle of support—the professionals who are committed to the family. These include the primary family therapist; the professionals with whom the primary therapist consults (whether in a treatment facility or outpatient setting); caseworkers and in-home aides; the family's primary health

Friends, other adoptive families, and professionals are all part of an effective support network, if they can all be coordinated in their efforts

care provider; specialists in occupational therapy, psychiatry, and other neurologically-related specialties whose services are needed by the child and the family; academic professionals, including all school personnel, tutors, speech therapists, and other learning-support professionals; respite providers; legal support to facilitate permanency; and recreational professionals who work in concert with the team to support the child's healing.

Finally, the community at large—including church members, club members, those who live and work in the neighborhood, and everyone else with whom the child may come in contact—provides the holding environment for not only the child but also the family. Communities can either be generally safe and supportive or unsafe and fragmented; thus, it is important that parents carefully consider this broad-based aspect of their support circle and make any changes necessary to provide the right growth environment for their family and child.

Unfortunately, extended family and friends also can hinder progress when they are not on board, critical of the parents, or misguided in their attempts to help. If parents are struggling in bringing their child into relationship, they need to review their circles of support for gaps both in the numbers of supporters they have in each level and in the quality of support they are receiving from those trying to be supportive. Making adjustments in their circles of support where necessary, even if it means the family changes location, will serve the child and the family in their healing process in the long run, which, after all, is the objective of the work.

Coordination of the members of a family's circles of support is necessary so that the support is organized, continuous, and focused on the phase of healing the child and family are working through. Usually, it is the parents and the main support professional guiding the course of the intervention who define the role each circle of support plays in the healing process. Referring to the "working through" model, this core team determines where they are in the process at any given time, what needs to happen in that stage, and who carries out what part of the plan. It is crucial that all members of each circle of support understand the general process of working through, the roles each circle must play for the support to be effective, and the way that support can be best delivered.

With so many people involved in the emotionally distressed child's life, it is easy for the "team" to struggle with being pulled in different directions, led by their conflicting values and priorities. However, each person involved in the child's life needs to communicate openly in service of the child's best interests. We know that the stress of raising a distressed child can fracture a family along its existing fault lines and at times those closest to the child experience and see things that others who are more removed do not. This can cause the primary attachment figure to "look" crazy and at times to behave erratically. Additionally, the child's distress may "leak" into the support team, causing high emotions and stark opinions to arise that take the focus off of the task at hand. Understanding and managing your team can provide the structure to contain the stress. The team must be there to support, sometimes "provide the cortex" for, give feedback to, and embrace the primary family.

Collaboration as a team enables parents, family, friends, helping professionals, and the community at large the ability to view the child as a whole, thus preventing potentially competing approaches, which fragment and dilute treatment. It is wise for the whole team to meet on a regular basis—perhaps quarterly—to reconnect to reinforce the team philosophy and goals, review the progress, and set the priorities for the upcoming portion of the intervention. Not only does this approach coordinate efforts, it reinforces for the parents that they are not alone and that with the team's support they can sustain hope for healing.

Inevitably, though, as much as a coordinated, effective team may be desirable, it is easy for conflicts to ensue and rifts to form amongst the team members. What works best to avoid these potential pitfalls, as well as to repair problems once they have arisen, is relying on a set, semiformal structure within which the team can operate during all types of communication, whether that be at the one-on-one, partial team, or full team level. The following are aspects of a helpful protocol for communication that can be employed throughout the intervention.

Your child's distress may "leak" into your support team. Understanding and managing your team can provide the structure to contain the stress.

Suggested Protocol for Team Communication

➤ Set a place, time, and dates for support meetings, informing all involved well in advance so they can prioritize the events as their calendars fill. This can often be done by the case manager or therapy professional involved.

➤ Provide refreshments, including hot beverages, to set a nurturing tone for the meeting.

➤ After everyone arrives, as a group compile an agenda for the meeting that allows time for all concerns to be heard.

➤ Email and phone contact are fine for eliciting and receiving help when an in-person meeting is not possible, but if you are addressing a problem or conflict, only use these forms of communication to set up a time when you can meet in person. *It is too easy to depersonalize those with whom you need to find common ground and to speak regrettable words if you are not face to face.*

➤ If you need to contact someone individually to solve a problem, ask when it would be a good time to talk, and communicate your intention to work together to solve the problem.

➤ If you are tempted to write an angry email, even if you are not intending to send it, do not even type it. Too often, the automatic motion of pressing "send" after writing an email will foil your plan to "just put it down on paper." If writing when you are angry helps, do it by hand.

➤ Define the problem in a way that places no blame (using "I" statements is helpful): write it down; then, point by point, write out exactly what you want to say and stick to your script.

➤ If you know that resolving a personal conflict is chancy, arrange for a neutral third party to conduct the meeting; choose someone who can assure each person is heard and who is capable of staving off personal attacks.

➤ If you are on the receiving end of a conflict, remain objective by writing down and repeating back to the person what you hear them saying point by point. When the person with a problem feels heard, animosity dissolves; and your role as an active listener helps prevent you from taking what you are hearing personally. After all, a person with a problem is a person who needs something, so it helps not to make it about you.

➤ As you are talking with a professional, write down the salient points

of the conversation for later reference. Inevitably, emotional interference will prevent most of the information you are hearing from
making it to memory.

➤ If you are a professional, ask the parents to write down salient
points for themselves. Going over these highlights with them at the
end of the session can help clarify meaning and help embed the
information in memory.

Underlying all team communication, there needs to be a shared and
unified philosophical base that is established at the beginning. The "common ground" for the entire team is supporting the welfare of the distressed child, and it may help to reiterate this often. Each team member
has something of value to add as the group develops its objectives. Along
with the conviction that a child needs a primary relationship and family
to thrive, a commitment to the child's safety, well-being, and permanent
family can constitute the core of any approach to helping a child heal. The
child's core needs drive the group process and decisions, while respect for
the parents as the child's primary advocates in the process must remain
paramount, because no one knows the child like his parents.

Through a one-on-one or group meeting, parents can then clarify with
the committed team members exactly how each can be of help to the child
and family. Finally, frequently communicating appreciation for the value
and importance of each person's contribution to creating success is essential as the process unfolds. Supporters need this "thank-you" to affirm
that their efforts are acknowledged and valued, as well as to fuel their
future actions on behalf of the family and child.

Who Do You Want on Your Team?

When raising an emotionally distressed child, families are involved with
multiple professionals and systems, which is inevitable and desirable. The
parents play the dual role of treatment team member and part of the treated
parent-child dyad; they are at once the treaters and the treated. This dual-
ity can become especially difficult when the child's disturbance begins to
evoke disturbances in the parents. Walking that line with professionals—
understanding and following through with treatment recommendations
while simultaneously being a voice for the direction of treatment—can be
like walking a tight rope. When parents are upset or angry at the treatment

team, the question should be, "Is my upset more about me or more about my child's needs?" Establishing ahead of time that this dynamic may occur, and if it does, that this question will be considered to clarify the focus of the action that needs to be taken, will lay the groundwork for successful resolution.

Even if the child is in legal limbo as he enters his intended permanent home, the professionals and systems in the child's life need to be working in concert with the parents as treatment proceeds. If this is not the case, parents need to approach the problem rationally and objectively because emotional and demanding behavior on their part will reflect negatively upon them as they move toward permanency. Sometimes other professionals on the team can be advocates for the parents as well, conveying their concerns to those who have legal control. Information about some of the professionals and systems that may be involved follows; parents need to understand these roles, powers, and potential as advocates for their child.

Psychotherapeutic Advocacy

It is uncommon for a family that is working toward permanency with an emotionally distressed child to be going it alone. Inevitably, issues and challenges arise that require the expertise of therapists or counselors who specialize in the problems these families face. It is important, however, that families seek and obtain the exact help they need, lest they flounder with a professional who means well but who is unfamiliar with pre- and post-adoption interventions. Specialists in facilitating attachment and in helping traumatized children and families heal are relatively common now, thanks to the work of researchers and therapists over the last twenty years who have applied and expanded the work of attachment-focused theorists such as John Bowlby and Mary Ainsworth, Daniel Hughes, Daniel Siegel, and Mary Dozier.

To find an attachment-focused therapist, many families rely upon recommendations of friends, family, and other professionals with whom they are involved. Thus, word of mouth is the most common way families get connected with a specialist who can meet their needs. Attachment-specific treatment centers can either provide services for the family or recommend someone in the area who can. Social workers, school counselors, adoption agencies, and other parents with challenging children are all good sources

The right therapist is someone who uses the attachment-focused therapy approach to treat the *relationship* between you and your child, not your child alone

of referrals to specialists with the right expertise for an emotionally distressed child and his family.

Additionally, parents may be able to find attachment-specific sites online that list therapists who have specific training for and experience with trauma-attachment issues. After parents find a potential therapist for their family, they need to be assertive in screening the professional to find out if s/he has adequate training and experience in helping families seeking permanency, and if the therapist seems to "click" with the family. The following are essential aspects of a professional's approach that families working to secure permanency need to seek.

Essential Elements of Effective Therapy for the Distressed Child and His Family

➤ Effective therapy for the distressed child and his family is attachment-focused *family* psychotherapy, which emphasizes developing relationships between the child and the primary and secondary caregivers. Therapists using this approach will align with the principles of "family systems," "attachment," "relationship-based therapy," "dyadic developmental psychotherapy" (DDP), and "Circle of Security," and they will advertise and describe their services as such.

➤ The therapist will specialize in working with children with attachment difficulties and their families, will be open about her/his strengths, weaknesses, and "success" rates, and will engage in professional consultation or receive supervision on cases.

➤ The therapist will work primarily with the parents and child together, sometimes with the parents alone, and only occasionally with the child alone.

➤ The therapist will not promote interventions such as point and reward systems and will not espouse the use of parental power and authority at the expense of emotional connection.

➤ The therapist will understand and teach "therapeutic parenting," a distinct paradigm that emphasizes parents attuning to the needs of the child by translating the meaning of behavior.

➤ The therapist will support the parents in observing and controlling their own anxieties and reactive behaviors so they can be truly present for the child.

➤ Ultimately, the therapist will use the same empathic attunement with the parents that s/he is teaching the parents to use with the child.

The quality of the therapeutic interface with the family will determine the effectiveness of the treatment. Clear definition of the problem in terms of relational development should precede any intervention and will be accompanied by a description of the specific relational outcome that is the treatment's goal. More important than the frequency of sessions is the depth of experience the family immerses in during sessions. Interventions should not just be discussed; they need to be practiced under the supportive guidance of the therapist such that the parents have a firm grasp of the treatment they will be carrying out when they leave the session.

Therapist availability between sessions is a crucial aspect of treatment, for it is often through this in-the-moment support that parents find the wherewithal to push through a stuck pattern in the relationship with their child. Families may live far from their therapeutic support system, but the availability of various media makes it possible for treatment to be carried out effectively nonetheless. Travel to attend in-person sessions with a therapist can be scheduled at the family's convenience, and between-session phone or Internet contact can be arranged to take place at set times so the family feels continuous support even if they reside a substantial distance away.

Department of Child and Family Services Advocacy

The Department of Child and Family Services (DCFS), most often administered at the state level by the Department of Public Health and Human Services (DPHHS), may be the legal guardian of the child until the child is adopted or provided legal guardianship by the family. The child will have an assigned caseworker, who works under the guidance of a supervisor, who works under the auspices of a local manager, who reports to a regional supervisor, who reports to a state DCFS manager, who reports to the department head of the state office of DPHHS. At times, because of an overtaxed and understaffed system, social workers are overwhelmed with

Understanding the lines of supervision within a massive bureaucracy like the Department of Child and Family Services may help you get what you need for your child and your family

the number of cases they have to manage, and the child can get lost in the shuffle. Parents should keep in mind that there is a hierarchy in place that they can access to address the child's needs. It behooves parents to know the names and contact information not only for their child's caseworker but also for that worker's up-line superiors.

In addition to the DCFS caseworker, parents may also be working with the adoption coordinator in their local DCFS office, who reports to a local manager, who reports to a state-level adoption supervisor, who reports to the state DCSF manager, who reports to the department head of the state DPHHS office. Already, adoptive permanency parents working through government-run offices have quite a few professionals whose job it is to support temporary and permanent placement of their child and with whom they must work. Yet there are many more affiliated professionals involved in a child's case with whom parents must work, such as therapists, doctors, specialty providers, and court personnel—most, if not all, of whom they did not choose—possibly adding another layer of stress to the family's life.

One potentially helpful service DCFS may offer is case coordination via family-group decision-making meetings. These meetings bring together family, friends, social workers, and service providers to share concerns, knowledge, and skills, and can be used throughout the child protective process as a way to support a child's current placement, help the placement progress toward permanency, and keep members of the team unified via goal setting and conflict resolution. This type of meeting may also serve as a helpful prototype for parents developing their post-adoptive support team.

Parents are sometimes required to take a series of parenting classes aimed at preparing them for fostering or adopting an emotionally distressed child. After completing mandatory classes, parents are required to obtain a number of continuing education credits (CEs) until permanency is achieved. DCFS usually runs the mandatory parenting classes, while parents fulfill their continuing education requirements by attending workshops, presentations, and trainings given by approved providers. The educative material provided in classes and subsequent CE events can vary in quantity, depth, and quality depending upon regional standards and the presenter's style. However, there will always be something of value gained by parents who pursue the requirements with interest, including meeting other parents in similar circumstances who may eventually become part of the family's circles of support.

Adoption Agency Advocacy

The quality, comprehensiveness of service, and reliability varies greatly among adoption agencies in terms of both pre- and post-adoptive services. Some agencies specialize in out-of-country adoptions and some in in-country adoptions. Evaluating an agency's operational model, its costs, its turnaround time, and its outcome statistics, in addition to speaking with other families who have adopted from the prospective agency, is a crucial first step for families wishing to adopt through a private agency. One of the most telling things about the quality of the agency is whether it offers substantial post-adoption support. More and more agencies are including this service as part of the adoption package because more parents are now speaking out about their need for support due to the trials and tribulations associated with raising their adopted child.

An adoption process is not over when the court grants approval, and this concept is becoming more widely recognized. Getting quality post-adoption support is a critical part of successful adoptions. Quality is determined by the type, regularity, and accessibility of services offered and the experience, knowledge, and availability of the professionals delivering the services. Parents need access to an adoption-specific, professionally facilitated parenting group that meets regularly, preferably at least once per month. They need access to professionals upon whom they can rely when a pressing question or problem arises.

As part of adequate post-adoption services, parents need to be encouraged to network with other permanency families in order to surround

Be sure that the adoption agency you choose provides and supports post-adoption services

themselves with experienced support. There is an adoption community within most localities that adoptive parents come to rely upon, and that sometimes even becomes the family's "extended family." Once a family becomes a part of such a community, knowledge about and referrals to all services related to adopted children's needs, such as those relevant to the child's educational, medical, and mental health needs, can become available to them. Access to respite may be available through the post-adoptive services of the adoption agency; however, within the adoptive community, parents often organize a respite-trading system to give families that much-needed hiatus that they will all need at times throughout their adoptive journey.

Educational Advocacy

Whether an emotionally distressed child is homeschooled or attends a private or public school, he will invariably have some difficulty with some or all aspects of receiving his education—the academic work, the physical setting, the educational staff, or the interface with other students. Once the behavior that is getting in the way of learning is identified and the underlying need(s) enumerated, adjustments can be made that will enhance the child's learning experience, allowing the child to be more successful. The identified behavior(s) can be emotional, psychological, cognitive, or physiological in nature, and can be assessed through in-school educational testing and/or a neuropsychological examination, which can evaluate the brain's processing functions. Once the testing is complete and the needs are identified, services can be put into place that support the child in his educational setting.

Grounded in the state's legal responsibility to provide education for every child, an individual education plan (IEP) may be recommended by the child study team (CST)—an entity consisting of school personnel, parents, community professionals, and occasionally also the child, if appropriate. Based on the results of testing, the IEP includes the reason the child needs support, the accommodations to be made, and the personnel that will carry them out. If a child does not qualify for an IEP, he still may be eligible for supportive services based on recommendations of the CST. In this case, a non-legally-binding document may be drawn up by the CST containing information similar to that in the IEP, and the accommodations can be carried out voluntarily by the school in service of the child.

Some states have a professional advocacy group whose members work with the parents and the CST to ensure that the child's needs are identified and adequately met. If this service is not available, parents can enlist the services of one or more of the child's community professionals and have them attend the CST if they feel they need backing for their efforts to get their child appropriate support. For the most part, however, schools are willing to do what it takes to help a child get the education he needs. Therefore, parents are apt to be better served if they maintain an attitude of cooperation and respect in all of their dealings with the school professionals. This does not mean parents sit back and wait for action to be taken; rather, they need to be supportive and persistent and help the school professionals wherever they can in the process.

Homeschooling is a choice parents make for their child, especially the first year or so that the child is in their home. This can enhance the attachment process and allow the child to begin to feel the security of his new home base, but it can also set up a confusing relationship with his parent. You will need to ask yourself, "Who do I need to be for my child right now—his teacher or his parent?" Does homeschooling this child allow you to switch roles from someone who rocks him to someone who grades his papers? It may be too much for both of you as you establish your relationship with one another. On the other hand, your child may be facing enough challenges as he adapts to his new surroundings and family dynamics, such that sending him to a community school would push him over the top in terms of his capacity to adjust. Only you, with feedback from your child and your support network, can make the final decision. The same services that are legally mandated to provide an appropriate education for a child attending a community school should be accessible to the homeschooled child; however, parents may need to advocate more heartily for their child to receive them.

Everyday advocacy in the public school system is necessary to help the child successfully interface with his academic challenges. For example, you may help the teacher understand that if she is willing to take a

---

**Your child's distress is likely to influence school success.
Decisions about homeschooling and advocating
for special supports in the public school are vital.**

few minutes first thing in the morning to reestablish the relationship with your child, he renews the connection he needs to feel safe and grounded at school and will do better in the classroom.

Clear, simple expectations with consistent adult follow-through, predictability of schedule, and frequent checking in with the child, such as during times of transition from one activity to the next, all serve to lessen the child's fear and anxiety (the source of difficult behaviors) and to allow him to become more trusting that he is safe and his needs will be met.

From the start, set up a simple, effective, and swift system of communication between parents and teachers, one that does not rely on the child as emissary. This cooperation can be done via a quick, daily email exchange of status updates between parent and teacher. Parents can initiate this process by introducing themselves and their child to the teacher and school personnel before the academic year begins. The introduction can include parents sharing with the school something about the child's interests, hobbies, and relationships to others, along with what is helpful to their child in the academic setting. Revisiting the school on a regular basis, such as on a weekly schedule, can help parents and teacher stay united in their efforts to help the child. There is no substitution for parents building good relationships with those with whom the child works every day at school.

Legal Advocacy

Prior to the establishment of legal adoption or guardianship, the child may be involved with professionals who legally represent his best interests. This may include the child's attorney, guardian ad litem, court-appointed special advocate (CASA), and foster parents, as well as those who have legal custody of the child, such as DCFS, and must interface with the legal system. The way a child in custody is taken care of while the legal system is involved can have great impact on the child's long-term ability to be placed for adoption. The longer a child is in a home where he experiences neglect and abuse, the more severe the damage will be. The younger the neglected/abused child is, the more severe the harm. Yet removing a child from his birth home comes with it the risk of multiple placements and potential abuse in those placements.

Those who work in the legal system must help the child by making decisions as quickly as possible and standing by the decisions that have

Legal support is available and necessary for complex questions of guardianship and adoption

been made. The most harmful out-of-home plan for a child is being moved from place to place because each disruption convinces him that the world is unsafe, that adults are not to be trusted, and that he must take care of himself. This is equally true for the child's relationships with his legal and custodial advocates; thus, professionals must make a standing commitment to the child in their care to see him through to permanency and to follow up with the child in his new home, so he can experience continuity of relationship with all important figures in his life.

Most professionals working with a child disrupted from his birth family's home are caring and competent, but they work in a cumbersome system that does not provide for an adequate, timely response to the child's present and ongoing needs. Most children want to return to their birth families and miss their birth parents deeply, even if they have experienced neglect or abuse at their parents' hands. This longing, the insecurity of living with relative strangers, and the history of traumatization create needs in the child which require special, consistent, and well-timed responses.

Medical Advocacy

There is a direct link between adverse childhood events and physical health (Anda, et al., 2006), and parents need to find medical practitioners who understand and embrace this perspective in order to get treatment for the whole child, not just his symptoms. A child's grief may be expressed physically through stomachaches, encopresis, enuresis, muscle aches, headaches, colds, runny noses, short-term memory problems, and other symptoms. Viewed from the perspective that the distressed child has been living with significant ongoing stress, these ailments take on a whole new meaning. Short-term responses like taking medicine, drinking

Choose a physician who can treat the whole child and understands the results of adverse childhood experiences on your child

more fluids, or other commonly prescribed interventions may help some in the present, but they do not help in the long run.

Ongoing stress elevates cortisol levels, and cortisol, a stress hormone, affects all body systems negatively if its flow never gets "turned off." Normally, cortisol is released in immediate response to stress of any kind—the definition of which differs with the individual—and then its flow is inhibited when the stress passes. In the distressed child, the stress has been ongoing, so the cortisol flow has remained "turned on," depleting the adrenal glands, which cripples the body's immune response, rendering the child extra-receptive to viral and bacterial infections. Thus, the child may be ill more often than his peers, suffer more frequently from some kind of physical illness, and spend more time in medical appointments.

The emotionally distressed child cannot self-regulate to attain a more restful, less stressful state, so his parents need to do this for him. For parents to be able to respond, they must be present. This may entail one parent staying home full time, or two parents alternating schedules to share the childcare role so there is always an attachment figure available. The attachment figure's presence, attunement, and active response to the child's every need in the present comprise the long-term "cure" for the child's ongoing physical maladies. The parent's timely, accurate care lessens the child's chronic, heightened cortisol response, as well as reduces the effects of temporary, acute stress on the child's system.

Community Agency Advocacy and Supports

Communities vary in the types of services available to families who are working to make a permanent home for an emotionally distressed child, but most offer some kind of support, even if it is only a neighbor who is able to provide respite for a few hours a month. Large communities may have the potential to offer extensive services to families, from early childhood intervention to teen mentoring programs. Families need to be proactive in scouring their localities for any and all services that might be helpful and valuable to them as they traverse the healing journey. It really does "take a village," and the more community members who understand

Connecting with other adoptive families through groups or Internet forums can be an invaluable resource for you and your child

your family's situation and needs, the more the family can feel supported and accept the help that is offered.

Programs that can be especially helpful to families include support groups geared to parents who are raising emotionally distressed children; in-home therapeutic services that offer in-the-moment support to parents learning new ways of intervening with their child that are both pro-relational and effective in meeting the child's behaviorally obscured needs; and respite services that are oriented toward meeting the needs of a child who requires high structure coupled with a protective, relational approach that does not interfere with his developing primary attachment.

Agencies that offer a variety of services such as family therapy, in-home support, children's therapeutic activities geared to teaching pro-social skills, and access to community professionals providing psychiatric, medical, and physical/occupational therapies can provide a "one-stop shop" for families who are in need of multiple interventions that can be coordinated by an assigned case manager. When the services available in such an agency are of good quality, the family can bypass the need to search out each service separately and coordinate all of the appointments necessary on their own, yielding less stress and time-consuming travel and more time for relational development.

Other services families can find useful in the middle to later stages of treatment, when the child has established a stable core attachment to his primary caregiver, include Big Brothers Big Sisters, various children's enrichment programs, group sports activities, and multifamily gatherings during which parents and child can practice using their secure-base, safe-haven interactions within a safe context. Families may benefit from participation in social collaboration groups such as foster/adoptive parent associations at the local, state, and national levels.

Specialized Internet forums are available for families in all kinds of situations, and there are many to choose from in the foster/adoptive online community. Participating in these forums allows parents to connect with other families who are experiencing the same stage of treatment as they are, rendering support that is specific, timely, and flexible. Because these forums generally operate in the present, there may always be someone online with whom parents can communicate regardless of time zone differences. Accessibility and availability are crucial aspects of support families come to rely upon, and web-based sources can often fit the need.

Treatment Center Advocacy

A child will sometimes be entering a family from a treatment center such as Intermountain, which will oversee the healing process from the beginning when a child is evaluated for treatment through adoption. In such cases, family involvement may begin at any point in the child's treatment trajectory deemed appropriate for his healing and readiness for family integration. This situation can be ideal for both child and parents because support is continuous throughout the process and is provided by a fixed set of professionals on whom the child and family can depend over the long haul. This arrangement sets the stage for the relational development that is occurring between the child and his parents because the parent–treatment team relational development process lays the fertile ground and provides the model for the child-parent process.

Although not available to most families working toward permanency, a facility like Intermountain can and does provide an anchor for the philosophy central to effective relational development in its immediate community, in the surrounding communities, and in the regional area as a whole. This philosophical anchor attracts professionals who desire to work in the relational development paradigm, not only within the institution but also within the area at large, thus creating an accessible professional community of specialists for all families.

With the ever-growing realization that creating and maintaining a permanent home requires ongoing services, institutions such as Intermountain are expanding community treatment programs to broaden their availability to even those families whose child did not attend the inpatient treatment program. The efficacy of the developmental/relational approach is also becoming more well known, and as a result there are more professional specialists than ever making their services available to families (Kohlstaedt, 2010).

Treatment centers grounded in a unified philosophy and goals offer a wide range of services, including inpatient care, day treatment, in-home services, respite, psychiatry, and school-based services and can provide optimal support for you, your child, and your family

There is now a network of institutions, agencies, and private practitioners developing on regional levels throughout the country that is beginning to provide a much-needed sense of trust and security to families needing support in their quest for permanency. Not only are more family therapists now espousing the relational development approach, but so is a growing cohort of private and public agency professionals who are striving to stay current with treatment protocols based on the leading-edge research so they can provide interventions that specifically target the needs of those children and families reaching for permanency.

Parent Self-Advocacy

The permanency journey begins as parents discuss the pros and cons of taking on an emotionally distressed child, as we examined in Chapter 1. After becoming unified in their decision to proceed with the integration of a child with high needs, parents work as a team as they go forward. Parents then wind their way through the process, seeking advice, expertise, and services from family, friends, and professionals. Thus, parents are acting as their own advocates from the beginning.

Inevitably, however, somewhere along the road to adoption, parents' leadership in the process can wane or dissolve due to stress, feeling overwhelmed, or a sense of powerlessness. Identifying the parent actions and behaviors that enable them to continue to lead the way can help prevent this demise. After all, the parents are the child's primary caregivers and know the child better than anyone involved, so they should be the ones to maintain control of the process. As primary advocates for themselves, their child, and their family, parents need to

➤ know the legal rights of parents
➤ be assertive and persistent when seeking services for the child
➤ prepare for all meetings and appointments with whatever tools work best
➤ write down comments, questions, and requests, and refer to them when in a meeting or on the phone
➤ enlist the help of a support person who can attend meetings and who is prepared to take over for the parents as necessary

You are your child's and your family's best advocate!

- ➤ know that there will be many opportunities to get it right or for repair if it does not go well
- ➤ prepare closure statements for ending a meeting or phone call if it feels unproductive, such as, "I need time to think about the issue at hand and would like to continue this conversation after I have thought about it."
- ➤ make direct, specific requests when asking for services and say "no" clearly when services are not judged to be in the family's or child's best interests
- ➤ ask questions when something is confusing, for definitions of unknown terms, and for descriptions of suggested procedures
- ➤ reiterate your desire to maintain a unified team that is working toward common goals
- ➤ frequently express appreciation for or compliment the actions of others who are trying to help
- ➤ believe in the knowledge and power of being the child's parent(s)

Advocacy for your child is a long-term proposition. This can be both empowering and daunting for parents new to the process, but they must always keep in mind that although they are the coaches of the team, parents will not be undertaking this endeavor on their own.

There will be times when parents will wish they could abdicate their role as chief advocate for their child. These are times when the professionals on the team can respond by stepping in closer behind the parents to support them as well as to decipher the opportunity in the crisis. The greatest moments of difficulty and frustration in creating permanent relationships reflect the presence of core issues that must be dealt with if the relationship is to succeed. Rather than seeing deeply challenging situations as negative indicators for the prognosis of the process, professionals on the team can look at what is happening objectively to discover the issues that are presenting themselves for resolution.

The aim of assembling a committed team is to create a consistent network that provides a secure base and safe haven for the *family* as a whole so they have the support they need to move into adoption with their emotionally distressed child. Your team serves as the hands that hold you and your child, from which you can journey out and to which you can return safely with increasing confidence.

Key Points for Chapter 13

1. Friends, other adoptive families, and professionals are all part of an effective support network that is coordinated in its efforts.

2. Your child's distress may "leak" into your support team. Understanding and managing your team can provide the structure to contain the stress.

3. The right therapist is someone who uses the attachment-focused therapy approach to treat the *relationship* between you and your child, not your child alone.

4. Understanding the lines of supervision within a massive bureaucracy like the Department of Child and Family Services may help you get what you need for your child and your family.

5. Be sure that the adoption agency you choose provides and supports post-adoption services.

6. Your child's distress is likely to influence his school success. Decisions about homeschooling and advocating for special supports in the public school are vital to your child's success.

7. Legal support for children still in the system is available and necessary for complex questions of guardianship and adoption.

8. Choose a physician who can treat the whole child and understands the results of adverse childhood experiences on your child's physical well-being.

9. Connecting with other adoptive families through groups or Internet forums can be an invaluable resource for you and your child.

10. You are your child's and your family's best advocate!

Epilogue

A core belief at Intermountain is that to be alive means to continually grow and change. We never have it all perfectly understood. Nor can we intervene perfectly each time. Each new child and family that we treat, each new group of professionals that we train, each new staff member that comes on board presents us with new challenges and new ways of seeing the world.

And so it is with this book. We have tried to present the many-faceted ways in which we have come to understand a child's and a family's view of the world, and how to progress from hope into intimacy and a permanent, healing relationship.

We don't expect that you will read through this book from cover to cover (unless you are taking the *Relational Development* course—see below), but we do anticipate that you can use the information and the exercises in this text when you feel stuck, or when you want to understand your child better, or when you want to help another team member better understand your child and your experience.

Just as we believe that what is harmed by relationship must be healed by relationship, we also believe that what is learned is learned most effectively through relationship. Each bump, each problem, each conflict can present a new way of seeing the same reality.

Your journey will take time. To quote Jim FitzGerald, CEO of Intermountain, one final time, "Understand that there are no short-term solutions to long-term problems." Therefore, please stick with the process and commit for the long run. You are your child's greatest hope for joy, and he is your greatest hope for doing something magnificent in the world.

A Few Resources for Further Information

From books to magazine articles to trainings to the Internet, resources abound for parents and extended family members of children struggling to develop relationships. The following is just a sample of the available resources that might launch parents into the process of seeking further knowledge and support they may need to succeed with their prodigious undertaking.

Adoption support groups: http://www.adoptionservices.org/parenting /parenting_support_groups.html (scroll down to the bottom of the web page for Montana foster/adoption support groups)

Adoption Today magazine: http://www.adoptinfo.net

Attachment Parenting International: http://www.attachmentparenting .org

Child Trauma Academy: www.childtrauma.org

Circle of Security International: http://www.circleofsecurity.org

Education for extended family members: http://www.adopting.org /adoptions/what-adoptive-parents-need-by-rita-laws-phd-what-i-need -now.html

Relational Development, SW 472, online course, the University of Montana, available to parents, professionals, and students. See description at www.umt.edu/catalog and register at http://www.childwise.org /um-course

Trust-Based Relational Intervention: http://www.child.tcu.edu

Zero to Three: http://www.zerotothree.org

References

Ainsworth, M. D. S., Blehar, M., Waters, E., and Wall, S. (1978). *Patterns of attachment: A psychological study of the strange situation*. Hillsdale, NJ: Erlbaum.

Anda, R., Felitti, V., Bremner, J., Walker, D., Whitfield, C., Perry, B., Dube, S., and Giles, W. (2006). The enduring effects of abuse and related adverse experiences in childhood: A convergence of evidence from neurobiology and epidemiology. *European Archives of Psychiatry and Clinical Neuroscience, 256*, 174–86.

Berger, K. S. (2014). *Invitation to the lifespan, 2nd ed.* New York: Worth Publishers.

Berk, L. (2004). *Development through the lifespan, 3rd ed.* New York: Allyn & Bacon.

Bowlby, J. (1982). *Attachment.* Tavistock, UK: Institute of Human Relations.

Bowlby, J. (1988). *A secure base.* New York: Basic Books.

Chess, S., Thomas, A., Birch, H. G., and Hertzig, M. (1960). Implications of a longitudinal study of child development for child psychiatry. *American Journal of Psychiatry, 117*, 434–41.

Chess, S., Thomas, A., and Birch, H. (1965). *Your child is a person: A psychological approach to childhood without guilt.* New York: The Viking Press.

Child Development Institute (2015). http://childdevelopmentinfo.com /about/. Retrieved July 22, 2015.

Chugani, H. (1998, November). Biological basis of emotions: Brain systems and brain development. *Pediatrics, 102*(5), 1225–29.

Cremer-Vogel, K. (2009, April). Handling chronic misbehavior: A therapeutic approach that works. PowerPoint presentation, *Mental Health America of Montana 2009 Conference.* Great Falls, MT.

Cremer-Vogel, K., Richards, C., and Richards, D. (2008). *What every adoptive parent needs to know: Healing your child's wounded heart.* Bozeman, MT: Mountain Ridge Publishing.

Dobbs, D. (2009, December). The science of success. *Atlantic Monthly.* http://www.theatlantic.com/magazine/archive/2009/12/the-science -of-success/307761/. Retrieved July 22, 2015.

Erikson, E. (1993). *Childhood and society.* New York: W. W. Norton Co.

Fahlberg, V. (1990). *Residential treatment: A tapestry of many therapies.* Indianapolis, IN: Perspectives Press.

FitzGerald, J. (1996). Attachment and the impact of trauma for foster parents and emergency respite parents. Videotaped series sponsored by Montana Council for Families.

FitzGerald, J. (2001, September). Skewed developmental trajectories of abused and neglected children. *13th Annual Conference on Services for Children & Adolescents with Emotional Disturbances and Their Families.* Montana Department of Public Health and Human Services. Fairmont, MT.

FitzGerald, J. (2015, April). Sustaining empathy. PowerPoint presentation, *Why They Do What They Do* Training. Bozeman, MT.

Hoffman, K., Marvin, R., Cooper, G., and Powell, B. (2006). Changing toddlers' and preschoolers' attachment classifications: The circle of security intervention. *Journal of Consulting and Clinical Psychology, 74*(6), 1017–26.

Horner, A. (1989). *Object relations and the developing ego in therapy.* Northvale, NJ: Jason Aronson.

Hughes, D. A. (2004). An attachment-based treatment of maltreated children and young people. *Attachment & Human Development, 6,* 24–40.

Hughes, D. A. (2007). *Attachment focused family therapy.* New York: Norton & Co.

Johnson, T. C. (1996, 2005, 2007, 2009, 2011, 2013, 2015). *Updated— Understanding children's sexual behaviors—What's natural and healthy.* www.tcavjohn.com.

Johnson, T. C. (1998, 2001, 2006, 2009, 2011, 2014). *Helping children with sexual behavior problems—A guidebook for professionals and caregivers, 4th Edition.* www.tcavjohn.com.

Kohlberg, L. (1974). *Moral development.* Austin TX: Holt, Rinehart & Winston.

Kohlstaedt, E. (2005). Godzilla meets Mother Theresa: Child development for parents of children with serious emotional disturbance. Keynote, *Montana State Foster and Adoptive Parents Association Annual Conference.* Helena, MT.

Kohlstaedt, E. (2010). What is harmed by relationship can be healed by relationship. *Scottish Journal of Residential Child Care, 9*(2), 44–53.

Mahler, M., Pine, F., and Bergman, A. (1975). *The psychological birth of the human infant.* New York: Basic Books.

Miller, S. (2011, April). On the gains and losses of adoption. *Adoption Today*, 62–64.

Neufeld, G. (2005). *Hold onto your kids*. New York: Ballantine Books.

Perry, B. (1995). *Maltreated children: Experience, brain development and the next generation*. New York: Basic Books.

Piaget, Jean (1992). *The child's conception of the world*. Lanham, MD: Rowan & Littlefield.

Public Broadcasting Services (2015). The whole child: The ABC's of child development. http://www.pbs.org/wholechild/abc/physical.html. Retrieved July 22, 2015.

Schore, A. (1994). *Affect regulation and the origin of the self: The neurobiology of emotional development*. New Jersey: Lawrence Erlbaum Associates.

Shatz, C. J. (1992). The developing brain. *Scientific American, 267*(3), 60–67.

Siegel, D. J. (2001). Toward an interpersonal neurobiology of the developing mind: Attachment, "mindsight" and neural integration. *Infant Mental Health Journal, 22*(1–2), 67–94.

Siegel, D., and Hartzell, M. (2003). *Parenting from the inside out: How a deeper self-understanding can help you raise a child who thrives*. New York: Tarcher/Putnam.

Silverstein, D., and Roszia, S. (1999). Openness: a critical component of special needs adoption. *Child Welfare, 78*(5), 637–51.

Sroufe, L. A. (1995). *Emotional development: The organization of emotional life in the early years*. New York: Cambridge University Press.

Teicher, M., Andersen, S., Polcari, A., Anderson, C., and Navalta, C. (2002). Developmental neurobiology of childhood stress and trauma. *Psychiatric Clinics of North America, 25*, 397–426.

Tronick, E. Z. (2003). Of course all relationships are unique: How co-creative processes generate unique mother-infant and patient-therapist relationships and change other relationships. *Psychoanalytic Inquiry, 23*(3).

Zero to Three (2003). Charting your child's healthy development: 6 to 9 months. http://www.zerotothree.org. Retrieved June 2015.